The ICCA Handbook on Corporate

Social Responsibility

The ICCA Handbook on Corporate Social Responsibility

Edited by

Judith Hennigfeld
Manfred Pohl
Nick Tolhurst

John Wiley & Sons, Ltd

Other Wiley Editorial Offices

Library of Congress Cataloging in Publication Data

The ICCA handbook on corporate social responsibility / [compiled by] Judith Hennigfeld,
Manfred Pohl, Nick Tolhurst.
    p. cm.
Includes bibliographical references and index.
ISBN-13: 978-0-470-05710-0 (cloth : alk. paper)
ISBN-10: 0-470-05710-6 (cloth : alk. paper)
1. Social responsibility of business—Handbooks, manuals, etc. I. Hennigfeld, Judith.
II. Pohl, Manfred, 1944–   III. Tolhurst, Nick. IV. Institute for Corporate Culture Affairs.
HD60.I23 2006
658.4'08—dc22   2006018008

British Library Cataloguing in Publication Data

A catalogue record for this book is available from the British Library

ISBN-13 978-0-470-05710-0 (HB)
ISBN-10 0-470-05710-6 (HB)

Typeset in 11.5/15pt Bembo by Integra Software Services Pvt. Ltd, Pondicherry, India
Printed and bound in Great Britain by TJ International Ltd, Padstow, Cornwall, UK
This book is printed on acid-free paper responsibly manufactured from sustainable forestry in
which at least two trees are planted for each one used for paper production.

Contents

List of Contributors

Takis Arapoglou

Chairman and CEO, National Bank of Greece, Athens, Greece; Member, World Corporate Ethics' Council/ICCA's Advisory Board

Takis Arapoglou is chairman and CEO of National Bank of Greece, Athens. Prior to this he served on the board of directors of Egyptian American Bank, a subsidiary of American Express in Egypt (1994–6), and on the asset and liability committee of Citigroup Europe. Takis Arapoglou was a member of the supervisory board of Citibank Sweden (1984–5) and of the supervisory board of Chase Manhattan Bank Finland (1989–90) as well as of the Hellenic Bank Association (1991–3). In 2000, Takis Arapoglou returned to Citigroup in London as managing director and Global Banks Industry head after having served as general manager of Citibank/Citigroup in Greece in 1997.

Christopher Avery

Director, Business Human Rights Resource Centre, London, United Kingdom

Christopher Avery is founder and director of the Business Human Rights Resource Centre. He worked at the International Secretariat of Amnesty International in London, as legal adviser, then as deputy head of the 130-member research department. His work included representing Amnesty at the United Nations. After leaving Amnesty, Christopher Avery conducted independent field research in Africa and Asia on companies' involvement in development and human rights projects. He researched and wrote *Business and Human Rights in a Time of Change*, a report published by Amnesty International UK in 2000. In 1997 Christopher Avery was Stanford University's seventh Visiting Mentor – a Haas Center for Public Service programme that 'brings distinguished professionals in public service to a week-long residency on campus'. Christopher Avery was educated at Columbia University School of Law (LLM), University of California Davis School of Law (JD; Order of the Coif; Corpus Juris Secundum Award) and Stanford University (BA, Honours).

Dr Arno Balzer

Editor in Chief, Manager Magazin, Hamburg, Germany
Arno Balzer, born in 1958 in Biedenkopf, was appointed the new chief editor of the *Manager Magazin* on 1 July 2003. After studying economics at the Mainz and Nuremberg universities, and obtaining his doctorate in 1986, Arno Balzer started his career at the German business magazine *Wirtschaftswoche* as an editor before joining the *Manager Magazin* in 1990. In 1999 Arno Balzer was made deputy chief editor for financial markets and investment and since 2000 he has also been responsible for companies and finance.

Dr Rolf-E. Breuer

Chairman, Supervisory Board, Deutsche Bank AG, Frankfurt am Main, Germany; President of the World Corporate Ethics' Council/ICCA's Advisory Board
Rolf-E. Breuer has been chairman of the supervisory board of Deutsche Bank AG since May 2002 after holding positions of

spokesman of the board of managing directors and chairman of the group executive committee, member of the board of managing directors (until 1997), senior vice president and head of investment and trading department (until 1985). Rolf-E. Breuer is a member of the supervisory boards of Bertelsmann AG and E.ON AG. He holds additional non-executive memberships at Compagnie de Saint-Gobain SA, Kreditanstalt für Wiederaufbau, Landwirtschaftliche Rentenbank. He is also president of the Association of German Banks. Rolf-E. Breuer studied law at the Universities of Lausanne in Switzerland, Munich and Bonn before he received his doctorate from Bonn University.

Sir Geoffrey Chandler CBE

Founder-Chair, Amnesty International UK Business Group 1991–2001, former Director General, UK National Economic Development Office, and a former Director of Shell International

Sir Geoffrey Chandler is Chair Emeritus of the Amnesty International UK Business Group, having been founder-chair from 1991 to 2001. He began his career as a journalist on the BBC and *Financial Times*, subsequently spending 22 years with the Royal Dutch/Shell Group. He was a director of Shell Petroleum, Shell Petroleum NV and Shell International and the initiator of Shell's first Statement of General Business Principles in 1976. Sir Geoffrey Chandler was director general of the UK National Economic Development Office 1978–83, director of Industry Year 1986 and leader of the subsequent campaign of Industry Matters, and chaired the National Council of Voluntary Organisations 1989–96. Sir Geoffrey Chandler has honorary degrees from a number of universities and is the author of books on Greece and Trinidad and of numerous articles on corporate responsibilities and human rights.

Dr Hans-Ulrich Doerig

Vice-Chairman of the Board of Directors, Credit Suisse Group, Zurich, Switzerland; Member, World Corporate Ethics' Council/ICCA's Advisory Board

Hans-Ulrich Doerig studied at the St Gallen Graduate School for Business Administration and Economics (HSG). In 1968, Hans-Ulrich Doerig began his banking career with J.P. Morgan in New York. In 1973 he joined Credit Suisse in Zurich, where he held several management positions in the fields of international capital markets and corporate finance. From 1981 to 1982 Hans-Ulrich Doerig took over the responsibilities of chief executive officer ad interim of Credit Suisse First Boston in London. From 1982 to 1992 Hans-Ulrich Doerig was, as a member of the executive board, in charge of the multinational division, stock exchange and securities, capital markets Switzerland and overseas, corporate finance Switzerland and commercial business Far East and Australia. From 1993 until July 1996 he served as executive vice chairman of the board, heading the credit and finance committee as well as the audit committee of the board. Hans-Ulrich Doerig was appointed president of the general management of Credit Suisse in July 1996 and chief executive officer of Credit Suisse First Boston in 1997. Since April 2003 he has been vice chairman of the Credit Suisse Group Board of Directors and chairman of the risk committee. He lectured at Zurich University for 10 years and is the author of various books and publications.

Judith Hennigfeld

Managing Director, Institute for Corporate Culture Affairs eV, Frankfurt am Main, Germany

Judith Hennigfeld is Managing Director of the Institute for Corporate Culture Affairs (ICCA), which she joined in 2004. Previously she worked for more than ten years in international relations/affairs, focusing on social and environmental sustainability issues. From 1995 to 1999 she served at the UN Development

Programme in New York, where she was Programme Officer for the Bureau for Development Policy. Following this, she worked as an advisor to the European Commission and German Technical Cooperation.

Margaret Hodge MP

CSR Minister, Department of Trade and Industry, UK Government, United Kingdom

Margaret Hodge is Minister of State for Industry and the Regions. This includes responsibility for Business Relations, the Small Business Service, the Regions, the Company Law Reform Bill, Companies House, the Shareholder Executive and Corporate Social Responsibility. Margaret was elected Member of Parliament for Barking in 1994 and has carried out a number of roles in Government including Minister of State for Lifelong Learning and Higher Education, Department for Education and Skills, 2001–2003; Minister of State for Children, Young People and Families, Department for Education and Skills, 2003–2005; Minister of State for Employment and Welfare Reform in the Department for Work and Pensions 2005–2006. Margaret entered politics in 1973 as a councillor for the London Borough of Islington where she was Chair of the Housing Committee from 1975 to 1979 and Deputy Leader from 1981 to 1982, before becoming Leader from 1982 to 1992. She spent two years as a consultant for Price Waterhouse from 1992 to 1994. Prior to her appointment to the DfEE she was Joint Chairman of the House of Commons Education and Employment Select Committee.

Dr Markus Holzinger

Programme Manager, Volkswagen AutoUni, Wolfsburg, Germany

Markus Holzinger studied philosophy, sociology and German language and literature at the universities of Bamberg and Munich. A spell as scientific member of the project team 'The future of work' at the Ludwig-Maximilian University in Munich and a teaching position at the Technical University of Munich (sociology) were followed in 2000 by the award of a doctorate of philosophy with specialisation in sociology of science and technology on the basis of an examination of realism and constructivism in scientific and sociological theory. In November 2003 he took up the post of programme manager at the School of Humanities and Social Sciences of the Volkswagen AutoUni.

Dr Michael Kröher

Editor, Manager Magazin, Hamburg, Germany
Michael Kröher, born in Pirmasens in 1956, is editor of the *Manager Magazin* based in Hamburg, Germany. Michael Kröher obtained his doctorate from Hamburg University in 1990 and has written for many of Germany's leading publications including *Stern*, *Die Woche*, *Die Zeit* and *Geo* among others. He is responsible for the organisation and editorial content of the 'Good Company Ranking' published in the *Manager Magazin*.

Barbara J. Krumsiek

President and CEO, Calvert Group Ltd, Washington DC, United States
Barbara J. Krumsiek is president and CEO of Calvert, a mutual fund firm with over $11 billion in assets. Barbara J. Krumsiek is a 31-year veteran of the financial services industry having spent 23 years with Alliance Capital Management, LP. She graduated Phi Beta Kappa with honours from Douglass College, Rutgers University, receiving a bachelor's degree in mathematics. Barbara J. Krumsiek received a masters' degree in mathematics from the Courant Institute of Mathematical Sciences, New York University. In May 2002 Georgetown University awarded Barbara J. Krumsiek the degree of Doctor of Humane Letters, Honoris Causa, citing her work in advancing the critical dialogue regarding the role of business in society. Since joining Calvert in April 1997, Barbara J. Krumsiek has been active in domestic and international initiatives focused on encouraging corporations to adopt sustainable business practices,

often times with an emphasis on women's issues. Established in 2004, The Calvert Women's Principles are a code of corporate conduct focusing on gender equality and women's empowerment. In 2003, Calvert created a model charter language for corporate nominating committees focused on attaining diversity in corporate boardrooms.

Charito Kruvant

President and CEO, Creative Associates International Inc., Washington DC, United States

Charito Kruvant is president and CEO of Creative Associates International, Inc. a firm with more than 25 years of experience building capacity for education, civil society and communities in transition, especially in conflict and post-conflict situations. Charito Kruvant is chair of the board of the Community Foundation for the National Capital Region and of the advisory board of the US Small Business Administration Washington DC office. She also serves on the boards of Calvert, Venture Philanthropy Partners, Acacia Federal Savings Bank and the Summit Fund of Washington. Charito Kruvant has received numerous awards including the 2003 Entrepreneurial Visionary Award from the Women's Business Center of Washington DC; the US Small Business Administration's Women Business Owner of the Year in 1985 and 1988; Avon's Women of Enterprise Awards in 1988 and the National Association of Women Business Owners' Top Women Business Owners. Prior to founding Creative, Charito Kruvant was a prominent advocate for, and designer of, the Advisory and Learning Exchange in Washington DC, which provides bilingual education and learning disabled programmes. Born in Bolivia and raised in Argentina, Charito Kruvant has been a resident of metropolitan Washington DC for more than 30 years. She received a Bachelor of Arts from Colegio Ward in Argentina and a Master of Arts in early childhood development from the University of Maryland.

Professor Dr Ulrich Lehner

CEO, Henkel, Düsseldorf, Germany

Ulrich Lehner is chairman of Henkel. He was born in 1946 in Düsseldorf, and after training as an accountant, graduated in business and engineering at the Technical University of Darmstadt. Ulrich Lehner has had a career with Henkel stretching back to 1981, when he joined their tax department. He has been chairman at Henkel Düsseldorf since May 2000. He is on the board of various companies including Novartis, Switzerland; Ecolab Inc., USA, E.ON and HSBC. He is also honorary professor at the University of Münster.

Professor Dr Dirk Matten

Director, Centre for Research into Sustainability, Royal Holloway, University of London, United Kingdom; Member, World Corporate Ethics' Council/ICCA's Advisory Board

Dirk Matten is Professor of Business Ethics at Royal Holloway, University of London, UK. He is director of the Centre for Research into Sustainability (CRIS) which he joined in 2005 from the International Centre for Corporate Social Responsibility (ICCSR) at Nottingham University. He has published three books, more than 40 refereed journal articles and book chapters as well as over 60 conference papers on a wide range of topics in corporate environmental management, international management and business ethics. He is the author (with Andrew Crane) of *Business Ethics*, the first European text on business ethics, published in 2003 by Oxford University Press. He holds a PhD from Düsseldorf University and has taught business ethics and related topics at universities in Britain, Germany, Belgium, France and the Czech Republic. Prior to taking up an academic post in the UK, Dirk Matten spent more than three years in industry at the Frankfurt-based consultancy firm Newman Väth & Partner, where he was a senior consultant.

Fujio Mitarai

President and CEO, Canon Inc., Tokyo, Japan

Fujio Mitarai is president and CEO of Canon Inc. Born in 1935 in Kyushu, Japan, he graduated in 1961 in the department of law at Chuo University, Tokyo. Fujio Mitarai joined Canon in April 1961 and held a variety of positions both in Japan and the USA over the next four decades before being appointed president and CEO of Canon Inc. in March 1997. Fujio Mitarai also has a distinguished public service career, including being president of the Japanese Camera Industry Association, chairman, Japanese Federation of Economic Organisations (Keidanren) Committee on Corporate Governance, member of the Strategic Council on Intellectual Property, vice chairman, Japan Business Federation (Nippon Keidanren) and member of the Intellectual Property Strategy Headquarters (Cabinet Office). Fujio Mitarai has been awarded many honours during his career including the Officier de la Légion d'Honneur (France) in 1999, the Medal of Honour with Blue Ribbon (Japan) both in 1999 as well as the Commendation for Business Reformers (Japan) in 2002.

Liz Mohn

Member, Executive Committee, Bertelsmann Foundation, Gütersloh, Germany; Member, World Corporate Ethics' Council/ICCA's Advisory Board

Liz Mohn is the chair of the board of the Bertelsmann Verwaltungsgesellschaft mbH, member of the supervisory board of Bertelsmann AG and member of the executive committee of the board of the Bertelsmann Foundation. This Foundation, under the guidance of Liz Mohn, has focused on such areas as international dialogue among cultures, combining work and family as well as studies into successful corporate culture. Liz Mohn also supports the Bertelsmann aid fund, the medical information service, charities and information services for retirees, secretaries or spouses of employees in managerial positions. As founder and president of the Stiftung Deutsche Schlaganfall-Hilfe (foundation stroke patients in Germany), she engages in the areas of education, research and the creation of national and international networks.

Jan Oosterwijk

Founder and Managing Director, Natural Solutions, 's-Graveland, The Netherlands

Jan Oosterwijk, a Dutch national, is the founder and managing director of Natural Solutions, a company specialising in ecosystem/indigenous culture-friendly natural products. Jan Oosterwijk has previously been behind two of the most remarkable success cases of social responsible businesses, The Body Shop and Ben & Jerry's homemade ice cream. Jan Oosterwijk was one of the first entrepreneurs to establish a Body Shop franchise in Europe by establishing it in Belgium, Holland and Luxembourg. He then brought Ben & Jerry's into the same countries and has seen these businesses grow and develop into well-known and respected brands. Jan Oosterwijk is one of the foundersof the Social Venture Network Europe and also of the socially responsible venture capital fund for start-up ventures PYMWYMIC (Put Your Money Where Your Mouth Is Company).

Professor Dr Manfred Pohl

Founder and CEO, Institute for Corporate Culture Affairs eV, Frankfurt am Main, Germany; Member, World Corporate Ethics' Council/ICCA's Advisory Board

Manfred Pohl is founder and chief executive officer of the Institute for Corporate Culture Affairs. He is also founder of the European Association for Banking and Financial History, the Institute for Business History, Konvent für Deutschland, the Gesellschaft für Unternehmensgeschichte as well as the Frankfurter Kultur Komitee. Since 1997 he has been Honorary Professor at the

University of Frankfurt. In October 2001 he received the European Award for Culture at the European Parliament in Strasbourg. Manfred Pohl's most recent publications include *Bayernwerk (1921 bis 1996), Die Strabag (1923 bis 1998), VIAG (1923 bis 1998)*, Die Rentenbank, *Philipp Holzmann (1849 bis 1999), Von Stambul nach Bagdad – die Geschichte einer berühmten Eisenbahn* and *Hochtief und seine Geschichte. Von den Brüdern Helfmann bis ins 21. Jahrhundert.*

Gregory Tzeutschler Regaignon

Senior Researcher and North America Manager, Business & Human Rights Resource Centre, London, United Kingdom

Gregory Tzeutschler Regaignon is senior researcher and North America manager at the Business & Human Rights Resource Centre. He is an international lawyer with a background in African studies and international economics. He was previously an associate at Cleary, Gottlieb, Steen & Hamilton, a leading international law firm based in New York. Gregory Tzeutschler Regaignon has worked with human rights organisations in the United States and Indonesia, including Human Rights Watch, the National Endowment for Democracy and Legal Aid Institute of Indonesia, on corporate responsibility, labour rights and civil/political rights. Gregory Tzeutschler Regaignon was educated at Columbia Law School (JD, Harlan Fiske Stone Scholar), Johns Hopkins School of Advanced International Studies (SAIS) (MA, African Studies and International Economics) and Amherst College (BA, magna cum laude).

Birgit Riess

Head of Corporate Social Responsibility, Bertelsmann Foundation, Gütersloh, Germany

Birgit Riess is the head of corporate social responsibility, Bertelsmann Foundation. After studying business, law and social science, Birgit Riess organised and undertook a number of research projects in business and social studies at the Law and Economics Institute at the University of Kassel. In 1996 Birgit Riess joined the Bertelsmann Stiftung in Gütersloh, and led projects in the area of corporate culture and co-determination. Since 2004, Birgit Riess has managed the corporate social responsibility department and is now a member of the extended management council of the Bertelsmann Stiftung.

Klaus Richter

Module Manager, Volkswagen AutoUni, Wolfsburg, Germany

Klaus Richter studied German language and literature, sociology and philosophy at the Georg August University in Göttingen (Germany), majoring in theories of society and epistemology. He joined Volkswagen AutoUni's School of Humanities and Social Sciences in 2003. He developed the study module 'Corporate ethics and corporate governance', taught for the Volkswagen TOP management and the students of the Volkswagen AutoUni. Since May 2005 he has been studying for a PhD in philosophy entitled 'Corporate social responsibility in multinational corporations considering Volkswagen Corporation as example'. His research focus is on corporate social responsibility, corporate strategy, theories of democracy and business ethics implementation.

Anita Roper

Director of Sustainability, Alcoa, Pittsburgh, United States

Anita Roper, born in 1960 in Melbourne, studied management at the Monash University in Melbourne, Australia. She joined Alcoa as director of sustainability in January 2004. Anita Roper came to Alcoa after serving as acting secretary general of the International Council on Mining and Metals (ICMM) in London from November 2002 until September 2003. Prior to that post, she served as deputy secretary general of ICMM, where her role as chief operating officer gave her the responsibility for managing the council's day-to-day operations. Leading up to her role with the ICMM, Anita Roper went on assignment in November 1999 from WMC Resources Ltd, an Australian-based mineral resources company, to serve on the Global Mining Initiative (GMI). The world's leading mining, metals and minerals companies sponsored the GMI to develop their industry's role in the transition to sustainable development. The GMI contributed to preparations for the World Summit on Sustainable Development held in South Africa in September 2002 and resulted in the creation of the ICMM. From June 1998 until January 2001, Anita Roper was on another temporary assignment from WMC to the International Council on Metals and the Environment (ICME) in Ottawa, Canada, and served as its vice president of external relations. Prior to being sent on temporary overseas assignments, Anita Roper managed WMC's public policy unit at the company's headquarters in Melbourne. Anita Roper has recently joined as a member of the board of the Women's Network for a Sustainable Future and is also on the editorial board of the publication *Corporate Responsibility Management*.

Andreas von Schumann

Director, GTZ AgenZ Gesellschaft für Technische Zusammenarbeit, Eschborn, Germany

Andreas von Schumann is the director of GTZ AgenZ. He is a social scientist with 20 years of experience in international cooperation. Andreas von Schumann sees understanding sustainability as the nexus for politics, the private sector and society as one of the major challenges for the coming generation. As founder of AgenZ, he is responsible for the management of complex and highly political processes. Before founding AgenZ he was deputy director of the GTZ Expo 2000 Office, which bore the overall responsibility for a German government programme worth 100 million DM for the World Exposition EXPO 2000 in Hanover. From 1991 to 1997 he was press spokesman and head of press and editorial section of the GTZ and special-task manager for communication projects in Croatia (reconstruction), Russia (business promotion in West Siberia) and Romania (privatisation).

Yoshio Shirai

Senior Managing Director, Toyota Motor Corporation, Tokyo, Japan
Yoshio Shirai is senior managing director of the Toyota Motor Corporation. Yoshio Shirai completed the master's course in mechanical engineering at Hokkaido University in 1973 and joined Toyota that year. He has held a number of positions related to his degree. Yoshio Shirai was appointed general manager of Body Engineering Division 2 at the Vehicle Development Centre 2 in 1997. In June 2001 he was made a director, a title that was changed to managing officer in June 2003, and in June 2005 he became a senior managing director. In Yoshio Shirai's point of view, the key to Toyota succeeding against strong competition and maintaining its role as a world leader, in this time of rapid change, is its technology, rapid implementation and a strong commitment to research and development. He also stresses the importance of setting a good example and teaching younger personnel how to think and act globally.

Annabel Short

Senior Researcher and International Outreach Manager, Business & Human Rights Resource Centre, London, United Kingdom
Annabel Short is senior researcher and international outreach manager at the Business & Human Rights Resource Centre. She has worked as an environmental journalist; her academic background includes Spanish, French and development studies. Before joining the Resource Centre Annabel Short was a specialist in corporate social and environmental reporting at Context Group consultants in London. As a freelance journalist she has written for magazines such as *Geographical, Ethical Corporation* and *Tomorrow*, and wrote *Go Make A Difference!*, a book of environmental tips, for *The Ecologist*. She reported on the World Summit on Sustainable Development

for a UNEP-sponsored media project. Annabel Short spent one year working in Lima, Peru, with the Reuters news agency and as a campaigns volunteer at Amnesty International. She has an MSc in development studies from Birkbeck College (University of London), a postgraduate diploma in periodical journalism from City University, London, and an MA Joint Honours in Spanish and French from Edinburgh University.

Frank Straub
President, BLANCO, Oberderdingen, Germany
Frank Straub, born in 1945 in Oberderdingen, Germany, is the grandson of Heinrich Blanc, founder of BLANCO and co-founder of the components for electrical appliances company – EGO. After serving as a military service officer in the Air Force, Frank Straub studied business administration in Munich, before moving on to work for the EGO company. In 1975 he became a member of the board of directors of the advisory board and of the supervisory board of the EGO group. Since 1976, he has been head of the finance department of BLANCO and since 1985 managing director of finance and accounting of BLANCO. In 1993 he became the president of BLANCO. Frank Straub has been a member of the state board of the Baden-Württemberg Business Council (Wirtschaftsrat) since 1995 and since 2002 he has also been a member of the global governing board of the Caux Round Table.

Katja Suhr
Deputy Director, GTZ AgenZ Gesellschaft für Technische Zusammenarbeit, Eschborn, Germany
Katja Suhr is the deputy director of GTZ AgenZ responsible for the area of sustainable management and strategic marketing. Katja Suhr has a masters in business administration with working experience in industrialised and developing countries, combining issues of international cooperation with those of globally active companies. As a founding member of AgenZ since 2000, she bundles GTZ's instruments and international experience in the field of sustainable

management in order to improve the situation of companies in both developing and industrialised countries. From 1998 to 2000 she worked with small and medium-sized companies in Zimbabwe and South Africa. Katja Suhr started her career in 1996 with the international consulting firm Kienbaum Development Service in the field of privatisation in Eastern Europe and Germany.

Dr Dirko Thomsen

Module Manager, Volkswagen AutoUni, Wolfsburg, Germany

Dirko Thomsen obtained his PhD in Münster and a Master of Science (econ.) in London, after previously completing his studies of art history in Bonn. From 1990 to 1992, after the fall of the Berlin Wall, Dirko Thomsen taught philosophy at the University of Rostock and worked thereafter for the advertising agency Scholz & Friends in Dresden. Since 1992 he has designed educational and sociopolitical projects at Volkswagen as well as developing strategies for education and training. Dirko Thomsen is responsible for the academic programmes 'Innovation and creativity' and 'Mobility and society' at the School of Humanities and Social Sciences of the Volkswagen AutoUni.

Nick Tolhurst

Director, Institute for Corporate Culture Affairs eV, Frankfurt am Main, Germany

Nick Tolhurst joined the Institute for Corporate Culture Affairs (ICCA) as director in April 2004. Before joining ICCA, Nick Tolhurst worked for the British Foreign Ministry in Germany, advising British companies in Germany and German companies investing in the UK. Before joining the UK Foreign Office, Nick Tolhurst served at the European Commission at DG II (Economics and Financial Affairs) preparing for the introduction of the euro in differing cultures and economic systems. Nick Tolhurst studied at London Metropolitan University (UK) and completed a masters' degree at Osnabrück University (Germany) both in European studies specialising in economics and cultural studies. His thesis dissertation was on the role of differing cultural and economic contexts with regard to the European monetary union process.

Ben Verwaayen
CEO, BT British Telecom Group, London, United Kingdom
Ben Verwaayen joined BT on 14 January 2002 as chief executive. Ben Verwaayen was born in February 1952, is a Dutch national and graduated with a master's degree in law and international politics from the State University of Utrecht, Holland. Before joining BT Group, Ben Verwaayen had been, since October 1997, with Lucent Technologies Inc. His position on leaving was vice chairman of the management board. Before this, Ben Verwaayen was executive vice president and chief operating officer, and before this, executive vice president, international. Prior to Lucent, Ben Verwaayen was with Koninklijke PTT Nederland (KPN). From 1988 to 1997, he was president and managing director of KPN's PTT Telecom. From 1996 to mid-1997, Ben Verwaayen was chairman of the Unisource European venture with Telia, Swisscom and Telefonica, and chairman of AT&T/Unisource. Between 1975 and 1988, he was with ITT Nederland BV and had become general manager after enjoying a series of positions in business development, HR and public relations.

Peter Walter
Managing Director, Beta Healthcare GmbH & Co. KG, Augsburg, Germany
After his Fachabitur (baccalaureate diploma) Peter Walter undertook vocational training to become an industrial sales representative. He subsequently studied business management and took over the management of the family business in the jewellery sector. He crossed over to the pharmaceuticals sector in 1974 and took up a post as a medical representative for Boehringer Ingelheim. Between 1978 and 1993 he was a medical representative and regional head

of division for Ciba-Geigy. He started to build up betapharm Arzneimittel GmbH in 1993 as the company's managing director. In 2002 Peter Walter received the *Freiheit und Verantwortung* (Freedom and Responsibility) award from former German president Johannes Rau, which is awarded to those companies which stand out in the area of social responsibility. Since June 2005, Peter Walter has been managing director of Beta Healthcare GmbH & Co. KG and has taken on the task of further development of the group's commitment.

Stephen B. Young

Global Executive Director, Caux Round Table, Saint Paul, United States
Stephen Young is global executive director of the Caux Round Table and president of Winthrop Consulting. He is a member of the Bar Association of the State of Minnesota. He graduated from Harvard Law School, JD cum laude 1974 and Harvard College, AB degree magna cum laude 1967. He was assistant dean at Harvard Law School and dean and professor of law at the Hamline Law School. He has written and taught on fiduciary theory, corporate law and finance, international law, law and religion and Chinese and Vietnamese jurisprudence and is the author of the book *Moral Capitalism*.

Professor Dr Walther Ch. Zimmerli

President, Volkswagen AutoUni, Member of the World Corporate Ethics' Council/ICCA's Advisory Board
Walther Ch. Zimmerli is a professor of philosophy and since 2002 founding president of the Volkswagen AutoUni in Wolfsburg and member of the management team of Volkswagen Coaching GmbH. He studied at Yale College (Connecticut/USA), at the University of Göttingen (Germany) and obtained his doctorate in Zürich (Switzerland) in 1971 where he became professor of philosophy. From 1978 till 1988 he was professor for philosophy at the Technical University of Braunschweig. And from 1988 till 1996 philosophy professor at the University of Bamberg und

Erlangen/Nuremberg and later from 1996 till 1999 professor for systems philosophy at Philipps University in Marburg. Walther Ch. Zimmerli became president of Universität Witten/Herdecke in 1999, before taking up his current position at Volkswagen AutoUni. He has been a visiting professor in the USA, Australia, Japan and South Africa, where he has been senate visiting professor at the Stellenbosch University for the last 10 years. In April 2003, Walther Ch. Zimmerli was made honorary professor of the Technical University of Braunschweig. In 1996, Walther Ch. Zimmerli received the International Humboldt Prize for research.

Foreword

Judith Hennigfeld, Manfred Pohl and Nick Tolhurst

*C*orporate social responsibility (CSR) – undertaking business in an ethical way in order to achieve sustainable development, not only in economic terms, but also in the social and environmental sphere – has become increasingly important in today's business world. However, much debate remains concerning the role of CSR and companies' CSR policies in society. For example, to what extent are companies responsible for how they go about their business, how they deal with employees and how they operate at both global and local levels? Sceptics of CSR question whether, so long as the activities of business operations are covered by existing legislation, then, there is really a business case for companies to make contributions beyond this.

The answer lies in the awareness of the role of businesses in society. The 'business case' for CSR involves corporations taking a broader perspective of company performance than merely concentrating on the short-term maximisation of shareholder value to the exclusion of everything else. Many companies see that to be successful in the long term they need not only to utilise the resources of society, but also to nurture those societies in which they operate, and with whom they are increasingly interdependent. As Charito Kruvant and Barbara Krumsiek note (see Chapter 13), 'Profitability is essential. However, many companies today are realising that a successful business is one that not only earns acceptable profits but also helps to build a sustainable future and enhance the quality of life.'

The new role of corporations as full partners in their communities is represented by this holistic approach including not only shareholder value as a driving force but also obligations toward stakeholders, such as employees, suppliers or society as a whole. This approach is well summed up by Ben Verwaayen (Chapter 12), CEO of the BT Group; 'CSR (...) requires a company to make a choice – whether to make it a "tick in the box" issue or to see it as something that, if practised on a day-to-day basis, at the heart of a company, can contribute to the bottom line.' Accepting and implementing these additional responsibilities in the form of CSR lies at the heart of today's discussions around the topic. Implementing CSR in companies' business processes remains an important challenge and one which companies cannot achieve without embedding this in their corporate culture, for as Sir Geoffrey Chandler (Chapter 3) observes '(...), so long as money to shareholders is seen as the purpose of the company, CSR will remain a diversion (...).'

The CSR movement has gained momentum and with it many organisations have been established focusing on environmental protection, sustainability, human rights and the implementation of CSR and corporate culture. The diversity of organisations and their services and activities cause additional confusion concerning the very concept of CSR and its implementation within companies. Therefore the Institute for Corporate Culture Affairs (ICCA) offers a comprehensive approach including its services as a knowledge broker, publications and events providing essential knowledge and experience in the field of CSR. As an independent not-for-profit organisation, ICCA specialises in primary research and enables companies to tap into its expertise, resources and networks benefiting from its overriding mission of combining the best theoretical grounding in the subject with practical examples of how companies implement CSR policies and strategies successfully. Leading CEOs, business people and academics work together on the key questions of CSR and corporate culture feeding back their experiences, newly gained knowledge and perceptions into their companies and organisations. Since its foundation in 2003, ICCA has worked together with the top companies operating in the world today, both to assist in the mainstreaming of CSR within corporations, as well as to bring the subject to a greater audience.

With *The ICCA Handbook on Corporate Social Responsibility*, the ICCA presents a unique source for good practice and lessons learned on the implementation of CSR as well as underlining the fact that CSR should arise from a corporate culture, implying values and norms which in themselves endorse ecologically sustainable and socially fair ways of doing business. This application-oriented handbook serves as a practical guide to CSR implementation as a cross-cutting task with respect to a corporation's past, its present behaviour and our future as a global society. The *Handbook* explores the general concept of CSR offering valid definitions and theories as a basis for future action, investigates implementation approaches and provides inside accounts of well-known CEOs, leading academics and CSR organisations. In their essays, contributors share their experiences, good practices and lessons learned, offering unique insights on how to put CSR into practice and make it part of the core business of companies.

The *Handbook* is divided into three parts, offering an introduction to the topic of CSR, sharing good practices and lessons learned and providing examples on ranking and auditing approaches.

As a reader you will find a variety of articles including topics such as microfinance, business ethics, measurement, ranking and auditing from companies such as Volkswagen AG, Alcoa, Canon, Toyota, British Telecom and many more.

The world's first and only CSR minister, appointed by the UK government, Margaret Hodge, shares the British strategy towards CSR and how his government supports companies' engagement in CSR in Chapter 5. In Chapter 13, Barbara Krumsiek, president and CEO of Calvert, and Charito Kruvant, president and CEO of Creative Associates International based in Washington DC, promote the empowerment of women in the business world who represent 'an untapped economic resource' in the development of societies and economies. Another example is Jan Oosterwijk (Chapter 11), former director of the executive board of The Body Shop International, who shares a remarkable success story of CSR mainstreaming at The Body Shop even before CSR was addressed and defined, as well as his own personal ideas and experience on combining business with a respect for nature.

These are just a few examples of the many excellent essays presented in this *Handbook* sharing insight into companies' approaches worldwide. ICCA is very proud to present these first-hand accounts of the CSR and business community and hopes to encourage further exchange of good practices and the creation of synergies among international corporations in this area.

The ICCA Handbook on Corporate Social Responsibility reflects the diversity of CSR experiences and creates an invaluable source of knowledge thereby strengthening the network of CSR leaders. Large-scale enterprises, such as those represented in this *Handbook*, influence stakeholders significantly and have an enormous impact on environments and social conditions of the societies in which they are active. Therefore, they, more than others, can act as catalysts in bringing about major changes for the better with regard to environmental sustainability, ethical behaviour and socially responsible business practices. This *Handbook* presents CEOs and companies that have seized the opportunities offered by CSR and is intended to encourage future exchange and development in the field of CSR.

The Institute for Corporate Culture Affairs would like to thank all participants who have contributed to this publication – our highly valued members as well as external partners. Your experiences and knowledge in the field of CSR and its implementation will support the creation of a common understanding and help shape the key aspects creating value for companies and societies alike.

Acknowledgements

The Institute for Corporate Culture Affairs (ICCA) would like to express its deepest thanks to all those who made the publication of *The ICCA Handbook on Corporate Social Responsibility* possible.

We would like to place on record our thanks, first of all, to all those who so generously offered their contributory articles, informed by their professional and personal experience. We are grateful that they chose to share their good practices and lessons learned on corporate social responsibility and corporate culture via our publication and thus provide examples of how companies can undertake their business in a sustainable and responsible manner to a wider audience. In particular we would like to thank our members and partners who have supported our work over the last two years and who have generously advised us. We would particularly like to thank Mr Haruo Funabashi, president of the Sirius Institute, for his good advice and assistance.

ICCA would also like to thank the many people who contributed towards the realisation of this publication including ICCA project manager Katja Böhmer as well as intern Julia Klamp and freelance adviser Jutta Vahrson who assisted in the research, compilation and contact work in setting up this publication.

Frankfurt am Main, 31 March 2006
Professor Dr Manfred Pohl
Judith Hennigfeld
Nick Tolhurst
Institute for Corporate Culture Affairs

PART I

INTRODUCTION AND BACKGROUND TO CSR

Why Do Companies Engage in Corporate Social Responsibility? Background, Reasons and Basic Concepts

Dirk Matten

INTRODUCTION

'The movement on corporate social responsibility has won the battle of ideas.' This was the opening line of a 20-page supplement on CSR in *The Economist* in early 2005 (Crook, 2005). In fact, for managers in today's global business world CSR is an acronym that can scarcely be avoided. Basically all of the world's top multinationals engage in CSR in some form and there is almost no country in which businesses have not taken up the challenge of CSR in some way. Even in a country such as India, in the West sometimes rather snobbishly dubbed an 'emerging economy',

The ICCA Handbook on Corporate Social Responsibility   Edited by J. Hennigfeld, M. Pohl and N. Tolhurst
© 2006 John Wiley & Sons, Ltd

a company such as the Tata Steel Corporation prides itself on a legacy of no fewer than 100 years in active CSR (Elankumaran, Seal and Hashmi, 2005). And the contributions by leaders from various companies compiled in this volume speak for themselves. CSR is one of the key challenges for today's business leaders globally.

There is, however, less clarity about what 'corporate social responsibility' actually means. Apart from the novelty of CSR, one of the key problems is the plethora and heterogeneity of actors in the CSR world. The corporate world is not the sole context in which CSR is addressed in rather different approaches and strategies across the globe. CSR provides an arena for political actors and key players in civil society. It is also top of the agenda on many high-profile political platforms, such as the World Economic Forum, and governments have increasingly tried to influence the agenda, be it at the national level (such as the UK's minister for CSR in the Department of Trade and Industry) or via supranational initiatives (such as the Green and White Papers on CSR issued by the European Union). Furthermore, a burgeoning jungle of consultants, NGOs, foundations and other activist groups is proof of the topic's growing profile. And last but by no means least, this development has been pushed further by a growing number of academic institutes and centres across the globe, which have not only produced more literature on CSR but have also contributed to making CSR a central element of today's and tomorrow's business leaders' education.

In this introductory chapter to the *ICCA Handbook* I will try to provide some clarity in the understanding of the concept and a few yardsticks for navigating through the contemporary debate on CSR with all its fancy jargon and daily growing inventions of buzzwords.[1] In doing so, I will also try to provide some idea about the reasons why companies have taken up the challenge of CSR. I will start with a basic definition of CSR based on what could be

---

[1] In doing so I will closely follow the more in-depth analysis of my textbook, co-authored with Professor Andrew Crane (Crane and Matten, 2004).

considered the most longstanding and broadly accepted definition of CSR from an academic perspective. Subsequently, I will sketch out key arguments for CSR, each approaching the topic from a different perspective. Finally, I will provide an assessment of how the debate is likely to unfold in the future.

WHAT IS CSR? THE TEXTBOOK ANSWER

There has been some debate as to whether CSR is such a novel phenomenon at all. If one talked to someone like Sir Adrian Cadbury, one of the leading voices in the contemporary CSR debate on responsible corporate governance in the UK and beyond, he might easily argue that his great-grandfathers in the nineteenth century were already seasoned practitioners of CSR – albeit without labelling their considerable philanthropic engagement for their workforces in and local communities around the Cadbury's chocolate factories in Bournville near Birmingham in this way. Similar cases could be made by the Thyssens and Krupps in Germany or the Rockefellers, Dukes and Carnegies in the USA – all of whom spent considerable sums of money on promoting the general well-being of their society in the nineteenth and early twentieth centuries, be it in social projects, education or the arts (Cannon, 1994).

It was, however, in the United States in the early 1950s that the role of the corporation in society became subject to a more systematic debate and many consider Howard R. Bowen's book *Social Responsibilities of the Businessman* (1953) to be the landmark contribution in the still ongoing debate on CSR (Carroll, 1999). Arguably, from this starting point, the US in particular led the debate on the role and responsibilities of companies in society and by the 1970s a growing consensus on the understanding of CSR had emerged. The most longstanding and authoritative voice in this debate is management professor Archie Carroll, based

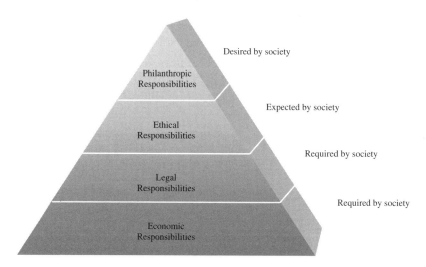

Figure 1.1 Carroll's (1991) Four-Part Model of Corporate Social Responsibility

at the University of Georgia, who suggested probably the most established and accepted model of CSR. It is the 'Four-Part Model of Corporate Social Responsibility' (Carroll, 1979), subsequently refined in later publications (Carroll, 1991; Carroll and Buchholtz, 2002). This model is depicted in Figure 1.1.

Carroll regards CSR as a multi-layered concept, which can be differentiated into four interrelated aspects – economic, legal, ethical and philanthropic responsibilities. He presents these different responsibilities as consecutive layers within a pyramid, such that 'true' social responsibility requires the meeting of all four levels consecutively. Hence, Carroll and Buchholtz (2000: 35) offer the following *definition*: 'Corporate social responsibility encompasses the economic, legal, ethical, and philanthropic expectations placed on organizations by society at a given point in time.'

- **Economic responsibility**. Companies have shareholders who demand a reasonable return on their investments, they have employees who want safe and fairly paid jobs, they have customers who demand good quality products at a fair price etc. This is by definition the reason why businesses are set up in society and thus a company's first responsibility is to be a properly functioning economic unit and to stay in business. This first layer of CSR is the basis for all the subsequent responsibilities, which rest on this (ideally) solid basis. According to Carroll (1991), the satisfaction of economic responsibilities is thus required of all corporations.

- **Legal responsibility**. The legal responsibility of corporations demands that businesses abide by the law and 'play by the rules of the game'. Laws are understood as the codification of society's moral views, and therefore abiding by these standards is a necessary prerequisite for any further reasoning about social responsibilities. In some sense, one might consider legal responsibility as a truism, which corporations have to fulfil just to keep their licence to operate. However, one only needs to open the business pages nowadays to see that the ongoing coverage of corporate scams, scandals and lawsuits reveals that abiding by the law, not bending the rules and not cutting corners, can hardly be taken for granted in today's business world. As with economic responsibilities, Carroll (1991) suggests that the satisfaction of legal responsibilities is required of all corporations seeking to be socially responsible.

- **Ethical responsibility**. These responsibilities oblige corporations to do what is right, just and fair even when they are not compelled to do so by the legal framework. For example, when Shell sought to dispose of the Brent Spar oil platform at sea in 1995, it had the full agreement of the law and the British government, yet still fell victim to a vigorous campaign against the action by Greenpeace as well as a consumer boycott. As a result, the *legal* decision to dispose of the platform at sea was eventually reversed, since the firm had failed to take account of society's (or at least the protestors') wider *ethical* expectations. Carroll (1991) argues that ethical responsibilities therefore consist of what is generally *expected* by society, over and above economic and legal expectations.

- **Philanthropic responsibility**. Lastly, at the tip of the pyramid, the fourth level of CSR looks at the philanthropic responsibilities of corporations. The Greek work 'philanthropy' means literally 'the love of the fellow human' and by using this idea in a business context, the model includes all those issues that are within the corporation's discretion to improve the quality of life of employees, local communities and ultimately society in general. This aspect of CSR addresses a great variety of issues, including matters such as charitable donations, the building of recreation facilities for employees and their families, support for local schools, or sponsoring of art and sports events. According to Carroll (1991), philanthropic responsibilities are therefore merely *desired* of corporations without being expected or required, making them 'less important than the other three categories'.

The *advantage* of the four-part model of CSR is that it structures the various social responsibilities into different dimensions, yet does not seek to explain social responsibility without acknowledging the very real demands placed on the firm to be profitable and legal. In this sense, it is fairly pragmatic.

However, its main *limitation* is that it does not adequately address the problem of what should happen when two or more responsibilities are in conflict. For example, the threat of plant closures often raises the problem of balancing economic responsibilities (of remaining efficient and profitable) with ethical responsibilities to provide secure jobs to employees. A second problem with the model, and indeed with much of the CSR literature, is that it is strongly biased towards the US context. And in fact the more interesting contributions to recent debates have emerged elsewhere, such as in Europe (Matten and Moon, 2004a), Africa (Visser, Middleton and McIntosh, 2005) and Asia (Birch and Moon, 2004).

As mentioned earlier, alongside the initial debate on CSR, which originated in the US, the increasingly global spread of the idea has resulted in a number of reasons and concepts for companies to become involved in CSR. In the following four sections of this chapter I will map out four main avenues in which CSR ideas have been talked about over the last couple of years.[2]

ECONOMIC DRIVERS OF CSR: THE BUSINESS CASE

A first, and arguably the most widely embraced, reason for companies to engage in CSR is based on the insight that in many cases it simply makes good business sense to behave in a fashion that is perceived as responsible by society. This is based on a number of distinct, but related arguments, many of which tend to be couched in terms of enlightened self-interest, i.e. the corporation takes on social responsibilities insofar as doing so promotes its own self-interest. For example:

- Corporations perceived as being socially responsible might be rewarded with extra and/or more satisfied customers, while perceived irresponsibility may result in boycotts or other undesirable consumer actions.
- Similarly, employees might be attracted to work for, and even be more committed to, corporations perceived as being socially responsible.
- Voluntarily committing to social actions and programmes may forestall legislation and ensure greater corporate independence from government.

---

[2] In using those four main directions, I refer to a categorisation recently developed by business ethicist Domènec Melé, based at the University of Navarra (Garriga and Melé, 2004), which I draw on substantially in the following sections of this chapter.

- Making a positive contribution to society might be regarded as a long-term investment in a safer, better-educated and more equitable community, which subsequently benefits the corporation by creating an improved and stable context in which to do business.

Interestingly, this group of arguments was raised initially by one of the harshest critics of CSR. In 1970, just after the first big wave of the CSR movement in the US, Nobel-prize-winning economist Milton Friedman published an article that has since become a classic among all those who question the alleged social role of corporations. Under the provocative title 'The social responsibility of business is to increase its profits' (Friedman, 1970) he vigorously protested against the notion of social responsibilities for corporations. He based his argument on three main premises:

- Only human beings have a moral responsibility for their actions. His first substantial point was that corporations are not human beings and therefore cannot assume true moral responsibility for their actions. Since corporations are set up by individual human beings, it is those human beings who are then individually responsible for the actions of the corporation.
- It is managers' responsibility to act solely in the interests of shareholders. His second point was that as long as a corporation abides by the legal framework society has set up for business, the only responsibility of the managers of the corporation is to make a profit, because it is for this task that the firm has been set up and the managers have been employed. Acting for any other purpose constitutes a betrayal of their special responsibility to shareholders and thus essentially represents 'theft' from shareholders' pockets.
- Social issues and problems are the proper province of the state rather than corporate managers. Friedman's third main point was that managers should not, and cannot, decide what is in society's best interests. This is the job of government. Corporate managers are neither trained to set and achieve social goals, nor (unlike politicians) are they democratically elected to do so.

In arguing against CSR, Friedman (1970) in fact does not dispute the validity of such actions, but rather says that they are not CSR at all when carried out for reasons of self-interest, but merely profit-maximisation 'under the cloak of social responsibility'. This may well be true, and to a large extent depends on the *primary motivations* of the decision maker (Bowie, 1991). It is not so much a matter of whether profit subsequently arises from social actions, but whether profit or altruism was the main reason for the action in the first place. However, corporate motives are difficult, sometimes impossible, to determine. Moreover, despite numerous academic studies, a direct relationship between social responsibility and profitability has been almost impossible to unambiguously 'prove' (Griffin and Mahon, 1997; Waddock and Graves, 1997). Even though the overall weight of evidence seems to suggest some kind of positive relationship, there is still the issue of causality. When successful companies are seen to be operating CSR programmes, it is just as reasonable to suggest that CSR does not contribute to success, but rather that financial success frees the company to indulge in the 'luxury' of CSR.

Looking at CSR then as a business case would chiefly embrace the first level of responsibility of Carroll's pyramid (Figure 1.1): simply because CSR enhances profitability, corporations should take the interests, concerns and demands of wider society around them into account and address these in a way that results in a (long-term) profitable business environment. In the following I will have a look at two key areas in which this CSR approach has been rather influential.

CSR as increasing shareholder value

Even the most vehement opponents of CSR admit that certain voluntary initiatives to meet the interests of groups beyond the immediate owners of the firm can have a long-term positive impact for owners themselves – even though they would then consider 'CSR' to be a misnomer. In particular agency theorists, such as

Harvard's Michael Jensen (2002), generally not the usual suspects in the CSR world, have recently made the case for CSR as 'enlightened value maximisation'. The criteria for CSR activities for the corporation then should be in how far the money spent on wider society's interest has a long-term positive effect on the maximisation of shareholder value.

For many companies, the stock market provides a further incentive to engage in CSR. With the general public apparently becoming increasingly concerned about CSR, a large and rapidly growing body of shareholders that specifically factors ethical concerns into investment decisions has emerged (Rivoli, 1995; Taylor, 2001). Ethical investment is thus the use of ethical, social and environmental criteria in the selection and management of investment portfolios, generally consisting of company shares (Cowton, 1994). For a growing number of companies CSR is not so much an agenda pushed by their community affairs or human resources department, but rather an imperative raised by their CFO who finds compliance with investors' CSR-related criteria to be a key to lucrative procurement of capital.

The criteria for choosing an investment can either be negative or positive. Investors can either exclude certain companies with undesired features (negative screening) or adopt companies with certain desired features (positive screening). Besides investment brokers and portfolio management companies, the key actors in ethical investment are funds that offer investment opportunities in company shares complying with certain defined ethical criteria.

Increasingly, analysts and investment firms question companies on their ethical policies, as the existence of ethical funds has proven to be not just simply a new niche in the market, but has drawn attention to a previously ignored issue. As Rob Hardy, an asset manager from the investment banker JP Morgan Fleming in London puts it: 'We monitor the environmental and social profiles of the companies we invest in and adopt an engagement approach with the worst performers. I like to think we're waking companies up to these issues' (Cowe, 2002). Ultimately, ethical investment obviously has an ongoing disciplinary effect on a wide range of companies, mainly because socially irresponsible behaviour makes them less attractive for a growing number of investors. This movement is further enhanced by the development of stock-market indexes, such as the US-based Dow Jones Sustainability Index or the UK-based FTSE4Good Index, which provide a performance ranking of a portfolio of companies listed in the index according to the fulfilment of certain CSR-related criteria.

CSR as competitive advantage

A growing number of voices link CSR activities directly to the competitive advantage of companies. For instance, strategy guru Michael Porter has applied his well-established model of competitive advantage to CSR (Porter and Kramer, 2002). He argues that in certain situations, CSR – in particular philanthropic investment into societal causes – will create a long-term competitive advantage not only for the individual company but also for the entire cluster in which the company operates. A classic example would be a software company that provides its software to schools or libraries for free. This will not only give students and local communities access to a scarce resource but in the long term will enhance computer literacy in society with long-term beneficial effects for the future market opportunities of the company itself, as well as for its competitors and other players in the industrial cluster. Furthermore, Porter and Kramer would argue that companies can do certain jobs better than governments, because they have the skills for specialised tasks, meaning that strategic philanthropy by companies would also contribute to making society competitive in a far more effective manner than government money could.

A similar win–win approach has gained unprecedented currency with the 'bottom of the pyramid' (BOP) concept developed by

C.K. Prahalad and others (Prahalad and Hammond, 2002; Hart, 2005; Prahalad, 2005). At the core of this approach is the simple insight that most Western multinationals, particular those producing mass consumer products such as food, detergents, cars, mobile phones etc., serve merely the upper 5 to 10% of consumers in emerging or developing markets such as China, India, Brazil or Nigeria. A huge market of potentially up to four billion consumers has, however, remained untapped just because, these authors argue, Western corporations simply transfer their longstanding business models to countries in which consumer behaviour follows completely different patterns. Rather than, for instance, selling a 20-kilogram box of detergent to a consumer, a company should switch to selling its detergent in little sachets geared to income levels and consumption patterns, allowing consumers to buy just the amount of detergent they need for the day. One could cite a long list of successful examples from other industries, such as banking, communication technology, consumer electronics or transportation – to name but a few.

From a CSR perspective, the proponents of the BOP approach argue that a business model attuned to the needs and contingencies of emerging markets does not only provide these formerly disenfranchised people access to much coveted products taken for granted in the developed West, but also allows these people a much greater stake in the process of actual wealth creation. The latter is because much of the BOP thinking is predicated on the assumption that successful business models would also necessarily call for significantly larger parts of the value chain to be located within these markets. At the same time, by adopting the BOP approach these companies would also pursue their business interest, as this model would provide access to a larger global market.

It should be mentioned, however, that the BOP model has led to considerable controversy. While the CSR-related arguments of its proponents seem tantalising, critics have argued that BOP is in fact producing exactly the opposite of its intended effects: it will make these countries even more dependent on the West, will reproduce rather problematic Western consumption and production patterns in the developing world and will ultimately infringe the economic independence and success of these countries, as Western multinationals will easily be able to force local competitors out of the market.

MANAGERIAL DRIVERS OF CSR: BALANCING STAKEHOLDER INTERESTS

A second group of reasons for companies to engage in CSR is related to their day-to-day business challenge of balancing the diverse interests of stakeholders. CSR in this perspective offers strategies and tools to address the issues and demands faced by the company in its relations with a variety of groups in society. Though implicitly linked to the business-case arguments discussed above, many business leaders tend to talk about CSR in a far more pragmatic fashion: rather than musing about the ideological status of CSR as profit maximisation, they see CSR as a way of tackling the day-to-day issues of maintaining the company's licence to operate. Typical questions here would be, for instance, the use of new technologies, undesired side effects of products, outsourcing of jobs or the environmental and social impacts of business on local communities. CSR provides companies with solutions in situations where they have to address all these different interests and work towards solutions acceptable to all parties involved.

Closely related to this pragmatic challenge is stakeholder theory, one of the main buzzwords of CSR and indeed the most popular theoretical concept in business–society relations. Furthermore, this perspective has also kindled considerable interest in the question of how one can actually manage the company's success, its 'corporate social performance' with regard to these day-to-day challenges. In the following, I will briefly examine each concept in turn.

Stakeholder theory of the firm

The stakeholder theory of the firm is probably the most popular and influential theory to emerge in the CSR area (Stark, 1994). While the term 'stakeholder' was first recorded in the 1960s, the theoretical approach was in the main developed and presented by Edward Freeman (1984) in the 1980s. The stakeholder approach begins by looking at various groups to which the corporation has a responsibility. The main starting point is the claim that corporations are not simply managed in the interests of their shareholders alone but that instead a whole range of groups, or *stakeholders*, have a legitimate interest in the corporation as well.

Although there are numerous different definitions as to who or what constitutes a stakeholder, Freeman's (1984: 46) original definition is perhaps the most widely used: 'A stakeholder in an organisation is . . . any group or individual who can affect, or is affected by, the achievement of the organisation's objectives.'

But what is meant here by 'affects' and 'affected by'? To provide a more precise definition, Evan and Freeman (Evan and Freeman, 1993) suggest we can apply two simple principles. The first is the principle of corporate rights, which demands that the corporation has the obligation not to violate the rights of others. The second, the principle of corporate effect, says that companies are responsible for the effects of their actions on others. In the light of these two basic principles a stakeholder can be defined in the following slightly more precise way: 'A stakeholder of a corporation is an individual or a group which either is harmed by, or benefits from, the corporation; *or* whose rights can be violated, or must be respected, by the corporation.'

This definition makes clear that the range of stakeholders differs from company to company, and even for the same company in different situations, tasks or projects.

Using this definition, then, it is not possible to identify a definitive group of relevant stakeholders for any given corporation

(a) **Traditional managerial model of the firm**

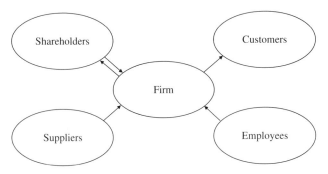

(b) **Stakeholder model**

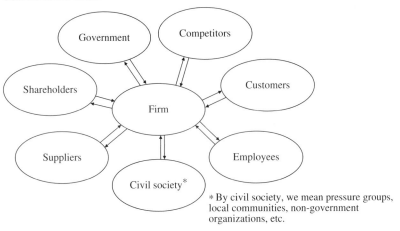

* By civil society, we mean pressure groups, local communities, non-government organizations, etc.

Figure 1.2 Stakeholder theory of the firm (adapted from Crane and Matten, 2004: 51)

in any given situation. However, a typical representation is given in Figure 1.2.

Figure 1.2(a) shows the traditional model of managerial capitalism, where the company is seen as only related to four groups. Suppliers, employees and shareholders provide the basic resources for the corporation, which then uses these to provide products for consumers. The shareholders are the 'owners' of the firm and are consequently the dominant group, in whose interest the firm should be run. In Figure 1.2(b) we find the stakeholder view of the firm, where the shareholders are one group among several others. The company has obligations not only to one group but also to a whole variety of other constituencies that are affected by its activities. The corporation is thus situated at the centre of a series of interdependent two-way relationships.

Returning to the discussion earlier in this chapter regarding Milton Friedman's arguments against social responsibility, his second main objection was that businesses should only be run in the interests of their owners. This correlates with the traditional managerial model of the corporation, where managers' only obligation is to shareholders. Indeed, in legal terms, we have already seen that in most developed nations managers have a special *fiduciary relationship* with shareholders to act in their interests. Stakeholder theory therefore has to provide a compelling reason why other groups also have a legitimate claim on the corporation.

Freeman (1984) himself gives two main arguments. First, on a merely descriptive level, if one examines the relationship between the firm and the various groups to which it is related by all sorts of contracts, it is simply not true to say that shareholders constitute the only group with a legitimate interest in the corporation. From a *legal perspective* there are many more groups other than shareholders that appear to hold a legitimate 'stake' in the corporation since their interests are already protected in some way. There are not only legally binding contracts with suppliers, employees or customers but also an increasingly dense network of laws and regulations enforced by society; these signify that it is simply a matter of fact that a large spectrum of different stakeholders has certain rights and claims on the corporation. For example, in many countries legislation protects certain employee rights in relation to working conditions and pay, suggesting that, from a CSR point of view, it has already been agreed that corporations have certain obligations toward employees. Of course, among this broader set of obligations and rights, there are also obligations toward investors, but from a legal perspective this does not remove the obligations the corporation also has to other stakeholders.

A second group of arguments comes from an *economic perspective*. First and foremost we find the problem of *externalities*: if a firm closes a plant in a small community and lays off the workers, it is not only the relation with the employees that is directly affected – shop owners will lose business, tax payments to fund schools and other public services will also suffer – but since the company has no *contractual* relation to these groups, the traditional model suggests that these obligations do not exist. Another even more important aspect is the *agency problem*: one of the key arguments for the traditional model lies in the fact that shareholders are seen as the owners of the corporation, and consequently the corporation's dominant obligation is to them. This view, however, only reflects the reality of shareholder's interests in a very limited number of cases. The majority of shareholders invest in shares not predominantly to 'own' a company (or parts of it), nor is their aim necessarily that the firm will maximise its long-term profitability. In the first place, shareholders often buy shares for speculative reasons, and are primarily interested in the development of the share price rather than in an 'ownership' stake in a physical corporation. Hence, it is not evident why the highly speculative and mostly short-term interests of shareowners should take precedence over the often long-term interests of other groups such as customers, employees or suppliers (for further details see the landmark contribution by Goshal, 2004).

According to Freeman, this broader view of responsibility towards multiple stakeholders assigns a new role to management. Rather than being simply agents of shareholders, management must take the rights and interests of all legitimate stakeholders into account. While they still have a fiduciary responsibility to look after shareholders' interests, managers must balance this with the competing interests of other stakeholders for the long-term survival of the corporation, rather than maximising the interests of just one group at a time. Furthermore though, since the company is obliged to respect the rights of *all* stakeholders, this automatically implies that, to a certain extent, stakeholders should be able to participate in those managerial decisions that substantially affect their welfare and their rights. In a more developed form, Freeman has argued in favour of a *stakeholder democracy* where every corporation has a stakeholder board of directors, giving stakeholders the opportunity to influence and control corporate decisions. This also includes the idea of a model or a legally binding code of *corporate governance*, which codifies and regulates the various rights of stakeholder groups. Though under different labels, this appears to be more prevalent in Europe where, for instance, employee influence in corporate governance is far more developed than it is in the US, where stakeholder theory originated.

Corporate social performance

In this section I look at companies that view CSR pragmatically as a new area of management, which helps them to tackle new business challenges. From this perspective, it is only too natural to ask − if we are able to measure, rate and classify companies on their *economic* performance − why should it not be possible to do the same for a company's *societal* performances as well? The answer to this question has been given by the idea of *corporate social performance* (CSP) and again, the debate about adequate constructs has been long and varied in output. Donna Wood (1991) has presented a model many regard as the state-of-the-art concept and that has been extensively cited in the CSR literature. In terms of her model, corporate social performance can be observed as the *principles* of CSR, the *processes* of social responsiveness and the *outcomes* of corporate behaviour. These *outcomes* are delineated in three concrete areas:

- Social policies − explicit and pronounced corporate social policies stating the company's values, beliefs and goals with regard to its social environment. For example, most major firms now explicitly include social objectives in their mission statements and other corporate policies. Some corporations even have rather explicit goals and targets in relation to social issues, such as Royal Dutch/Shell's commitment to reduce greenhouse gas emissions by 10% below 1990 levels by 2002.

- Social programmes – specific social programmes of activities, measures and instruments implemented to achieve social policies. For example, many firms have implemented programmes to manage their environmental impacts based on environmental management systems, such as ISO 14000/1 and EMAS, which include measures and instruments that facilitate auditing of environmental performance.

- Social impacts – social impacts can be traced by looking at concrete changes the corporation has achieved through the programmes implemented in any period. Obviously this is frequently the most difficult to achieve, since much data on social impacts is 'soft' (i.e. difficult to collect and quantify objectively), and the specific impact of the corporation cannot be easily isolated from other factors. Nevertheless, some impacts can be estimated reasonably well. For example: policies aimed at benefiting local schools can examine literacy rates and examination grades; environmental policies can be evaluated with pollution data; employee welfare policies can be assessed with employee satisfaction questionnaires; and equal opportunity programmes can be evaluated by monitoring the composition of the workforce and benchmarking against comparable organisations.

Clearly then, while the outcome of CSR in the form of CSP is an important consideration, the actual measurement of social performance remains a complex task. Many of the chapters authored by practitioners in this volume provide further details on how companies address the implementation of CSP in practice. One would expect that the more companies invest considerable resources into their stakeholder relations and attempt to have a positive impact in society, the stronger their interest in actually having some yardstick to assess their effectiveness and their efficiency in this area.

ETHICAL DRIVERS OF CSR: 'DOING THE RIGHT THING'

A third motivation to engage in CSR, and in a sense the converse of the aforementioned reason, is that companies look for ways of doing business that are consistent with society's fundamental moral values. CSR here serves as a way to solve ethical dilemmas both within the company, such as discrimination or bribery, and in the company's business environment, such as human rights issues in suppliers' factories or the impact of the company's activities on global climate change. In some cases, these ethical issues are raised by society as a whole; in other instances it may be an individual manager or employee who raises these ethical concerns.

Below I will analyse two areas driven primarily by this particular motivation. The first is the concept of business ethics, arguably one of the most longstanding areas of practical concern and academic inquiry in the CSR area. The concept of sustainability is the second CSR topic inspired largely by ethical assumptions that has been rather powerful in particular in the business world.

Business ethics

In many ways, business ethics is the most longstanding pillar of CSR and in many business schools CSR would be taught as part of a business ethics course (Matten and Moon, 2004b). Business ethics can be defined as the study of business situations, activities and decisions addressing issues of right and wrong. Normally, one would argue that the legal framework of a society deals with these issues by forbidding and sanctioning behaviour considered as morally wrong by the majority of society. The key reason then why companies engage in business ethics is that laws only cover a limited number of the situations in which firms are confronted with questions about right and wrong. For example, in many countries legislation does not prevent businesses from testing their products on animals, selling landmines to oppressive regimes, or forbidding their employees to join a union – issues which many business people might feel very strongly about in one way or the other.

Traditionally, business ethics – in particular in its American tradition – has chiefly focused on situations within the company and on ethical dilemmas individual managers might face. The typical approach would be to use certain ethical theories from philosophy and apply those principles to a particular business situation. For example, in the preceding section I discussed the *stakeholder concept* of the firm. Evan and Freeman (1993) argue that the ethical basis of this concept has been derived in essence from Immanuel Kant's ethics of duty. Drawing on Kant's 'categorical imperative', companies should treat employees, local communities, or suppliers not only as a means, but also as an end in themselves, e.g. as constituencies with rights, goals and priorities of their own. Evan and Freeman therefore suggest that firms have a fundamental *duty* to allow these stakeholders some degree of influence on the corporation. By doing this, they would be enabled to act as free and autonomous human beings rather than being merely factors of production (employees), or sources of income (consumers), etc.

Recently, in particular in the context of multinational corporations in developing countries, the issues of business and human rights has gained increasing momentum (Sullivan, 2003). Typical issues have been labour standards, the rights of indigenous populations, corruption and bribery or the relation of companies to oppressive regimes. Among the key CSR tools deriving particularly from the business ethics debate are corporate codes of ethics or codes of conduct.

As recent research has shown, virtually all multinational corporations in Europe and North America use some form of code (Bondy, Matten and Moon, 2004). Codes of ethics are voluntary statements that commit organisations, industries or professions to specific beliefs, values and actions and/or that set out appropriate ethical behaviour for employees. There are four main types of ethical codes:

- Organisational or corporate codes of ethics. These are specific to a single organisation. Sometimes they are called codes of conduct or codes of business principles, but basically these codes seek to identify and encourage ethical behaviour at the level of the individual organisation.
- Professional codes of ethics. Professional groups also often have their own guidelines for appropriate conduct for their members. While most traditional professions, such as medicine, law and accountancy, have longstanding codes of conduct, it is now also increasingly common for other professions, such as marketing, purchasing or engineering, to have their own codes of ethics.
- Industry codes of ethics. As well as specific professions, particular industries also sometimes have their own codes of ethics. For example, in many countries, the financial services industry has a code of conduct for companies and/or employees operating in the industry. Similarly, at the international level the World Federation for the Sporting Goods Industry (WFSGI) developed a code of conduct for its members in 1997 'to ensure that member companies satisfy the highest ethical standards in the global marketplace' (van Tulder and Kolk, 2001).
- Programme or group codes of ethics. Finally, certain programmes, coalitions or other subgrouping of organisations also establish codes of ethics for those participating in the specific programmes. For example, a collaboration of various business leaders from Europe, the US and Japan resulted in the development of a global code of ethics for business, called

the CAUX Roundtable Principles for Business. Sometimes, conforming to a particular programme code is a prerequisite for using a particular label or mark of accreditation. For instance, companies wishing to market their products as 'fairly traded' will have to abide by the code established by the relevant fair trade body, such as the Fairtrade Foundation in the UK, or Max Havelaar in the Netherlands.

Sustainability as a new normative agenda in CSR

Following the Rio Earth Summit of 1992, one concept in particular appears to have been widely promoted (though not unilaterally accepted) as the essential new conceptual frame for assessing not only CSR activities specifically, but also industrial and social development more generally. That concept is *sustainability*. Sustainability has become an increasingly common term in the rhetoric surrounding CSR, and has been widely used by corporations, governments, consultants, pressure groups and academics alike.

Despite this widespread use, sustainability is a term that has been utilised and interpreted in substantially different ways (Dobson, 1996). Probably the most common usage of sustainability, however, is in relation to *sustainable development*, which is typically defined as development that meets the needs of the present without compromising the ability of future generations to meet their own needs (World Commission on Environment and Development, 1987). The concept clearly rests on a fundamental ethical assumption, whereby it is considered to be morally wrong to use resources in a manner that threatens the existence of future generations.

This, however, is only the core idea of an elusive and widely contested concept – and one which has also been subject to a vast array of different conceptualisations and definitions (Gladwin,

Kennelly and Krause, 1995). At a very basic level, sustainability appears to be primarily about system maintenance, as in ensuring that our actions do not impact upon the system − for example the earth or the biosphere − in such a way that its long-term viability is threatened. By focusing sustainable development on the potential for future generations to satisfy their needs, sustainability concentrates on considerations of *intergenerational equity*, i.e. equality between one generation and another. In this, the concept rests substantially on fundamental moral values concerning fairness and justice between and within generations of the earth population.

With its roots in environmental management and analysis, sustainability as a concept was for a long time largely synonymous with environmental sustainability. More recently though, the concept of sustainability has been broadened to include not only environmental considerations, but also economic and social considerations (Elkington, 1998). This is shown in Figure 1.3.

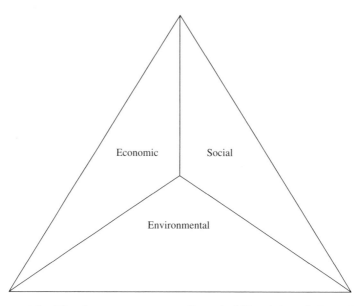

Figure 1.3 The three components of sustainability (adapted from Crane and Matten, 2004: 22)

This extension of the sustainability concept arose primarily because it is not only impractical, but even sometimes impossible, to address the sustainability of the natural environment without also considering the social and economic aspects of relevant communities and their activities. For example, while environmentalists have opposed road-building programmes on account of the detrimental impact of such schemes on the environment, others have pointed to the benefits for local communities, namely less congestion in their towns and extra jobs for their citizens. As I see it then, sustainability can be regarded as comprising three components – environmental, economic and social. This suggests the following definition: 'Sustainability refers to the long-term maintenance of systems according to environmental, economic and social considerations.'

While I regard this definition as sufficient for determining the essential content of the sustainability concept, it is evident that sustainability as a phenomenon also represents a specific goal to be achieved. The framing of sustainability as a goal for business is encapsulated most completely in the notion of a 'triple bottom line'.

The triple bottom line (TBL) is a term coined by John Elkington, the director of the SustainAbility strategy consultancy, who also vigorously advocates this idea and has written a number of influential books on corporate environmentalism. His view of the TBL is that it represents the notion that business does not have just one single goal – namely adding economic value – but that it has an extended goal set, which necessitates adding environmental and social value too (Elkington, 1998). In order to develop a clearer picture of just what the three components of sustainability actually represent in terms of a core idea in CSR, I shall examine each in turn.

- Environmental perspectives. As I mentioned briefly above, the concept of sustainability is generally regarded as having emerged from the environmental perspective, most notably in forestry management (Hediger, 1999). The basic principles of sustainability in the environmental perspective concern the effective management of physical resources so that they are conserved for the future. All biosystems are regarded as having finite resources and finite capacity, and hence sustainable human activity must operate at a level that does not threaten the health of those systems. Even at the most basic level, these concerns suggest a need to address a number of critical business problems, such as the impacts of industrialisation on biodiversity, the continued use of non-renewable resources such as oil, steel and coal, as well as the production of damaging environmental pollutants like greenhouse gases and CFCs from industrial plants and consumer products. At a more fundamental level though, these concerns also raise the problem of economic growth itself, and the vexed question of whether future generations can really enjoy the same living standards as we do without a reversal of the trend towards ever more production and consumption.

- Economic perspectives. The economic perspective on sustainability initially emerged from economic growth models that assessed the limits imposed by the carrying capacity of the earth (Meadows *et al.*, 1974). The recognition that continued growth in population, industrial activity, resource use and pollution could mean that standards of living would eventually decline led to the emergence of sustainability as a way of thinking about how to ensure that future generations would not be adversely affected by the activities and choices of the present generation.

  The implications of such thinking for CSR are situated on various different levels. A *narrow* concept of economic sustainability focuses on the economic performance of the corporation itself: the responsibility of management is to develop, produce and market products that secure the corporation's long-term economic performance. This includes a focus on strategies which, for example, lead to a long-term rise in share price, revenues and market share rather than on short-term 'explosions' of profits at the expense of the long-term viability of a firm's success. An example of an unsustainable approach in this perspective would be the 'dot.com bubble' at the beginning of this century. A *broader* concept of economic sustainability would include the company's attitude towards and impacts upon the economic framework in which it is embedded. Paying bribes or building cartels, for instance, could be regarded as economically unsustainable, because these activities undermine the long-term functioning of markets. Corporations which attempt to avoid paying corporate taxes through subtle accounting tricks might be said to behave in an unsustainable manner: if they are not willing to fund the political–institutional environment (such as schools, hospitals, the police and the justice system) they erode one of the key institutional bases of their corporate success.

- Social perspectives. The development of the social perspective on sustainability has tended to trail behind the evolution of the environmental and economic perspectives (Scott, Park and Cocklin, 2000) and remains a relatively new phenomenon. The explicit integration of social concerns into the business discourse around sustainability can be seen to have emerged during the 1990s, primarily it would seem in response to concerns regarding the impacts of business activities on indigenous communities in less-developed countries and regions. It would be wrong to assume though that this means that local community claims on business (and other social issues) went entirely unheard by business, or unexamined by CSR scholars until this period.

The key issue in the social perspective on sustainability is *social justice*. Despite the impressive advances in standards of living that many of us have enjoyed, the UN *2001 Report on the World Social Situation* (UN, 2001) identified growing disparities in income and wealth within many countries, including much of Latin America, Eastern Europe and almost two-thirds of OECD countries. Similarly, the report highlighted a constantly growing divide between richer and poorer countries. The UN also identified general under-provision and widespread deterioration of basic services in many countries, coupled with an inability to keep pace with even basic needs. As one of the main engines of economic development, business is increasingly bound up in such debates. Therefore a more just and equitable world, whether between rich consumers in the West and poor workers in developing countries, between the urban rich and the rural poor, or between men and women, remains the central concern in the social perspective on sustainability.

POLITICAL DRIVERS FOR CSR: BEING A GOOD CORPORATE CITIZEN

A fourth and more recent group of arguments advocates CSR as a way in which corporations can be accepted, responsible and well-integrated members of society. The key backdrop for corporations' thinking about these issues and their decisions to resort to CSR as a solution is the ongoing debate on the economic and political power of (mostly multinational) corporations in the global economy.

The rise in corporate power and influence over the past 20 years or so has been receiving growing attention from business, academics and the general public alike. We have seen various street demonstrations against growing corporate power, as well as targeted attacks on specific corporations, such as McDonald's, Monsanto, Coca-Cola, Nestlé or Shell. Moreover a number of influential books, such as David Korten's *When Corporations Rule the World* (2001), Noreena Hertz's *The Silent Takeover* (2001a) and Naomi Klein's best-selling *No Logo* (2000), have argued that the 'big brand bullies' have increasingly exercised more and more influence and control over society. There has also been a growing interest in these issues in recent films, the most prominent being *The Corporation*, based on Joel Bakan's book (2004). There is, however, considerable controversy in the literature about this thesis: while this growing body of work sees a problem in the extended power residing in the corporate sector, some mainstream business writers still contend that even large MNCs are rather weak and politically dependent on national governments (e.g. Rugman, 2000).

The crucial point in the critical view is the argument that people's lives across the globe appear increasingly to be controlled and shaped no longer by governments but by corporations. Let us have a look at some examples:

- The liberalisation and deregulation of markets and industries during the rule of centre-right governments throughout the 1980s and the early 1990s (as exemplified by 'Thatcherism' and 'Reaganomics') has given more influence, liberty and choice to private actors. The more the market dominates economic life, the less scope there is for governmental intervention and influence.
- The same period has resulted in sweeping privatisations of major public services and formerly public-owned companies. Private actors now dominate major industries such as the media, telecommunications, transport, and utilities.
- Most industrialised countries have to varying degrees struggled with unemployment. Although governments are made responsible for this, at the same time their scope to influence these figures is increasingly constrained, since corporations take the decisions on employment, relocation or lay-offs.
- Globalisation facilitates relocation and means that companies can engage governments in a 'race to the bottom', i.e. corporations have tended to relocate to 'low-cost' regions where they are faced with only limited regulation (or at least enforcement) of pay and working conditions, environmental protection provisions and corporate taxation.
- Since many of the new risks emergent in industrial society are complex and far-reaching (often beyond the scope of individual countries), they would require very intricate laws, which in

turn would be very difficult to implement and monitor. Hence, corporations have increasingly been set the task of regulating themselves rather than facing direct government regulation. For example, in various legislative projects the European Union has set incentives for companies or industry to come up with self-regulation and self-commitments rather than imposing a law upon them from above. Consequently, companies – or bodies of organised corporate interests – are increasingly assuming the role of political actors in the sphere of social and environmental issues.

The central problem behind these trends, however, is clearly visible: the idea of democracy is to give people control over the basic conditions of their lives and the possibility to choose those policies that they regard as desirable. However, since many pertinent decisions are no longer taken by governments (and hence, indirectly by individual citizens) but by corporations (who are not subject to democratic election), the problem of corporate transparency and accountability to society becomes crucial.

Corporate citizenship as a new label for CSR

The main reaction by corporations with regard to this particular challenge has been to couch CSR strategies in the new terminology of 'corporate citizenship' (CC) or being a 'good corporate citizen'. There are a number of good reasons why this shift in terminology has taken place.

- As van Luijk (2001) has pointed out, industry has never been completely happy with some of the language used in CSR. To start with, the very notion of business *ethics* might be seen as somewhat suspicious, as it implies that 'ethics' is something that is not originally present in business, or even worse, which is opposed to business; 'ethics' as such for many practitioners already has quite an elitist, even patronising slant to it.

- A similar argument can be made for corporate social *responsibility*: this, from a business point of view, could be seen to suggest a very admonishing and even reproachful connotation, apart from the fact that it was used by many proponents in the sense of reminding business of something *additional* they should do.

- It is also worth noting that most of the existing terms were initially introduced into the debate by academics, making it more difficult to establish legitimacy and a lasting place in the business world.

- 'Citizenship', on the other hand, has a rather different connotation for business. Not only was CC initially coined by practitioners, but it can also be said to highlight the fact that the corporation sees – or recaptures – its rightful place in society, alongside other 'citizens', with whom the corporation forms a community. Citizenship then focuses on the rights and responsibilities of all members of the community, who are mutually interlinked and dependent on each other (Waddell, 2000).

In many ways then CC represents a new label to describe practices encompassed by the label of CSR for more than 30 years. There is a slight emphasis on corporate giving, philanthropy and investments in the local community to enhance 'social capital' and in general companies use the CC terminology to emphasise their membership of a political, social and cultural community. However, on balance most companies and 98 % of the academic literature in essence use CC as a new label for CSR. It is no surprise then that many managers, in particular those who do not have an academic background in management, are often somewhat suspicious about a discipline which easily comes up with new buzzwords and catchphrases, without necessarily providing any new content or meaning. Unfortunately, CSR is no exception here and the new terminology of CC is chiefly a new way to market old ideas.

Corporate citizenship as a political concept

There is, however, a growing debate in the CSR literature concerning a better understanding of the new challenges in relations between society and business from a political perspective and addressing how to make better use of the citizenship concept to solve imminent and new CSR challenges facing corporations (Matten and Crane, 2005; Moon, Crane and Matten, 2005; Crane, Matten and Moon, 2006). The starting point of this debate is the idea that 'citizenship' is a concept that conceptualises roles, responsibilities and tasks for all members of a political community. In simplified terms, those communities consist of those who govern ('the government') and those who are governed ('the citizens'). Corporations are to be found on both sides of this dichotomy, as they increasingly assume roles similar to those of governments, as well as attempting to assume the role of a responsible and 'good' citizen in the community. Below I will briefly discuss both roles in turn.

First, if one considers *corporations as governments* (Matten and Crane, 2005) one could argue that they partly take over certain of the fundamental roles of governments. A key task of a government with regard to its people is to uphold and guarantee their basic rights as citizens. Corporations then may enter the arena of citizenship at the point where traditional governmental actors start to fail to be the only 'counterpart' of citizenship, the only actor to guarantee the governance of citizenship rights. Quite simply, they can be said to partly take over those functions with regard to the protection, facilitation and enabling of citizens' rights – formerly an expectation placed solely on the government. Let us consider some examples:

- Social rights (access to basic commodities such as education, healthcare, welfare, etc.). Many CSR activities, in particular in the developing world, pursue initiatives formerly within the province of the welfare state. Feeding homeless people, improving working conditions in sweatshops, ensuring employees a living wage, providing schools, medical centres and roads, or even providing financial support for the schooling of child labourers are all activities in which corporations such as Shell, Nike, Levi Strauss and others have engaged under the label of CC.

- Civil rights (guarantee of free markets, private property, freedom of speech, etc.). Governmental failure again becomes particularly visible in developing or transforming countries. Drastic examples, such as the role of Shell in Nigeria and its apparent contribution to restricting the civil rights of the Ogoni people (Boele, Fabig and Wheeler, 2000), show that corporations might play a crucial role in either discouraging (as Shell) or encouraging governments to live up to their responsibility in this arena of citizenship. A positive example for the latter might be General Motors and other, mostly US, corporations in South Africa during the apartheid period, who, after being pressurised by their own stakeholders, eventually exerted some pressure of their own on the South African government to desist from violating the civil rights of black South Africans (De George, 1999).
- Political rights (right to vote, to hold office, etc.). Voter apathy in national elections has been widely identified in many industrialised countries, yet there appears to be a growing willingness on the part of individuals to participate in political action *aimed at corporations rather than at governments* (Hertz, 2001). Whether through single-issue campaigns, anti-corporate protests, consumer boycotts or other forms of sub-political action, individual citizens have increasingly sought to effect political change by leveraging the power, and to some extent vulnerability, of corporations.

The key consequence of this shift in roles is thus that corporations have to live up to certain demands that were originally made solely of governments. Incidentally, this is one of the key differences between modern CSR and nineteenth-century philanthropy: while the activities of the latter led to some form of welfare state and government guarantees, modern CSR picks up these issues as a consequence of governments gradually retiring from the governance of these rights. I will discuss the implications in greater detail in the concluding section below.

Second, if one considers *corporations as citizens* (Moon, Crane and Matten, 2005) one can draw upon a rich heritage of ideas in political science, which has discussed contemporary and innovative forms of citizenship. These ideas have been informed by the developments discussed at the start of this section and focus on the possibilities for citizens to participate in the governance of societies. Here, corporations could indeed assume a more citizen-like role by taking part in societal governance. Again, let us consider some examples:

- Participation in governance: a key obligation of citizens is to participate in the governance of society and to advance the common good. Corporations enter the picture here in various ways. For instance, many corporations are involved in lobbying political actors, or through industry associations, attempt to influence and shape regulations. Furthermore, many corporations engage in extensive processes of stakeholder engagement and form partnerships with civil society actors on a variety of issues (Bendell, 2000).
- Contributing to social development: there is a growing claim on citizens to initiate social progress and development in civil society by becoming involved in a dense network of links to fellow citizens, rather than simply waiting for the welfare state to intervene. Many CSR programmes of corporations can be understood in exactly this fashion. An example is Hewlett-Packard's conceptualisation of itself as an organisation that 'is helping people overcome barriers to social and economic progress' and is 'learning to compete better in the region [South Asia] and around the world' (Dunn and Yamashita, 2003) as a

result of its engagement in the Kuppam region of India. This is not only described as the company's responsibility to this AIDS-infected area but also in terms of the value that the Kuppam community will contribute to Hewlett-Packard.

- Deliberation: citizens have the obligation to participate in society by directly engaging in processes from which a collective will can emerge. This aspect of citizenship particularly stresses the need for governance not to be merely exerted top-down by governments but instead to be embedded in extensive debate and deliberation in society if a democratic society is to flourish. Again, a considerable amount of CSR activities discussed in this book show that corporations have become quite active in this arena as well.

The citizenship perspective, however, raises some severe conditions for corporations wanting to be like citizens. One of the key conditions would be that corporations, in participating in society, do not just represent their own interests but to some degree also respect and advocate the general welfare of society. Among the key conditions, however, would be the need to be transparent and accountable to fellow citizens, which I will discuss in the next section.

Accountability and transparency as prerequisites for corporate citizenship

One central point in the CSR debate more recently is the question as to *who controls corporations* and *to whom are corporations accountable*. There are those like Friedman, as discussed above, who see it as a given that corporations are only accountable to their shareholders, and furthermore, are accountable to obey and comply with the laws of the countries in which they do business. However, there are also good arguments to support the view that since 'corporate citizens' now shape and influence so much of public and private life in modern societies, they in effect are political actors, and thus have to become more accountable to society.

One argument, offered by Hertz (2001b) and others, is that, given the power of big corporations, there is more democratic power in an individual's choice as a consumer (for or against certain products) than in voters' choices at the ballot box. As Smith (1990) contends, consumption choices are to some extent 'purchase votes' in the social control of corporations. However, one should also recognise the limitations of the individual's power to affect corporate policy through purchase choices. There is little guarantee that consumers' social choices will be reflected in their consumer choices, nor that such social choices will be even recognised, never mind acted on, by corporations. After all, not only do corporations benefit from a massive power imbalance compared to individual consumers, but consumers are also constrained in executing their voting rights by the choices offered by the market. Perhaps most importantly, consumers are just one of the multiple stakeholders that corporations might be expected to be accountable to.

This has led to further questions regarding how corporations can be made more accountable for their actions to the broad range of relevant stakeholders. One important consequence for corporations seeking to become more accountable is to audit and report on their social, ethical and environmental performance through new accounting procedures, such as environmental accounting and social reporting (e.g. Gray *et al.*, 1997; Zadek, Pruzan and Evans, 1997; Livesey, 2002). Another important stream of literature has looked at broader issues of communication with stakeholders, together with the development of stakeholder dialogue and stakeholder partnerships (Bendell, 2000; Crane and Livesey, 2003). The key issue here is that corporate social activity and performance should be made more visible to those with a stake in the corporation in order to enhance corporate accountability. The term usually applied to this is transparency.

Although *transparency* can relate to any aspect of the corporation, demands for transparency usually relate primarily to *social* as opposed to *commercial* concerns, since traditionally corporations have claimed that much of their data are commercially confidential. However, it is evident that many social issues cannot be easily separated from commercial decisions. For example, Nike long claimed that the identity and location of their suppliers could not be revealed because it was commercially sensitive information that their competitors could exploit. However, concerns over working conditions in these factories led to demands for Nike to make the information public, which to some extent they have eventually agreed to do.

The tenor of current demands for greater corporate accountability and transparency, particularly as exemplified by the protest movement against global capitalism, MNCs and global governing bodies such as the IMF or the World Bank, suggests that these developments might no longer be an option for corporations. Increasingly, corporate accountability and transparency are being presented as necessities, not only from a normative point of view, but also with regard to the practical aspects of doing business effectively and maintaining public legitimacy. These topics then inform much of the contemporary debate in the CSR world.

CONCLUSION: WILL CSR BE MORE THAN AN EPHEMERAL MANAGEMENT FASHION?

In this chapter I have discussed four main arguments in favour of CSR as well as key concepts and ideas linked to these four ways of approaching CSR. Table 1.1 provides an overview of the main points.

Finally, one might want to ask to what extent CSR is just the buzzword of the era, which – like many other management fashions – will be forgotten in a few years. A number of arguments suggest that – while the language might change and 'CSR' might

Table 1.1   Reasons for engaging in CSR and basic approaches

Why CSR?	Motto	Nature of the drivers	Key ideas and concepts
CSR is enhancing the long-term profitability of the company.	'There is a clear-cut business case in CSR!'	Economic	• Shareholder value maximisation • Socially responsible investment • Competitive advantage • Bottom of the pyramid strategies
CSR solves day-to-day management problems.	'CSR enables us to manage our stakeholder relations!'	Managerial	• Stakeholder theory • Corporate social performance
CSR is the morally right thing to do.	'CSR means doing the right thing!'	Ethical	• Business ethics • Sustainability
CSR is a way to be a legitimate and accepted member of society.	'CSR makes us a good corporate citizen!'	Political	• Corporate citizenship • Accountability • Transparency

quickly be given another label by corporate PR specialists – the fundamental business challenge is here to stay. I will confine myself to just one aspect, though admittedly the most important one. All four reasons, in some way or the other, are implicitly predicated on the assumption that companies assume responsibility for social issues – or in Carroll's words – seek to live up to various societal expectations, because, at least for the foreseeable future, they are not likely to face any major competitors in this specific social role. The biggest 'competitor' for many of the issues addressed nowadays by CSR has traditionally been the nation state and its institutions. The key reason, however, why CSR has grown in importance over the last decade in most industrialised democracies lies in the fact that the role of governments, in particular the welfare state, has been considerably reduced and constrained. This certainly applies to the birthplace of CSR, the US, where traditionally the state has assumed far less responsibility for social issues and where corporations have always been more exposed to social demands (Palazzo, 2002). Analysing the situation in Europe, it is unsurprising that the UK, after the Thatcher era and its impact on the British welfare state in the 1980s, has spearheaded the CSR movement in Europe (Moon, 2004). But even longstanding 'nanny states', such as Germany, Japan or Sweden, are increasingly facing pressures to reduce governmental provision of social services, to privatise more areas of public services and to devolve societal governance towards private actors.

These developments are underpinned by the fact that these governance deficits are even more pronounced in developing and emerging economies, one of the key drivers of CSR as discussed in this chapter. On top of that, an entirely new area is the increasing governance vacuum on the global level, where institutions such as the UN, the EU and others now increasingly involve private, most notably corporate, actors in addressing the most urgent social issues of our time. The UN Global Compact, discussed elsewhere in this book, is only one recent example.

Referring back to the four main reasons for CSR presented in this chapter (see again Table 1.1), from an *economic* perspective it is very likely that the areas where companies can make a profit by pursuing social causes, particularly at the 'bottom of the pyramid', will increase. *Managers* are very likely to discover that they will not be able to call on the state or the law to tackle issues and conflicts with their stakeholders in a growing number of their projects. With governments being reluctant to address issues such as global warming or to take a controversial stance on new technologies such as genetic engineering, companies are very likely to be confronted with a growing number of *ethical* controversies. And with corporations gaining more influence in the *political* process and ongoing efforts to privatise public services, the calls for more transparency and accountability will certainly not vanish.

Critics of CSR, from Milton Friedman to the recent survey on CSR in *The Economist* (Crook, 2005), normally overlook this completely and still assume that 'the proper guardians of the public interest are governments' (Crook, 2005: 18). It is, however, understandable why they prefer to do so: if the driving forces leading to increasing CSR continue to develop, this could easily generate even greater exposure of corporations particularly to the political aspects of CSR. One might arguably see the CSR debate developing in this direction over the next few years. Growing demands for political control, accountability and transparency might, however, steer the ship of the corporate world into rather uncharted territories, where CSR will be increasingly appreciated as a guideline and framework for action.

References

Bakan, J. 2004. *The Corporation – The Pathological Pursuit of Profit and Power*. New York: Free Press.

Bendell, J. (Ed.). 2000. *Terms for Endearment: Business, NGOs and Sustainable Development*. Sheffield: Greenleaf.

Birch, D. and J. Moon. 2004. Corporate social responsibility in Asia, *Journal of Corporate Citizenship*, **13**, Special Issue, 18–149.

Boele, R., H. Fabig and D. Wheeler. 2000. The story of Shell, Nigeria and the Ogoni people – a study in unsustainable development. I – Economy, environment and social relationships, Paper presented at the Academy of Management Conference. Toronto.

Bondy, K., D. Matten and J. Moon. 2004. The adoption of voluntary codes of conduct in MNCs – a three countries comparative study, *Business and Society Review*, **109**(4), 449–77.

Bowen, H.R. 1953. *Social Responsibilities of the Businessman*. New York: Harper&Row.

Bowie, N.E. 1991. New directions in corporate social responsibility, *Business Horizons*, **34**, July/August, 56–65.

Cannon, T. 1994. *Corporate Responsibility*. London: Pearson.

Carroll, A.B. 1979. A three-dimensional model of corporate social performance, *Academy of Management Review*, **4**, 497–505.

Carroll, A.B. 1991. The pyramid of corporate social responsibility: toward the moral management of organizational stakeholders, *Business Horizons*, Jul–Aug, 39–48.

Carroll, A.B. 1999. Corporate social responsibility – evolution of a definitional construct, *Business & Society*, **38**(3), 268–95.

Carroll, A.B. and A.K. Buchholtz. 2000. *Business and Society: Ethics and Stakeholder Management*, 4th ed. Cincinnati: Thomson Learning.

Carroll, A.B. and A.K. Buchholtz. 2002. *Business and Society: Ethics and Stakeholder Management*, 5th ed. Cincinnati: South-Western College Publishing/Thomson Learning.

Cowe, R. 2002. Wanted: shareholders with a global conscience, *The Observer – Business*, 24 November, 2002.

Cowton, C.J. 1994. The development of ethical investment products, in A.R. Prindl and B. Prodhan (Eds.), *Ethical Conflicts in Finance*, pp. 213–32. Oxford: Blackwell.

Crane, A. and S. Livesey. 2003. Are you talking to me? Stakeholder communication and the risks and rewards of dialogue, in J. Andriof, S. Waddock, S. Rahman and B. Husted (Eds.), *Unfolding Stakeholder Thinking*. Sheffield: Greenleaf.

Crane, A. and D. Matten. 2004. *Business Ethics – A European Perspective. Managing Corporate Citizenship and Sustainability in the Age of Globalization*. Oxford: Oxford University Press.

Crane, A.W., D. Matten and J. Moon. 2006. *Corporations and Citizenship*. Cambridge: Cambridge University Press.

Crook, C. 2005. The good company, *The Economist*, **374**(8410), 22 January, 2005.

De George, R.T. 1999. *Business Ethics*, 5th ed. Upper Saddle River, NJ: Prentice Hall.

Dobson, A. 1996. Environmental sustainabilities: an analysis and typology, *Environmental Politics*, **5**(3), 401–28.

Dunn, D. and K. Yamashita. 2003. Microcapitalism and the megacorporation, *Harvard Business Review*, **81**(8), 46–54.

Elankumaran, S., R. Seal and A. Hashmi. 2005. Transcending transformation: enlightening endeavours at Tata steel, *Journal of Business Ethics*, **59**(1), 109–19.

Elkington, J. 1998. *Cannibals With Forks: The Triple Bottom Line of 21st Century Business*. Oxford: Capstone.

Evan, W.M. and R.E. Freeman. 1993. A stakeholder theory of the modern corporation: Kantian capitalism, in W.M. Hoffman and R.E. Frederick (Eds.), *Business Ethics: Readings and Cases in Corporate Morality*, 3rd ed., pp. 145–54. New York: McGraw-Hill.

Freeman, R.E. 1984. *Strategic Management. A Stakeholder Approach*. Boston: Pitman.

Friedman, M. 1970. The social responsibility of business is to increase its profits, *The New York Times Magazine*, 13 September, 1970.

Garriga, E. and D. Melé. 2004. Corporate social responsibility theories: mapping the territory, *Journal of Business Ethics*, **53**(1–2), 51–71.

Gladwin, T.N., J.J. Kennelly and T.S. Krause. 1995. Shifting paradigms for sustainable development: implications for management theory and research, *Academy of Management Review*, **20**(4), 874–907.

Goshal, S. 2004. Bad management theories are destroying good management practices, *Academy of Management Learning and Education*, **4**(1), 75–91.

Gray, R., C. Dey, D. Owen, R. Evans and S. Zadek. 1997. Struggling with the praxis of social accounting: stakeholders, accountability, audits and procedures, *Accounting, Auditing and Accountability Journal*, **10**(3), 325.

Griffin, J.J. and J.F. Mahon. 1997. The corporate social performance and corporate financial performance debate: twenty-five years of incomparable research, *Business & Society*, **36**(1), 5–31.

Hart, S.L. 2005. *Capitalism at the Crossroads: the Unlimited Business Opportunities in Solving the World's Most Difficult Problems*. Upper Saddle River, NJ: Wharton School Publishing.

Hediger, W. 1999. Reconciling 'weak' and 'strong' sustainability, *International Journal of Social Economics*, **26**(7/8/9), 1120–43.

Hertz, N. 2001a. *The Silent Takeover*. London: Heinemann.

Hertz, N. 2001b. Better to shop than to vote? *Business Ethics: A European Review*, **10**(3), 190–3.

Jensen, M.C. 2002. Value maximization, stakeholder theory and the corporate objective function, *Business Ethics Quarterly*, **12**(2), 235–56.

Klein, N. 2000. *No Logo: Taking Aim at the Brand Bullies*. London: Flamingo.

Korten, D.C. 2001. *When Corporations Rule the World*, 2nd ed. Bloomfield, CT: Kumarian Press.

Livesey, S. 2002. The discourse of the middle ground: citizen Shell commits to sustainable development, *Management Communication Quarterly*, **15**(3), 313–49.

Matten, D. and A. Crane. 2005. Corporate citizenship – towards a theoretical conceptualisation, *Academy of Management Review*, **30**, 166–79.

Matten, D. and J. Moon. 2004a. A conceptual framework for understanding CSR in Europe, in A. Habisch, J. Jonker, M. Wegner and R. Schmidpeter (Eds.), *CSR across Europe*, pp. 339–60. Berlin: Springer.

Matten, D. and J. Moon. 2004b. Corporate social responsibility education in Europe, *Journal of Business Ethics*, **54**(4), 323–37.

Meadows, D.H., D.L. Meadows, J. Randers and W.W. Behrens. 1974. *The Limits to Growth*. London: Pan.

Moon, J. 2004. CSR in the UK: an explicit model of business – society relations, in A. Habisch, J. Jonker, M. Wegner and R. Schmidpeter (Eds.), *CSR across Europe*, pp. 51–65. Berlin: Springer.

Moon, J., A. Crane and D. Matten. 2005. Can corporations be citizens? Corporate citizenship as a metaphor for business participation in society, *Business Ethics Quarterly*, **15**(3), 427–51.

Palazzo, B. 2002. US-American and German business ethics: an intercultural comparison, *Journal of Business Ethics*, **41**, 195–216.

Porter, M.E. and M.R. Kramer. 2002. The competitive advantage of corporate philanthropy, *Harvard Business Review*, **80**(12), 56–69.

Prahalad, C.K. 2005. *The Fortune at the Bottom of the Pyramid*. Upper Saddle River, NJ: Wharton School Publishing.

Prahalad, C.K. and A. Hammond. 2002. Serving the world's poor, profitably, *Harvard Business Review*, **80**(9), 48–57.

Rivoli, P. 1995. Ethical aspects of investor behaviour, *Journal of Business Ethics*, **14**, 265–77.

Rugman, A.M. 2000. *The End of Globalisation*. London: Random House.

Scott, K., J. Park and C. Cocklin. 2000. From 'sustainable rural communities' to 'social sustainability': giving voice to diversity in Mangakahia Valley, New Zealand, *Journal of Rural Studies*, **16**, 443–6.

Smith, N.C. 1990. *Morality and the Market: Consumer Pressure for Corporate Accountability*. London: Routledge.

Stark, A. 1994. What's the matter with business ethics? *Harvard Business Review*, May–June, 38–48.

Sullivan, R. (Ed.). 2003. *Business and Human Rights*. Sheffield: Greenleaf.

Taylor, R. 2001. Putting ethics into investment, *Business Ethics: A European Review*, **10**(1), 53–60.

UN. 2001. *2001 Report on the World Situation*. New York: United Nations Publications.

van Luijk, H.J.L. 2001. Business ethics in Europe: a tale of two efforts, in R. Lang (Ed.), *Wirtschaftsethik in Mittel- und Osteuropa*, pp. 9–18. Munich: Rainer Hampp.

van Tulder, R. and A. Kolk. 2001. Multinationality and corporate ethics: codes of conduct in the sporting goods industry, *Journal of International Business Studies*, **32**(2), 267–83.

Visser, W., C. Middleton and M. McIntosh. 2005. Corporate citizenship in Africa, *Journal of Corporate Citizenship*, 18, Special Issue, 17–124.

Waddell, S. 2000. New institutions for the practice of corporate citizenship: historical, intersectoral, and developmental perspectives, *Business and Society Review*, **105**(1), 107–26.

Waddock, S.A. and S.B. Graves. 1997. The corporate social performance–financial performance link, *Strategic Management Journal*, **18**(4), 303–19.

Wood, D.J. 1991. Corporate social performance revisited, *Academy of Management Review*, **16**, 691–718.

World Commission on Environment and Development. 1987. *Our Common Future*. Oxford: Oxford University Press.

Zadek, S., P. Pruzan and R. Evans (Eds.). 1997. *Building Corporate Accountability: Emerging Practices in Social and Ethical Accounting, Auditing and Reporting*. London: Earthscan.

CHAPTER 2

Corporate Culture and CSR – How They Interrelate and Consequences for Successful Implementation

Manfred Pohl[1]

INTRODUCTION

Globalisation has changed the world and has created awe-inspiring opportunities for both consumers and companies alike. Considering globalisation from a consumer point of view, availability and consumption of products from around the world come to the fore. For corporations, a new and almost unlimited growth potential becomes accessible, not only in terms of sales but also in manufacturing. But globalisation has not yet receded from demanding revolution in the areas of technology as well as politics, the economy and society, enclosed in the all-embracing term of culture.

---

[1] Manfred Pohl would like to thank Katja Böhmer for the research undertaken in preparation for this chapter.

The ICCA Handbook on Corporate Social Responsibility Edited by J. Hennigfeld, M. Pohl and N. Tolhurst
© 2006 John Wiley & Sons, Ltd

Because of this worldwide expansion the role of multinational companies has changed and they can no longer deny their own significant influence, not only in relation to consumers and suppliers but also in relation to the environment and society as a whole. Additionally, the public has been sensitised and increasingly demands responsible business practices. Consequently it is not astonishing that most companies have recognised the importance of engaging in corporate social responsibility (CSR), encompassing not only their economic but also their legal, ethical and philanthropic responsibilities to society. That is why the CSR movement has gained momentum over the years, and the concept is now implemented around the world.

But where does this development come from?

There are five main fields of concern shaping the world today and in the future; they can be briefly stated as follows:

1. Shorter innovation times help companies reap financial rewards and revenues earlier, supporting their growth and the worldwide dissemination of products. The development of communication, information and medical technologies is realised more quickly, reducing the time span between research and implementation and enabling companies to enter markets faster while working on new products to be introduced shortly after. Shorter product lifecycles as described above represent a challenge to companies that have to stay abreast of innovations in order to survive among competitors and must also consider their impact on environments and societies.

2. Countries are losing ground *vis-à-vis* greater unity, as for example represented by the European Union, or a possible 'United States of Africa' or 'United States of South America' in the future. At the same time, new identities and structures are increasingly arising in regions. Today Europe amounts for an estimated 13 % of the world's population; in 20 to 30 years it will be reduced to approximately 5 %. At that time approximately

60 million people of Muslim origin will live in Europe. China and India may represent relatively poor countries, but with about 2.5 billion people they amount for approximately 40 % of the world population. These developments represent a new cultural diversity with a multitude of attitudes, experiences, ways of living and working, offering new possibilities and insights into different cultures and how they affect people's behaviour. How will this affect people's individual culture? Will it foster the development of a new culture with universal shared values and norms? How will companies' way of doing business change within this new constellation?

These adjustments will not only have consequences for countries' identities by increasing cultural diversity, they will also affect agreements, trade and ethical standards – and consequently the way corporations do business around the world.

3. For decades the world has turned to the USA to benefit from political, economic and cultural ideas and theories. Economic theories such as Friedman's theory of monetarism (economic activity dependent on the monetary supply and demand) (Wöll, 2000) were adopted by European countries, and other theories followed, such as shareholder value or sociopolitical topics, namely corporate social responsibility. Europe has up to now accepted and absorbed US theories without critique, also accepting their superior role in the world. But the twenty-first century should not be shaped only by the USA. Europe has gained a stronger position in the world and should further develop its own identity and strengths to shape our culture. This way, one culture will not rise to eliminate another, but will coexist and find new ways of cooperation to survive.

4. The world faces new threats. Terrorism such as the 9/11 attacks and epidemics such as SARS threaten the lives of people around the world and have a disastrous influence on the economies. If a country like China were not able to participate

in world trade because of an epidemic such as SARS, this would cause major damage to the world economy. All in all, terrorism and epidemics have a cultural background, finding their implementation through religious beliefs and traditional ways of life. Being aware of these cultural influences will become of increasing importance in the future.

5. As part of our culture, religion and values are experiencing a renaissance. People's trust in politics, economies and companies has been shattered by scandals portrayed by the media, causing them to return to what they know. Their own values and religious beliefs provide them with a sense of security and truth, emphasising again the importance and significance of culture.

But what role do companies play in this constellation, and how does it relate to corporate culture and CSR? And what do they have to do to survive in the era of globalisation and participate in creating a peaceful world?

The described changes, processes and developments are not only of a political, economic or social nature; the process as a whole is a cultural process, in that it encompasses political, economic and social changes which are part of culture.

Relating this to corporations, we can observe that corporate culture is of increasing importance.

Multinational companies play a crucial role in shaping globalisation. At this point American, European or Japanese companies may dominate the world economy, but their behaviour will determine whether they rank among the winners or whether other nations replace them. This will be determined by the cultural make up of the companies. In India, for example, corporate culture encompasses different values, norms and beliefs, and therefore creates a different basis for action. One example for a possible rise of Indian companies is the fact that people have a higher tolerance of forbearance, resulting in a completely different approach to work and company performance.

The proportion of companies of different nationalities will therefore shift, and a range of underrepresented nationalities will improve their position in the world economy.

This change in market constellation describes a cultural shift, emphasising again the importance of corporate culture. Companies have to consider cultural issues on an international and national as well as on a regional and local basis to create a corporate culture that will help them survive among other cultures.

The impact of globalisation on corporations is reflected in their search for a new cultural identity that enables them to survive in the era of globalisation. This search has lately been characterised by a number of activities related to CSR and sustainability. Therefore it is worthwhile to take a closer look at corporate culture and how it influences companies, especially in their current effort to implement CSR.

WHAT IS CORPORATE CULTURE?

As we have learned, culture is the driving force in changing the world. The question of how companies find a new identity in this world can only be answered by considering their corporate culture.

Corporate culture is a 'set of distinctive spiritual, material, intellectual and emotional features of society or a social group, and (it) encompasses, in addition to art and literature, lifestyles, ways of living together, value systems, traditions and beliefs' (UNESCO, 2002).

In other words, corporate culture comprises the attitudes, values, beliefs, norms and customs of a company, defining the way it acts, how it achieves its economic success and how it interacts with employees and suppliers. Therefore culture is the result of an evolutionary process, being established throughout the history of a company and formed through its leaders' beliefs and attitudes. These corporate leaders are responsible for communicating, defining and translating culture into the corporations. But corporate culture can only be effective and sustainable when all parts of it, including corporate history (the cultural memory), CSR and research into future corporate culture issues, are considered and transferred into everyday business processes. A purely economic view would be incomplete, because all actions and decisions are made in respect of corporate culture. Therefore, corporate culture defines 'good' and 'bad' behaviour, and is not implemented only in 'good times', but instead represents the underlying force for all action – especially in 'bad times'.

Just as culture generates all change processes in the world, corporate culture has the same influence in relation to activities and changes within companies.

Companies are consequently required to consider and preserve their corporate culture, because it is their only instrument for survival. This can be achieved by implementing an overall cultural strategy, particularly with regard to the future developments in CSR.

WHAT IS CORPORATE SOCIAL RESPONSIBILITY (CSR)?

'Corporate social responsibility is defined as the ongoing commitment by businesses to behave ethically and contribute to economic development, while improving the quality of life of its employees and that of the community within which it operates as well as society at large' (Institute for Corporate Culture Affairs, 2005).

Put into practice, CSR is the practical steps developed out of a company's set of values, beliefs and norms – namely its corporate culture. CSR should be embedded in and can only be realised through corporate culture to overcome the misrepresentation of being another 'add-on'. Although today CSR as a concept seems to be accepted around the world, the individual implementation is far from effective. One explanation may be the lack of a universal approach, resulting in a variety of theories and concepts all summarised under terms such as corporate citizenship, community relations, corporate responsibility or sustainability. These terms may all reflect the intention of integrating CSR, but in lack of an effective strategy, CSR is implemented without focus, resulting in a multi-project approach. The current implementation of CSR is limited to sponsorships or volunteer activities, mainly for theatre, opera, the arts or sports events. Furthermore, companies make donations to organisations such as UNESCO or support the work of the World Bank, thereby not assuming the necessary responsibilities themselves.

The top 500 companies spend an estimated US$30 to 50 billion annually on sponsoring activities. The implementation of CSR is currently still reduced to more or less uncoordinated, ineffective spending, without any strategy or achievable goals. Companies basically sponsor many small projects with little effect. But being a 'good citizen' includes more than just sponsoring activities, it includes taking economic responsibilities into account, and at the same time considering the company's responsibility to society. Monetary support for organisations and current activities has to be continued, but corporations are also required to deploy their regional and local presence to make an even larger contribution to societies and environments.

To make a meaningful contribution and have an effective approach to CSR, companies need to understand that CSR is inextricably linked to the company's corporate culture. Therefore, understanding the relationship between CSR and the company's cultural memory is of importance to the developments in the field and in the companies themselves.

Corporate social responsibility is the practical instrument to help companies understand their culture, translate it into every business process and live out the underlying values and beliefs. In order to achieve complete integration, transparency and effectiveness, and to make a meaningful contribution to sustainability, activities need to be integrated strategically into the organisational structure of the company, and must be afforded the same importance and status as for example economic departments. Organising and integrating CSR activities will be the task of corporate culture departments (CCDs) formally established within the company. CCDs are intended to provide a focus and strategy to the company's CSR approach and initiatives, thereby guaranteeing its importance and aligning CSR goals with overall business goals.

Although strategies need to be aligned, corporate culture and CSR require an independent strategy covering activities and goals, focusing initiatives to achieve the best possible contribution to society and environments. The need for an independent strategy is also expressed in the communication of CSR. Communication is an essential component of corporate culture, and companies do not only have the right to communicate their successes and failures but also the obligation to do so. Corporate social responsibility must be actively communicated in order to achieve the most success. Effective implementation represents only the first step to overall success; awareness among stakeholders such as suppliers, employees and the public represents an equally important factor.

Accounting rules and procedures have been established for controlling companies' actions and impacts. Such rules also exist for CSR. Reporting guidelines such as the Global Reporting Initiative (GRI) (www.globalreporting.org) are already available to guide communication to stakeholders and interested parties, and they represent an important communication tool. Communication is part of corporate culture, and part of the requirements for integration and for achieving transparency. Therefore understanding the historical background and the relationship of CSR and corporate culture is indispensable to disseminating a universal concept and creating unity.

As mentioned before, CSR does not represent the content, but the tool to implement the values, beliefs, attitudes and norms, namely the corporate culture of a company. Establishing joint strategies as described above represents the only relevant and possible alternative to random approaches and ineffectiveness.

By using CSR as a tool, companies are able to meet the challenge of translating corporate culture into action, thereby taking into account the evolution of their culture and future challenges and opportunities without sacrificing business performance. Corporate culture is therefore the basis for all business activities and processes in a company, and needs an effective organisational structure.

But what are the practical consequences of this relationship?

In practical terms, corporate culture and CSR affect the way companies behave towards their stakeholders, and in turn influence how stakeholders perceive the company. Corporate culture represents the specific company's value system to be implemented with the help of CSR. Translated into everyday actions, a company's management – most of all top-level management – has to live up to its values and act as a role model. The implementation of this theory is best explained with an example such as the way CSR and corporate culture influence employees, suppliers and the society.

If a company values reliability and performance, managers have to portray these characteristics and behave accordingly, emphasising their values at the same time by offering rewards such as promotions or gifts, praise or other incentives to value their work; this will foster the desired behaviour and reflect the value system of the company.

Another example would be the integration of CSR in the supply chain.

Most companies have established codes of conduct or ethical norms to which employees must adhere. These rules for behaviour have been extended to suppliers, who are expected to accept and apply these rules in turn, thereby extending the reach of the company's corporate culture.

Companies value high performance levels corresponding to the theory of shareholder value. Performance results, however, are linked to the education level of the workforce. Investing and designing educational programmes and training measures will benefit the company as well as its employees and the people of the communities. Employees receive appropriate training to advance their careers, and people living in the communities have the chance to acquire the necessary skills required in today's business world. This way companies and employees live their values, disseminating them throughout the communities; companies and society as a whole both benefit from this mechanism. At this point, many critics argue that companies act out of self-interest, only providing assistance and support for programmes and activities that benefit the company itself. The debate about companies' reasons for implementing CSR will continue; but at this stage it is crucial to understand that companies will support initiatives reflecting their corporate culture and will use the tools offered by CSR to translate their values into action.

HOW CAN ICCA HELP COMPANIES UNDERSTAND THE IMPORTANCE OF CSR AND CORPORATE CULTURE?

Defining and creating the basis for future action in terms of CSR represents an insurmountable task for companies. Therefore, companies should turn to institutions with experience and expertise in the field of corporate culture and CSR, such as the Institute for Corporate Culture Affairs based in Frankfurt am Main, Germany.

As an international not-for-profit association aiming at mainstreaming CSR, ICCA recognises companies' roots in corporate culture and offers a variety of services, material and events aimed at establishing the necessary foundation for future progress on CSR. In order to establish this basis for action, ICCA defines the concepts, theories and relationships underlying CSR and corporate culture. This institute stresses that CSR needs to be embedded in a corporate environment where values, beliefs and norms are cultivated (corporate culture), in order to ensure that CSR becomes not just an 'add on', but an integral part of companies' core business. Educating company representatives is therefore based on primary research, training, briefings, conferences and workshops, providing expert knowledge and experience to ultimately give CSR a physical appearance with the establishment of corporate culture departments. ICCA works to achieve this goal of strategic integration within the companies.

ICCA helps companies understand relevant concepts and theories and how to translate them into their everyday business. With its services and projects, the Institute helps companies integrate CSR effectively and efficiently.

Activities are aimed at cooperation between companies and academics, ensuring that participants and members carry newly gained knowledge, experience and their own perceptions back into their institutions, namely businesses and universities.

The Institute offers the tools for implementing a company's culture and considering its influence and importance, and works at the forefront of current developments and issues, creating a pioneer position on CSR projects and research.

IMPLICATIONS FOR THE FUTURE

We have learned that globalisation has caused many changes in our cultures and that these cultural changes are manifested in science, relationships between countries, the strengths of different cultures worldwide and the risks and threats they face. Most of all, culture always has an impact on companies and therefore their own corporate culture. Corporate culture comprises the values and beliefs lived throughout the companies, representing an impetus for change.

However, corporate culture can only be translated by using CSR as a practical tool for implementation. CSR is a concept that is familiar around the world but is currently characterised by a lack of coordination and effectiveness, since activities are carried out without an appropriate strategy. Implementing CSR effectively requires an understanding of how corporate culture and CSR are related, and an awareness of the practical consequences reflected in the relationship to employees, suppliers and the society.

Companies' current support should be expanded to include not only organisations such as the Institute for Corporate Culture Affairs, but companies should also increase their strategically integrated contributions both regionally and locally. The ICCA helps companies understand and benefit from its specialisation on primary research through its main task as a knowledge broker. Cooperation between the academic and the business world will guarantee the recirculation of experiences and knowledge into companies and universities, contributing to the dissemination of good practices and knowledge.

The developments in the field of CSR require a sound basis of understanding of the relationships of theories and activities; only then can multinational corporations contribute to a sustainable and peaceful world and create a cultural identity that will ensure their future survival.

References

Global Reporting Initiative. www.globalreporting.org accessed 9 February 2006.

Institute for Corporate Culture Affairs (ICCA) (2005). *What is Corporate Social Responsibility?* www.cca-institute.org accessed 5 February 2006.

Pohl, Manfred (2002). *Zukunftsorientierte Avantgarde gesucht. Corporate Culture System (CCS) – die geistige Grundlage der weltweit agierenden Unternehmen im 21. Jahrhundert*. Frankfurter Allgemeine Zeitung. 4 November 2002.

Pohl, Manfred (2004). *Strengthening Corporate Social Responsibility*. IHK WirtschaftsForum 09/04.

Pohl, Manfred (2005a). *Die unterschätzte Unternehmenskultur.* Frankfurter Allgemeine Zeitung. 6 August 2005.

Pohl, Manfred (2005b). *ICCA's Projects and Developments for 2006.* World Corporate Ethics' Council Meeting. Athens, Greece.

Pohl, Manfred (2006). *Globalisierung: Die Suche nach einer globalen Identität.* 125th anniversary of the founding of the Association of German Students.

UNESCO (2002). *UNESCO Universal Declaration on Cultural Diversity.* www.unesco.org accessed 9 February 2006.

Wöll, Artur (2000). *Allgemeine Volkswirtschaftslehre.* 13th edition. Verlag Vahlens.

CHAPTER 3

CSR – The Way Ahead or a *Cul de Sac*?

Sir Geoffrey Chandler

*T*he corporate world has never been more influential; it has rarely been less trusted. The globalisation of the world economy – new in degree, if not in principle – has offered unprecedented opportunity to companies. This they have seized with alacrity. Supermarkets and the consumer goods industries have spread their supply chains ever deeper and wider into the developing world. Transnational companies, in particular oil and mining, have moved into areas previously denied them by political or ideological barriers. But it is also a world of insecurity and of environmental and social risks for which companies have shown themselves unprepared and unequipped. As public awareness has grown of the collateral damage that can be done to the physical and social environment in the course of company business, and as high profile examples of environmental pollution or complicity in human rights violations

The ICCA Handbook on Corporate Social Responsibility   Edited by J. Hennigfeld, M. Pohl and N. Tolhurst
© 2006 John Wiley & Sons, Ltd

have hit the headlines and damaged corporate reputations, the issue of companies' responsibility for the totality of their impact has become a matter of public concern. It is clear that the benefits that the market economy can bring are too narrowly distributed and are often gained at the expense of the weakest. The good that companies bring has frequently been accompanied by harm. Companies are now under scrutiny as never before.

'Corporate social responsibility' (CSR), long part of the vocabulary of debate about the role of business in society, now heads the agenda, sustaining an academic industry, fostering innumerable conferences, spawning consultancies and engaging the attention of companies, non-governmental organisations (NGOs) and governments. That the phrase is for business a self-inflicted wound seems not to be recognised. It implies that business, uniquely among legal occupations, has no inherent social utility, but requires a sanitising 'add-on'. More thoughtful practitioners are now deleting the 'S' in 'CSR', recognising its tautology and the fact that the totality of business operations has social relevance. The business contribution to society is inseparable from its profit-earning activities. It is socially responsible to produce a quality product or service and thereby make a profit. It is socially responsible to act in a principled manner towards each of a company's stakeholders – those who contribute to the company's success or are affected by its operations. These responsibilities are indivisible; but it is the long corporate record of indifference to environmental and social impacts that has prompted the current debate. Moreover, in a world where the accelerating internationalisation of the world economy has put increasing influence into the hands of companies, it is clear that they have greater unfulfilled potential for improving the context in which they operate than any other constituency, including government.

That potential has yet to be recognised and fulfilled. Too much can be asked and expected of companies. They cannot solve world problems of political injustice, economic inequity, disease, poverty and lack of development. They cannot fill the gaps left by government. But it is in their power either to ameliorate or aggravate these problems through the manner in which they conduct their own operations: without appropriate policies and practices it is clear that they do the latter. They have a direct and inalienable responsibility for the health and safety of their employees and for their impact on the lives and livelihood and physical environment of the communities in which they operate.

The climate today is changing. There is now a diversity of initiatives pushing companies towards recognition of the full range of their responsibilities, pre-eminent among these being the OECD Guidelines for Multinational Enterprises and the United Nations Global Compact. There are frameworks, such as the Global Reporting Initiative and AA1000, for reporting the whole of a company's impacts. All in principle point the way ahead, but all are voluntary and only a small percentage of the corporate world so far subscribes to them.

The CSR debate has both helped and hindered. It has helped to raise awareness of the nonfinancial impacts of business. At its best, CSR is defined as the responsibility of a company for the totality of its impact, with a need to embed society's values into its core operations as well as into its treatment of its social and physical environment. Responsibility is seen as encompassing a spectrum – from the running of a profitable business to the health and safety of staff and the impact on the societies in which a company operates.

Such clear-cut definitions are, however, the exception. CSR is more frequently defined as voluntary activity, often no more than community development, which is indeed a traditional activity for any thinking company, but far from the whole. The agenda of any conference will reveal the confusion between principle and expediency: 'a strategy for CSR', 'CSR for competitive advantage', 'innovation for CSR', 'CSR as a marketing aid' are commonplace items. All imply that CSR is a useful additive to make an otherwise unpalatable activity more acceptable – an option, not a principled point of departure. The International Chamber of Commerce defines CSR as a 'voluntary commitment by business to manage in a responsible way' and argues that its exercise makes it 'a far-sighted and profitable business policy'. The European Commission's follow-up to its Green Paper on CSR emphasised its voluntary nature. The first UK government minister with a responsibility for CSR called it a 'highly creative activity'.

There is confusion between philanthropy, which should indeed be creative, and the application of principle to core operations and to the treatment of all stakeholders. The first is essentially voluntary and will necessarily differ between companies: one size cannot fit all. The second cannot be voluntary – the health and safety of employees for example should be a paramount concern for companies – and one size of principle must indeed fit all, even if its application will vary with circumstances. CSR has fostered the illusion that a supermarket's community project in a poor UK district, however valuable, is a substitute for ensuring that there are acceptable labour conditions in all its many thousand suppliers in Asia, Africa and South America, and that the millions of dollars that may be spent on such philanthropic projects have as much impact as the billions spent on a company's core business throughout the world.

Much breath and paper are spent on elaborating the 'business case' for CSR, though it must be a matter of astonishment to other walks of life that for the corporate world doing right or acting on principle needs to be justified by monetary reward. The 'business case' – the requirement of financial justification for any action – may provide the necessary tactical entrée into boardrooms, but is both unreal and essentially amoral. In an ideal world, doing right would indeed have its own reward. But in the real world, dominated by short-term financial yardsticks, the truth is that there is no 'win–win' situation for following principle rather than profit. Bribery can and does pay both in the short run and, if you get away with it, as many can and do, in the long run as well. Externalising the costs of pollution gives a competitive edge over those who accept responsibility for their impact on the environment. A purely financial calculation may show it is cheaper to pay a fine for polluting than to invest in preventive measures. Avoiding human rights abuses cannot be a voluntary activity, nor should it be a matter of competitive advantage. Fear of reputational damage, which has proved costly to companies with a high profile, is not a universal incentive to good behaviour. We have seen companies sensitive to external moral pressure pulling out from countries only to be replaced by less scrupulous competitors.

The fog of definition surrounding CSR can provide a smokescreen for companies which proclaim their adherence to it while failing to adopt appropriate principles for the conduct of their core business. At its worst, CSR becomes a public relations device reminiscent of Groucho Marx's famous dictum: 'Integrity and honesty are the foundations of success. If you can fake those, you've got it made.' It obscures the democratic deficit left today by governmental failure at national and international level to respond adequately to the implications of a globalised economy and to demand accountability from companies which can move freely across boundaries and change their corporate identity at will. It is a failure bolstered by the lobbying of companies which use their growing influence to oppose government regulation which would help to underpin good behaviour and assist market forces to sort out the good from the bad. As it is, market forces, dominated by short-term financial criteria, and the vitiating fallacy that the purpose of the company is simply to provide rewards to shareholders both militate against broader corporate responsibility.

The shift of corporate social purpose, from the provision of goods and services, with profit as an essential condition of success, to the maximisation of shareholder profit, constitutes the biggest barrier to corporate responsibility. Companies and directors are incentivised primarily by short-term financial considerations. Managers once concerned with the whole of performance, in particular with the quality and commitment of staff, have given way to the tunnel vision of accountants subservient to the short-term imperatives of the stock exchange. With inadequate protection from the law for stakeholders other than shareholders, CSR, however defined, is confronted with a Sisyphean task.

It is here that the CSR debate has done most damage in fostering the myth that regulation is unnecessary and voluntarism enough, though the whole of corporate history shows unequivocally that protection of the interests of stakeholders other than the shareholder has come not from voluntary corporate initiative, but from external pressure followed by legislation. This has been true of labour conditions, of protection of the environment and, today, observance of human rights. The market economy survives today because it is not a 'free' market, but one bounded by moral parameters enforced by law. The challenge is to extend those parameters to embrace the values of contemporary society without diminishing the dynamism which needs to underlie the corporate contribution.

If companies are to gain public trust, the most important requirements are, first, explicit adherence to principles reflecting society's values; and second, full disclosure of the manner in which these principles are observed in practice. For the first, the United Nations human rights norms for business offered a way forward. They provided a distillation of the many internationally agreed instruments, of which the foremost is the UN Universal Declaration of Human Rights, which are applicable to companies. They were not intended to be legally binding, but, reflecting as they did the values of international society, were more than voluntary in that they represented what companies could legitimately be expected to do. The spectrum they covered was no broader than the principles adopted already by leading companies. But the exercise was flawed by the compromises necessary to obtain the unanimous support required from 26 disparate country experts which led to increasing elaboration and the addition of clauses on monitoring. This provoked widespread opposition, most intemperately voiced by the International Chamber of Commerce which failed to perceive the value of a set of standards applicable to all businesses which lay at the heart of the norms exercise. The issue, however, remains firmly on the UN agenda. It will now be pursued by a special representative appointed by the UN Secretary General whose first objective is to identify and clarify the human rights responsibilities of all businesses.

An international regulatory framework will undoubtedly be required eventually for business which can cross national boundaries at will; but this, needing international treaties for its implementation, lies many years ahead. In the meantime, a UN-endorsed set of recognised standards, covering the whole of corporate activities and applicable to all companies regardless of size, nationality or ownership, would provide criteria against which investors, consumers and other stakeholders, and most importantly the market, could judge the performance of companies on a comparable basis.

Full disclosure of a company's impacts on its stakeholders is also essential if the market is to operate effectively and be able to judge both short- and long-term influences on performance. This, however, will remain a hope rather than a reality so long as the extent of disclosure depends on the discretion of directors, rather than on a mandatory framework providing comparable data.

We are now probably stuck with the phrase 'CSR'. If indeed it were to be accepted as no more than a synonym for corporate responsibility, enjoining care and principled treatment for all whom a company impacts through the conduct of its business, as well as covering the voluntary initiatives that CSR espouses, then its use could be a stimulus to appropriate action. Were this no more than an academic debate, the intellectual confusion and self-serving corporate arguments that characterise it would be of little matter. As it is, the absence of clear definition, sustaining as it does the myth of the efficacy of voluntarism, is likely to delay effective action to address the root causes of public distrust – lack of transparency and inadequate accountability. So long as companies resist full disclosure of all their impacts, so long as there are no accepted universal standards against which the market can measure nonfinancial performance, so long as money to shareholders is seen as the purpose of the company, CSR will remain a diversion – a device to bolster a voluntarism which has never worked – rather than a solution, a cul de sac rather than the way ahead. It does not have to be this way, but it requires better and more far-sighted leadership from the corporate world if it is to change.

CHAPTER 4

Why all Companies should Address Human Rights – and how the Business & Human Rights Resource Centre can help

Christopher Avery, Annabel Short and Gregory Tzeutschler Regaignon

INTRODUCTION

The Business & Human Rights Resource Centre is an independent non-profit organisation in partnership with Amnesty International and leading academic institutions. Our International Advisory Network is chaired by Mary Robinson, former United Nations High Commissioner for Human Rights and President of Ireland.

Our website (www.business-humanrights.org) and Weekly Updates bring news and reports about companies' human rights conduct – positive and negative – to a global audience. The site covers over 3000 individual companies, is updated hourly, and receives over 1.5 million

The ICCA Handbook on Corporate Social Responsibility   Edited by J. Hennigfeld, M. Pohl and N. Tolhurst
© 2006 John Wiley & Sons, Ltd

hits per month. Further information about our work, including tools that we provide to help companies understand and manage human rights, is under the 'How we can help' section of this chapter.

There is still a tendency to view human rights as a narrow range of issues, applicable to only a few sectors: for example security issues in the extractive sector; labour rights in clothing companies' supply chains. But in fact human rights cover many issues, from discrimination to health and safety, poverty alleviation to pollution affecting human health. This means all companies have an impact on human rights, both in their relationships with their employees and in their relationship with the wider society in which they operate.

Table 4.1, presented at the end of this chapter, provides examples of how companies in many different sectors have impacted positively and negatively on a range of human rights.

The focus on business and human rights is here to stay. Never before have development, environmental and civil/political rights organisations joined together with such determination on a single issue – not just international organisations, but also national and local grassroots groups. There is a long-term commitment by them to monitor and address the human rights conduct of companies. The attention being given to business and human rights is no more a passing fad than environmentalism was when it appeared on the corporate scene several decades ago.

WHY BUSINESS AND HUMAN RIGHTS?

In response to calls for companies to address human rights issues, some companies and business organisations maintain that human rights are the concern and responsibility of governments, not the private sector. While the primary responsibility for human rights does lie with governments, companies are not exempt from responsibility.

The following sections set out why human rights are relevant to all companies, and why it is important that all companies take human rights seriously.

International standards require companies to address human rights

The preamble of the Universal Declaration of Human Rights calls on 'every individual and every organ of society' to promote and respect human rights. Professor Louis Henkin, a leading international law scholar, notes that 'every individual and every organ of society excludes no one, no company, no market, no cyberspace. The Universal Declaration applies to them all' (Henkin, 1999).

International standards referring explicitly to the responsibility of *business* to respect human rights include the OECD Guidelines for Multinational Enterprises and the ILO Tripartite Declaration.

The United Nations (UN) Norms on the Responsibilities of Transnational Corporations and Other Business Enterprises with Regard to Human Rights, adopted by the UN Sub-Commission on Human Rights in 2003, set out with some degree of specificity the human rights responsibilities of companies. As Irene Khan, Secretary-General of Amnesty International, has said, 'Human rights are rooted in law. Respecting and protecting them was never meant to be an optional extra, a matter of choice. It is expected and required. It should be part of the mainstream of any company's strategy, not only seen as part of its corporate social responsibility strategy' (Khan, 2005).

The UN Global Compact, which as of May 2006 has over 2300 participating companies, recognises that companies should respect international human rights standards. Its first two principles are:

- Principle 1: businesses should support and respect the protection of internationally proclaimed human rights; and
- Principle 2: make sure that they are not complicit in human rights abuses.

For further information about what international standards require of companies, see *Beyond Voluntarism: Human Rights and the Developing International Legal Obligations of Companies*, International Council on Human Rights Policy, February 2002. http://www.ichrp.org/ac/excerpts/41.pdf.

Only human rights provide companies with a framework of globally recognised principles

Only human rights can provide international companies with the bedrock of internationally accepted principles on which to base their social conduct.

While aspects of consumer law, criminal law, environmental law or corporate law can all help companies decide what they should do and not do, 'only human rights standards provide the comprehensive normative guide about how human beings should be treated' (Howen, 2005).

Companies themselves are starting to recognise that it is useful to address their social responsibilities through a human rights framework. In the Business Leaders Initiative on Human Rights (BLIHR), 10 companies are working with Mary Robinson to help mainstream human rights within their operations: ABB, Barclays, Body Shop, Gap, Hewlett-Packard, MTV Networks Europe, National Grid, Novartis, Novo Nordisk and Statoil. BLIHR says it is encouraged by the 'increased numbers of businesses willing to talk seriously about their human rights responsibilities, perhaps recognising that human rights is the most legitimate and universal framework for determining the social dimensions of business responsibility and issues of corporate governance' (Business Leaders Initiative on Human Rights, 2004: 11).

There are increasing expectations for companies to manage human rights issues

There are increasing expectations for companies to address human rights issues in a serious way. These expectations come from a broad range of sources:

- **Non-governmental organisations** – from local to international – are paying increasing attention to the impacts of companies, and forming influential coalitions to campaign for corporate accountability. Major human rights organisations such as Amnesty International and Human Rights Watch that traditionally focused on the conduct of governments now also report and campaign on company conduct, recognising that with increased power and influence comes increased responsibility for human rights.
- **Consumers** are taking social and environmental issues into account in their purchasing choices. They have more readily accessible information about individual companies' conduct to help them do this.
- **Employees and prospective employees** want to work for a company with a good record on social and environmental issues. They raise challenging questions internally: if they do not like the response, they may start looking for employment elsewhere.
- **Investors** (primarily socially responsible investors, but increasingly mainstream investors too) want to invest in companies that are alert to human rights issues and less likely to become entangled in a crisis.
- **International financial institutions** increasingly apply social and environmental criteria to their investments. In a recent interview in the *Financial Times*, Rachel Kyte, environment and

social director of the International Finance Corporation, said that businesses that take social and environmental issues seriously will be best placed to gain access to capital in the future (Scott, 2005).

- **Governments** are embarking on initiatives to encourage companies to address human rights. In 2000, the US and UK governments, seven major oil and mining companies and nine international non-governmental organisations publicly expressed their support for the Voluntary Principles on Security and Human Rights, which they had drawn up over a year-long dialogue process convened by the US State Department and the UK Foreign Office. Since then the Norwegian and Dutch governments have joined the process, and 16 companies now participate (as of May 2006). Of course governments also signal what human rights conduct they expect of companies when they adopt and enforce regulations on health and safety, discrimination, sexual harassment, labour rights, etc.

Silence and inaction on human rights are no longer tenable options. Sir Geoffrey Chandler (Founder Chair of Amnesty International UK Business Group 1991–2001, former Director of Shell International, former Director General of UK National Economic Development Office) says the days when companies could remain silent about human rights issues are over: 'Silence or inaction will be seen to provide comfort to oppression and may be adjudged complicity...Silence is not neutrality. To do nothing is not an option' (Chandler, 1997, 1998).

In the words of *The Economist*: 'Today multinationals are under pressure as never before to justify their dealings with abusive regimes and their treatment of employees in developing countries. Firms used to brush off criticism, saying that they had no control over third-world suppliers, and that politics was none of their business anyway. This is no longer good enough' (*The Economist*, 1998).

The pressure and expectations are not just for companies to take action, but to take substantive action that holds up under scrutiny. There is growing impatience with firms that address human rights like a public relations issue, for example assigning the subject to one person in the PR department, or adopting a human rights policy or joining the UN Global Compact without any further action towards implementation. Too many companies have responded with approaches that are superficial, minimalist and short term, failing to reflect a genuine commitment to address human rights in their operations.

There are significant risks for companies that don't respect human rights

Companies that fail to respect human rights expose themselves to a wide range of risks, including legal action, negative media coverage, protests, shareholder action and boycotts – with all the reputational and financial costs that these can bring.

Our own website and Weekly Updates draw international attention to cases of companies' negative impacts on human rights (as well as positive steps). Cases abound of companies that have faced reputational and financial damage, for example:

- Human rights lawsuits against companies including BHP Billiton, Cape PLC, Chevron/Texaco, Coca-Cola, ExxonMobil, Occidental Petroleum, Rio Tinto, Shell, Talisman Energy, Union Carbide/Dow, Unocal, Wal-Mart.
- Protests against Dow Chemical over the Union Carbide disaster in Bhopal, India, and a criminal prosecution in India against the former CEO of Union Carbide – continuing more than 20 years after the event.
- Protests against Shell for years over its conduct relating to the hanging of Ken Saro-Wiwa and eight other Ogoni activists by Nigerian authorities in 1995.
- Resolutions filed by Chevron shareholders seeking a report on its steps to address the health and environmental concerns of

indigenous communities in Ecuador affected by pollution from Texaco's (now part of Chevron) past oil drilling.

- A boycott against Taco Bell over poor conditions faced by tomato pickers working for its suppliers; Taco Bell has now addressed the complaints and the boycott has ended; the workers are now making similar demands of McDonald's.

Every responsible company has mechanisms to ensure that it complies with applicable national and local laws. But more is required to help a company ensure it meets its human rights obligations and avoids the negative consequences listed above. Phil Rudolph of US-based law firm Foley Hoag writes, 'Literal compliance with the law is of course necessary – it is the "entry fee" for engaging in business. But mere compliance is no longer likely to be sufficient to protect companies from potential moral and legal liability' (Rudolph, 2004).

Companies are expected to apply the same standards consistently throughout their operations – they will be strongly criticised when they follow local laws that flout internationally agreed standards. Consumers, investors, local communities and other stakeholders are on the lookout for breaches of those international standards and are quick to bring them to global attention: this is what has been described as the 'goldfish bowl' world in which multinational corporations now operate.

Companies benefit from taking a proactive stance on human rights

An environment in which human rights are protected is clearly better for business than one in which widespread abuses take place. As Mary Robinson has said: 'Companies have always recognised the importance of the rule of law in the context of their investments and operations around the world. They are the first to stress the importance of a transparent, well-functioning and just legal system as a critical part of an enabling environment for investment and economic growth' (www.blihr.org).

Paying attention to human rights can present significant opportunities for businesses, beyond mere avoidance of the risks described in the above section. Amnesty International and the Prince of Wales International Business Leaders Forum (2005) point out a number of commercial benefits of integrating human rights into business practice, including:

- enhanced reputation;
- more secure licence to operate;
- improved employee recruitment, retention, motivation; and
- improved stakeholder relations.

Business for Social Responsibility mentions a number of other benefits, including that policies requiring suppliers to respect human rights can also 'serve as tools to help companies select business partners that are well managed, reliable and operate ethically' (http://www.bsr.org/CSRResources/IssueBriefDetail.cfm? DocumentID=49038).

These arguments making the 'business case' for respecting human rights are often accompanied by attempts to quantify in financial terms the benefits of taking a proactive stance on human rights and corporate responsibility. But it is difficult to argue that rights such as the right to life, to health and to freedom from discrimination and abuse should only be respected when it pays. Companies are obliged to respect human rights at all times, not just when it suits them.

The public perception that many companies put profit before principle has contributed to the mistrust that the business world is experiencing today. To rebuild that trust, companies are increasingly recognising that it's wise to put principles first: the best starting point for this is the set of internationally agreed principles that are human rights.

Human rights are universal standards that go beyond national laws

Over the decades since the adoption of the Universal Declaration of Human Rights in 1948, governments from all regions have expressed support for the Declaration and for the universality of the rights it sets forth, recognising that they apply to everyone, everywhere.

At the 1993 UN World Conference on Human Rights, 171 governments reaffirmed their commitment to the Universal Declaration as 'a common standard of achievement for all peoples and all nations'. They adopted by consensus the Vienna Declaration, which states 'All human rights are universal, indivisible and interdependent and interrelated. The international community must treat human rights globally in a fair and equal manner, on the same footing, and with the same emphasis' (UN World Conference on Human Rights, 1993). And at the September 2005 UN Heads of State Summit, governments again recognised that human rights are universal: 'We reaffirm the universality, indivisibility, interdependence and interrelatedness of all human rights' (UN World Summit Outcome, 2005).

Principles of the sacredness of life, of human dignity and of the importance of justice and fair treatment are reflected in the teaching of all religions and all cultures.

UN Secretary-General Kofi Annan stated in 1997: 'There is no one set of European rights, and another of African rights. Human rights assert the dignity of each and every individual human being, and the inviolability of the individual's rights. They belong inherently to each person, each individual, and are not conferred by, or subject to, any governmental authority. There is not one law for one continent, and one for another. And there should be only one single standard – a universal standard – for judging human rights violations' (http://www.un.org/News/Press/docs/1997/19970813. SGSM6301.html).

The cultural-relativist concept that human rights are 'Western values' is far more likely to be supported by human rights violators in non-Western countries than by victims in those countries. As Michael Ignatieff has said, 'Relativism is the invariable ally of tyranny' (Ignatieff, 2000).

While human rights are universal, there is a need for cultural sensitivity in deciding the time, place and manner of raising certain human rights issues, as well as the need to recognise that one's home country also has human rights shortcomings.

THE NEED FOR MINIMUM BUSINESS AND HUMAN RIGHTS STANDARDS

Each week we add to our website reports of positive initiatives undertaken by individual companies to promote human rights, protect the environment, combat poverty and contribute to conflict resolution. But each week we also add a large number of reports about the involvement of companies and their suppliers in significant abuses of fundamental human rights, in all regions of the world.

The facts speak for themselves. The current framework (lack of corporate accountability at the international level; varying and often weak systems of accountability within states; reliance on voluntary measures by companies) is not addressing extensive human rights abuses.

There is clearly a need for the UN to adopt a set of international principles, based on existing internationally agreed standards, spelling out the minimum human rights floor that no company should fall below.

Voluntary initiatives are important, but they are not enough. While voluntary codes and initiatives have been helpful in raising awareness of human rights issues and improving the conduct of some companies, at the end of the day voluntary codes are respected only by those firms that want to respect them. Respect for internationally accepted, fundamental human rights standards is mandatory, not voluntary.

National law is not the human rights floor. It is surprising that a few companies still argue that if they respect national laws, that is enough. If one accepts this argument, it would have been enough for a company to respect the laws of Nazi Germany, or of apartheid South Africa. National law and practice are sometimes contrary to internationally accepted human rights standards.

So what is the floor? The Universal Declaration of Human Rights, and the International Covenants on Human Rights. There is a need to spell out clearly for business people what these human rights instruments require of their firms. The UN Norms on Business and Human Rights is one set of principles designed to do this. Professor John Ruggie, the new special representative of the UN Secretary-General on Business and Human Rights, has been mandated by the UN Commission on Human Rights to 'identify and clarify standards of corporate responsibility and accountability for transnational corporations and other business enterprises with regard to human rights' (UN Commission on Human Rights, 2005).

A set of UN principles would not be the end of voluntary initiatives by business. Voluntary initiatives are positive steps by the private sector that go beyond the required minimum – stepping up above the floor. There is a need for a mix of enlightened voluntary initiatives and minimum standards.

The Business Leaders Initiative on Human Rights made the following statement about this issue: 'The polarisation of views on the respective merits of voluntary and regulatory approaches has been regrettable. For us it is a false dilemma, human rights have always required a combination of both voluntary and mandatory efforts in order to achieve sustainable change and to raise the minimum standard of acceptable behaviour. As businesses, we believe there is a "minimum" or "essential" level of behaviour below which no business should be allowed to fall' (Business Leaders Initiative on Human Rights, 2004: 5).

Responsible companies should welcome a set of international minimum human rights standards for business. These companies are already respecting human rights, while some of their competitors are not. A set of international standards would provide clarity and help 'level the playing field'. Kenneth Roth, executive director of Human Rights Watch, commented in the *Financial Times*: '[S]ome Western companies … have begun to recognise it might be in their interest to operate under enforceable standards that apply to all their competitors, rather than under voluntary ones that, for all practical purposes, apply only to prominent companies … The only thing [most multinational] companies have to fear is an end to unfair competition from less savoury competitors' (Roth, 2005).

Nicholas Howen, Secretary-General of the International Commission of Jurists, recently noted: 'Those [companies] genuinely committed to respecting rights should have nothing to fear from international standards. But when rules are voluntary, the best companies lose out to competitors who make no investment in compliance with human rights. When clear minimum standards exist, those that do more than the minimum can rightly claim to be even more socially responsible' (Howen, 2005).

HOW WE CAN HELP

Below we provide an introduction to our work, followed by details of specific resources that companies and others may find useful.

About the Resource Centre

The Business & Human Rights Resource Centre was founded in 2002 by a group of former business people, advocates from Amnesty International and Oxfam, academics and environmentalists (now our trustees).

Our aim is to encourage companies to respect human rights, avoid harm to people and maximise their positive contribution. We do this by providing easy, one-stop access to information on companies' human rights impacts via our website: www.business-humanrights.org.

The website draws wider international attention to alleged abuses, and provides increased recognition for positive steps by companies. Some key features of the site are:

- **Covers over 3000 companies, 160 countries, 150 sectors.**
- **Updated hourly.**
- **Over 1.5 million hits per month.**
- **Globally recognised**: the UN, ILO and business organisations have linked their websites to ours.
- **Balanced approach**: the website includes reports about positive initiatives as well as misconduct by companies. We welcome responses from companies.
- **Coverage in English, Spanish and French.**
- **A wide range of sources**, including NGOs, companies, journalists, governments, the UN. Many of the reports on our website are not available anywhere else.

The Resource Centre works in a collaborative partnership with Amnesty International sections and 20 leading academic institutions. Our International Advisory Network, chaired by Mary Robinson, consists of over 80 experts working in all areas of the business and human rights field.

3000 individual company sections

The website has individual sections on over 3000 companies, ranging from well-known multinational corporations to smaller national companies and suppliers.

The section that company representatives are most likely to visit first is the section on their own company, followed by those of their competitors and suppliers. We aim to include a balanced range of news and reports about all the companies on our website, and welcome any comments or clarifications regarding the material to which we link.

Introductory material on business and human rights

For a selection of material that provides an overview of business and human rights issues – and a good introduction for those who are new to the subject – we would recommend the following resources. All of them are available in the section of our website called 'Getting started – an introduction to the subject', accessible via the top navigation bar of our website:

- Business Leaders Initiative on Human Rights (www.blihr.org).
- *A Guide for Integrating Human Rights into Business Management* (Business Leaders Initiative on Human Rights, UN Global Compact and Office of the High Commissioner for Human Rights, February 2006).
- *Report of the United Nations High Commissioner on Human Rights on the Responsibilities of Transnational Corporations and Related Business Enterprises with Regard to Human Rights* (February 2005).
- *Embedding Human Rights into Business Practice* (Office of the High Commissioner for Human Rights and UN Global Compact, November 2004).

- Human Rights Compliance Assessment (assessment tool for companies, developed by Human Rights and Business Project of the Danish Institute for Human Rights, in association with Confederation of Danish Industries and Industrialisation Fund for Developing Countries).
- *Human Rights – Is It Any of Your Business?* (Amnesty International and International Business Leaders Forum, April 2000).
- *Business and Human Rights: A Management Primer* (Shell, 1998).

Running list of company policy statements on human rights

This section of our site, accessible via our homepage, links to company policy statements referring explicitly to human rights. As of May 2006 it included statements by 98 companies. If you know of a company with a human rights policy statement that is not yet included in our section, please let us know and we will add a link.

Top human rights reports by companies

This section profiles best practice company reports on human rights issues, recommended to the Resource Centre by a range of experts. They are included in the section for their strong references to some or all of the following:

- practical implementation;
- policies and management systems;
- specific challenges and limitations;
- commitments and targets for future improvement;
- monitoring and verification;
- involvement of external stakeholders;
- management of human rights and environmental issues in the supply chain.

As of May 2006, the section included reports by: ABB, adidas-Salomon, Anglo American, BHP Billiton, BP, BT, Carrefour, Chiquita, Co-operative Financial Services, Ford, Gap, Hewlett-Packard, ING, National Grid, Nike, Novartis, Novo Nordisk, Reebok, Rio Tinto, Shell, Statoil.

Key principles and United Nations initiatives

Our website includes the main international standards that are the basis for companies' human rights obligations, and various codes and sets of principles designed for business. Click on 'Quick links: Text of business & human rights standards', under 'Special Resources' on the right-hand side of the homepage.

We also track developments relating to these principles, including how individual companies are implementing (or failing to implement) them.

For example, we have a special section on the UN Global Compact, one on the UN Norms on business and human rights, and one on the Business Leaders Initiative on Human Rights which is 'road-testing' the Norms.

Professor John Ruggie, the Special Representative of the UN Secretary-General on Business and Human Rights, has a designated section of our website where he adds material related to his work as Special Representative and which he uses as a platform to request input on specific issues.

Free Weekly Updates

Our free Weekly Updates currently reach over 2500 opinion leaders worldwide, bringing them the week's top positive and negative stories on business and human rights. We invite companies to respond to items critical of their conduct that we plan to include in the Updates; this helps keep the Updates balanced, and encourages companies to address important concerns being raised by civil society. We have invited over 90 companies to respond and nearly all have done so. In some cases this has then led to comments by third parties on the company response, and then further comments by the company. In this way the Updates help keep issues alive until they have been addressed on the ground. To stay informed about breaking news and developments, you can sign up for these Updates via the red box on our homepage.

Custom Alerts

Our Custom Alerts are a paid subscription service for companies, investment firms, NGOs and others.

Subscribers select categories (companies/countries/issues etc.) from our website, and receive an automatic email alert each time we add something about their chosen topics to the site.

The alerts help subscribers to:

- **Keep track** of what is being said about individual companies' social and environmental conduct worldwide.
- **Keep informed by a wide range of sources**. Much of the material on our site and in the alerts goes beyond 'mainstream' sources and therefore is not picked up by news clippings services.
- **Save time**. Subscribers no longer have to search for relevant items on our site, but receive them directly in their inbox.
- **Be prepared for questions about their company and human rights**. The Custom Alerts serve as an early warning system for business people, letting them know as soon as news and reports about their company are added to our website where they reach a wide and influential audience.

Some examples:

- **adidas** might select 'adidas', 'Nike', 'Footwear', 'Clothing & textile', 'Labour rights', 'Supply chain', 'Monitoring', 'China', 'Indonesia'.

- **Nestlé** might select 'Nestlé', 'Danone', 'PepsiCo', 'Food & beverage', 'Baby milk', 'Access to water', 'Protests', 'Racial discrimination', 'Brazil', 'India'.
- **Dell** might select 'Dell', 'Toshiba', 'Technology', 'Supply chain', 'Labour rights', 'Environment', 'Health & safety', 'Digital divide', 'China'.
- **HSBC** might select 'HSBC', 'Credit Suisse', 'Banking & finance', 'Environment', 'Equator Principles', 'Project financing/ loans', 'Impact assessment', 'Protests'.
- **Investment firms and rating agencies** could select companies or sectors that are in their portfolio or that they are researching.

For more information see: www.business-humanrights.org/ CustomAlerts.

Contact us

As attention to business and human rights continues to grow, the Resource Centre will aim to remain the leading independent resource on the subject, tracking the latest developments in the field, and providing facts on the human rights conduct of individual companies worldwide. Increasingly we will be bringing international attention to 'under the radar' reports of companies' human rights impacts in developing countries.

If you, your company or organisation would like to suggest material for our website, or submit a response to material we already link to, please do not hesitate to get in touch: contact@business-humanrights.org.

References

Amnesty International and International Business Leaders Forum (2000). *Human Rights: Is it any of your business?* April, p. 25.
Business Leaders Initiative on Human Rights (2004). Report 2, December.

Chandler, Sir Geoffrey (1997). Oil companies and human rights. *Oxford Energy Forum*, November, p. 3.

Chandler, Sir Geoffrey (1998). Exploitation is our responsibility *Sunday Business* (UK), 16 August.

Economist, The (1998). Survey: human-rights law – the power of publicity. *The Economist*, 5 December, p. 13.

Henkin, Louis (1999). The Universal Declaration at 50 and the challenge of global markets. *Brooklyn Journal of International Law*, **25**(1): 25.

Howen, Nicholas (2005). Business, human rights and accountability. Speech delivered at the Business and Human Rights Conference organised by the Danish Section of the International Commission of Jurists, Copenhagen, 21 September.

Ignatieff, Michael (2000). Human rights as idolatry. Tanner Lectures on Human Values, 4–7 April.

Khan, Irene (2005). Should human rights be your business? Speech delivered to Japan Association of Corporate Executives, Keizai Doyukai, Tokyo, 2 June 2005, http://asiapacific.amnesty.org/apro/APROweb.nsf/pages/IreneKhan_KeizaiDoyukai.

Roth, Kenneth (2005). Rules on corporate ethics could help, not hinder, multinationals. *Financial Times*, 21 June, http://hrw.org/english/docs/2005/06/21/global11176.htm.

Rudolph, Phil (2004). Foley Hoag foreword, in *The Changing Landscape of Liability*, SustainAbility, December, p. 3, http://www.sustainability.com/insight/liability-article.asp?id=180.

Scott, Mike (2005). Project finance sparks change. *Financial Times*, 21 March.

UN Commission on Human Rights (2005). Human rights and transnational corporations and other business enterprises. Resolution 2005/69, adopted 20 April 2005, para. 1(a).

UN World Conference on Human Rights (1993). The Vienna Declaration and Programme of Action, adopted 25 June 1993, para. 5.

UN World Summit Outcome (2005). UN doc. A/60/L.1, 20 September, para. 13.

Table 4.1 lists a range of human rights issues for business. For each issue, it provides an example of a positive company initiative and an example of an alleged abuse.

The examples come from several sources, including the media, NGOs and companies. The source material for each example and further details about each case can be found on our website: http://www.business-humanrights.org/.

When we have received a company response to a particular allegation we have indicated this in the table: the responses are included alongside the original item on our website.

Table 4.1 Examples of companies' impact on a range of human rights issues

Issue	Positive initiatives	Abuses/alleged misconduct
Workplace health and safety	**Global:** Diverse coalition of companies commits to advance workplace safety over 3 years with a 'World Safety Declaration' – founding companies include **DuPont, BP, Tata Steel & Chemicals, Fluor, Aker Kvaerner, Cemex.**	**Thailand:** A fire in **Kader Toy Factory**, producing **Disney** dolls, kills 188 workers, seriously injures 469. The workers, mostly women, had been locked inside the factory 'to prevent them from stealing toys'.
Supply chain	**Global:** **Hewlett-Packard, Dell, IBM** develop Electronic Industry Code of Conduct and establish implementation working group to improve supply-chain conditions. **Cisco Systems, Microsoft, Intel** later endorse the code.	**Bangladesh:** 64 die and at least 74 are injured when **Spectrum-Shahriyar** apparel factory collapses – supplier to several Western retailers including **Carrefour, Inditex, Cotton Group, Scapino, New Wave Group** (all these companies provided a response regarding this incident).
Freedom of association/ Right to form and join trade unions	**China:** **Reebok** encourages democratisation of union at two supplier factories.	**Canada and USA:** Over 200 academics including international law experts sign statement of concern about **Wal-Mart**'s closure of unionised store in Quebec and other steps by Wal-Mart they say are contrary to international law on freedom of association and trade union rights.

Working conditions	**Cambodia:** **Adidas, Gap, Levi Strauss, Nike, Reebok, Sears, Wal-Mart, H&M, Children's Place, Disney** provide support for ILO workplace monitoring project.	**USA (American Samoa):** **Daewoosa Samoa** factory manager found guilty of human trafficking after workers found beaten and starved (supplied **Sears, JC Penney, MV Sport, Spalding/Jacques Moret**).
Child labour	**Global:** UNICEF guide on managing child labour issues responsibly describes codes of conduct and practical steps taken by **Ikea, Levi Strauss, Pentland, Reebok**.	**West Africa:** Lawsuit brought in US court against **Nestlé, Archer Daniels Midland, Cargill** over alleged use of forced child labour in production of cocoa by their suppliers in West Africa.
Forced labour	**Burma:** **Reebok** CEO Paul Fireman op-ed in *Wall Street Journal* condemns Burma's human rights record, including use of forced labour.	**China:** **Deutsche Bank, HSBC, ING, Merrill Lynch, Morgan Stanley, UBS** hold shares (on behalf of clients) in wig maker accused of using forced prison labour (responses to allegations provided by all these firms except Merrill Lynch).
Age discrimination	**UK:** **Pertemps Recruitment** is recognised by UK government for tackling age discrimination in the workplace.	**Australia:** Tribunal finds **Virgin Blue** airline discriminated against flight attendants on the basis of age.

Table 4.1 (Continued)

Issue	Positive initiatives	Abuses/alleged misconduct
Disability discrimination	**India:** **Tata Group's Titan Industries** (watch manufacturer) takes steps in hiring, tool-provision, training and housing to support disabled workers: 5.4 % of workforce has disabilities.	**USA:** Judge orders **United Airlines** to hire and compensate hearing-impaired mechanic.
Gender discrimination	**USA:** **Starbucks, Dell** are first firms to endorse Calvert Women's Principles – comprehensive code of conduct focused on promoting gender equality and women's empowerment.	**Saudi Arabia:** Swedish firms accused in SwedWatch report of adhering to local rules that violate workers' rights to gender equality.
Racial/ethnic/ caste discrimination	**France:** In effort to better detect workplace discrimination against immigrants and minorities, **Casino** supermarket chain creates diagnostic tool to be shared with other companies.	**USA:** Post–11 September workplace discrimination continues nearly four years after terrorist attacks – leads to lawsuits against hotels, car rental agencies, construction firms.
Religious discrimination	**Indonesia:** At its two Indonesian plants (where 90 % of staff are Muslim) **Mattel** provides prayer rooms, flexible schedules to accommodate Friday prayer, permission for Muslim employees who have three years of service to make a pilgrimage to Mecca, with 45 days leave of absence on full pay.	**UK:** Industrial tribunal finds Muslim bus cleaner unfairly sacked by **NIC Hygiene** for taking extended leave to make pilgrimage to Mecca: manager had told him to presume leave had been granted.

Sexual harassment	USA: **Barratt American** (California home builder) trains all its employees on sexual harassment.	USA: Hispanic farmworkers win $1 million sexual harassment case against **Rivera Vineyards.**
Unfair trial and rule of law	**Venezuela:** **Statoil,** Amnesty International and United Nations support human rights training programme for judges and public defenders.	**China:** Five workers who protested unpaid wages and excessive working hours at **Stella International** factory imprisoned after brief trial behind closed doors.
Genocide	**Rwanda:** Five years after the genocide, Hutus and Tutsis join forces to form **Abahuzamugambi coffee cooperative** with aim of promoting unity and reconciliation.	**Sudan:** Human Rights Watch report 'Sudan, Oil and Human Rights' alleges oil companies help fuel genocide by providing revenues for the government, displacing victimised groups, facilitating specific abuses.
Rape and sexual abuse	**Global:** **Body Shop** Ireland supports Amnesty International campaign to raise awareness of violence against women in conflict zones: helps customers take action in the case of Kavira Maraulu, raped and beaten by soldiers in Dem. Rep. of Congo.	**Kenya:** Women working at certain flower plantations (providing fresh flowers for European market) raped on a regular basis by male employers. AIDS is rampant.

Table 4.1 (Continued)

Issue	Positive initiatives	Abuses/alleged misconduct
Torture and ill-treatment	**China:** While a vice president of Occidental Chemical, John Kamm raises with a senior official the case of Yao Yongzhan, Tiananmen Square protester reportedly being tortured in prison. One month later Yao Yongzhan is released. John Kamm later establishes his own company, continues raising prisoner of conscience and torture cases with Chinese authorities.	**Iraq:** US army report says security firms **CACI, Titan** involved in cases of torture at Abu Ghraib prison.
Security and conflict	**Indonesia:** Observers welcome detailed independent human rights audit of Freeport-McMoRan's mining activities (commissioned by Freeport): audit examines and makes recommendations on the company's relationship with Indonesian security forces.	**Dem. Rep. of Congo:** Report by UN peacekeeping mission in Dem. Rep. of Congo suggests **Anvil Mining** representatives provided contradictory statements about their role in an army crackdown on an uprising near its operations in Kilwa, October 2004, which left over 100 dead.
Freedom of expression	**USA:** **Newman's Own** funds freedom of expression prize for 13th year. The $25,000 award is presented to a US resident who has fought courageously, despite adversity, to safeguard the First Amendment right to freedom of expression as it applies to the written word.	**China:** **Yahoo!** provides details to Chinese government that led to imprisonment of journalist Shi Tao – human rights experts criticise Yahoo!'s explanation of its conduct; Yahoo! fails to provide a response to their concerns.

Housing and displacement	**Sri Lanka:** Holcim partners with microfinance bank to address housing needs of the poor.	**Israel/Occupied territories:** Caterpillar criticised for selling modified bulldozers to Israel – used for destruction of Palestinian homes. Caterpillar says it has neither the legal right nor the means to monitor the use of its equipment.
Health	**Global:** Global Coalition on HIV/AIDS awards companies that have innovative approaches to tackling HIV/AIDS, both in workplace and in wider community: **Volkswagen, Getty Images, MAC Cosmetics, Bristol-Myers Squibb, Virgin Unite, De Beers.**	**Ecuador:** Medical study finds high levels of cancer risk to indigenous peoples and peasant farmers living in areas contaminated by **Texaco**'s former operations.
Access to medicines	**Latin America:** 11 countries reach agreement with **Abbott Laboratories, GlaxoSmithKline, Merck, Bristol-Myers Squibb, Roche, Bayer and 19 other pharmaceutical firms** on discounted pricing for HIV/AIDS drugs.	**Global:** Médecins Sans Frontiéres report says new HIV/AIDS medicines still being priced well out of reach of patients in poor countries – refers to **Abbott Laboratories, GlaxoSmithKline, Gilead, Merck.** (Abbott, GSK, Merck provided responses to these concerns.)

Table 4.1 (Continued)

Issue	Positive initiatives	Abuses/alleged misconduct
Poverty and development	**Global:** World Business Council for Sustainable Development features steps companies are taking to help meet Millennium Development Goals, including **Unilever, Procter & Gamble, Holcim, GrupoNueva, EDF, Philips, Vodafone, SC Johnson, Rio Tinto, BP, Eskom, Rabobank, ConocoPhillips.**	**Global:** Christian Aid report 'How tax policies fleece the poor' argues that global poverty commitments will not be met unless poor countries are allowed to stop companies from avoiding paying national taxes.
Disclosure/use of payments to governments (affecting poverty and development)	**Global:** **Statoil** publishes breakdown of all its tax payments to governments worldwide – move welcomed by Publish What You Pay coalition.	**Equatorial Guinea:** US Senate investigation into money laundering controls at **Riggs Bank** reveals misappropriation of at least US$35 million of oil revenues by President Obiang, his family and other officials. Most of the irregular payments came from **ExxonMobil, Amerada Hess, Marathon.**
Indigenous peoples	**Australia:** **Rio Tinto** Child Health Partnership with **Telethon Institute** aims to improve health and well-being of Aboriginal and Torres Strait Islander children and families.	**Guatemala:** Indigenous communities protest **Glamis Gold**'s mining project, saying they were not adequately consulted, and that the operations will harm natural resources, violate their religious and cultural rights – IFC ombudsman investigation finds that consultation was lacking.

Access to water	Mozambique, Nigeria, South Africa, Malawi, Tanzania, Kenya, Swaziland: World Economic Forum launches 'Africa Water Project Exchange' to create partnerships for the delivery, conservation and management of water. Companies involved include **Alcan, Thames Water/RWE**.	India: Villagers accuse **Coca-Cola** plants of depleting local drinking water supplies. (Coca-Cola provided a response to these allegations.)
Environment	Global: Over 4000 Chinese electronics manufacturers to face tough tests on environmental management as **Sony** adopts new 'Green Partner' programme.	Peru: Emissions from **Doe Run** smelter cause acid rain, pollute rivers with zinc and arsenic, and cause almost all young children in La Oroya mining town to have harmful levels of lead in their blood, say local community groups. (Doe Run provided a response to these concerns.)
Education	India: **Ballarpur Industries** works with civil society organisation 'Pratham' towards ensuring primary education for underprivileged children in urban slums in Delhi, Amravati, Nasik, Thane, Aurangabad and Nagpur.	China: In some estimates 10 million school-age children are at work. Director of China Labor Bulletin says this means 'the rural education system in many parts of the countryside is in a state of virtual collapse'.

CHAPTER 5

The British CSR Strategy: How a Government Supports the Good Work

Margaret Hodge

INTRODUCTION

I became responsible for the Government's Corporate Social Responsibility (CSR) brief in May 2006 when I joined the Department for Trade and Industry (DTI). Since then, I have got to know examples of how Corporate Social Responsibility can contribute to achieving sustainable development – how we can act to ensure that our economic and social aims complement each other. Fundamentally CSR is a business agenda – it is about the businesses' contribution to social and environmental progress. Activities are varied and with so much debate surrounding the subject, it is important to have a clear understanding of what CSR is, where the future lies and how government can contribute.

The ICCA Handbook on Corporate Social Responsibility Edited by J. Hennigfeld, M. Pohl and N. Tolhurst
© 2006 John Wiley & Sons, Ltd

We have an ambitious vision for CSR. Underpinning our approach is our belief that economic prosperity and social justice are interlinked and not competing objectives. We want to see businesses take account of their economic, social and environmental impacts, and take action to address key challenges – locally, regionally, nationally and internationally. This is not just because we see that as a moral and ethical approach. It makes business sense for businesses to act in a responsible way which ensures their longer term sustainability.

GOVERNMENT APPROACH AND POLICY FRAMEWORK

As the sponsoring department for business, DTI leads on Corporate Social Responsibility policy. Our aim is to improve the UK's national competitiveness and raise productivity. But there is no value in short-term growth at the expense of the long-term future for us all. The principles which inform our view of Corporate Social Responsibility also influence a range of Government policies.

Our approach is to strike the right balance between voluntary action and statutory regulation. We do not want new burdens on business which could hurt competitiveness and stifle innovation. We want a regulatory and fiscal framework which encourages entrepreneurial activities associated with responsible business behaviour. But we must also protect the long-term interests of our communities. We are committed to setting the right policy framework that stimulates companies to voluntarily raise their performance beyond minimum legal requirements, building on what we have learnt from things like health and safety and employment law for example. There are many examples of well-targeted intervention – one is the introduction of Statement of Investment Principles (SIPs). Since 2000, trustees have been required to disclose, as part of their SIPs, the extent to which social, environmental or ethical considerations are taken into account in the selection, retention and realisation of investments. This measure was introduced to encourage the market to take environmental and social considerations into account in pension investments. A light touch approach such as this can often be the most effective way to promote and extend the good work that business is already doing.

COMPANY LAW

Although the UK Government advocates limited regulation, we recognise that the regulatory framework will need to evolve to reflect changing circumstances. This framework provides the base line for corporate behaviour while CSR encompasses the voluntary actions that companies undertake over and above these minimum legal standards. We do not believe that a 'one size fits all' approach would necessarily benefit the business community, the environment or wider society.

One way to create the right balance is by setting out clearly the standards we expect of company directors. The Companies Bill includes a statutory statement of directors' general duties. This will for the first time set out how directors are expected to behave in an authoritative but accessible way. In line with the recommendation of the independent Company Law Review, that statutory statement will adopt an approach that the Review called 'enlightened shareholder value.' Under this approach the basic goal for directors should be the success of the company for the benefit of its shareholders. But we believe – as the Review did – that business prosperity and responsible business behaviour are two sides of the same coin. The duty will therefore go onto to say that, in seeking to promote the success of the company, directors must have regard to factors such as the interests of the company's employees and the impact of the company's operations on the community and the environment.[1]

REPORTING

One of the most powerful ways in which directors can be held accountable for their actions and behaviour is through improved corporate reporting. That is why in the Companies Bill we have streamlined the arrangements for narrative business reporting and introduced changes to the Business Review which all companies, other than small companies, are required to produce. The Bill sets out the explicit link between the directors' duties and the Business Review, stating that its purpose is to inform the shareholders and help them assess how the directors have performed their duty to promote the success of the company. The Business Review must be a balanced and comprehensive analysis consistent with the size and complexity of the company's business. In the case of quoted companies, the Bill will require the directors to report on matters such as employees, the environment and social and community issues where these are necessary for an understanding of the development, performance and position of the company. We hope that the Business Review will improve transparency and add value to the quality of reporting, as well as highlight the potential of these intangible and non-financial issues to impact on company performance.

A growing number of companies are recognising that greater transparency is vital to building trust and reputation. Reporting on CSR has increased significantly over the last few years. UK companies are now among the leaders reporting on their Corporate Social Responsibility. For example, in 2004, Sustainability, in partnership with UNEP and Standard & Poor's produced a report

---

[1] More information on the reform of company law can be found at www.dti.gov.uk/cld/facts/clr.htm

entitled 'Risk and Opportunity, Best Practice in Non-Financial Reporting'. This surveyed global companies and found that 7 out of 10 of the top global reporters were UK companies. A new Global Reporters survey is due to be published later this year.

In January this year, we published new guidelines on environmental reporting, which will help business prepare their CSR reports. These guidelines aim to help identify and address the most significant environmental impacts and report on these in a way which meets the needs of shareholders and stakeholders alike.[2] The Government has also published guidance on reporting on employee matters. The report of the Accounting for People task force on human capital management reporting is a distinct approach to people management that treats it as a high level strategic issue and seeks to systematically analyse, measure and evaluate how people policies and practices create value for the business.[3]

Indexing is considered by many as a very useful way for companies to demonstrate their CSR credentials. A key initiative is the FTSE4Good Index Series which is designed to measure the performance of companies that meet globally recognised corporate responsibility standards, and to facilitate further engagement from companies in the FTSE Exchange. Created in 2001, the FTSE4Good Index series covers a range of social and environmental impacts, including the environment, supply chain and human rights criteria and, more recently, countering bribery. It is designed as a means of meeting the needs of socially responsible investors to evaluate the quality of companies' approach to Corporate Responsibility and to provide a benchmark tool for financial instruments. Since its launch the number of companies in the index has increased from 700 to over 900.[4]

---

[2] More information on environmental reporting is available at: www.defra.gov.uk/environment/business.
[3] More information on Accounting for People is available at: www.accountingforpeople.gov.uk
[4] More information on FTSE4Good can be found at: http://www.ftse.com/Indices/FTSE4Good_Index_Series/index.jsp

DRIVERS FOR CSR

This Government encourages as many companies as possible to think about how CSR can be applied to their own operations. Both for small and medium sized companies and large-scale multinational enterprises. Key to promoting CSR is the need to promote the business case for proactive investment in CSR activities, and for better standards of business transparency with good reporting and codes of practice.

Many companies have found that acting in a socially responsible way can improve their competitiveness. They cite the higher levels of demand for their products resulting from an improved reputation with their customers, an increased ability to exploit new opportunities by developing products tailored towards niche markets and a greater ability to improve access and retain capital by mitigating against environmental and social risks to a company's assets.

Improvements in motivating staff and a better ability to recruit and retain employees can also lead to savings on recruitment costs. For example National Grid, an energy delivery business, has pioneered business involvement in the rehabilitation of offenders. The company has trained over 140 offenders in a range of gas industry specialisms and a further 100 have completed training and were in jobs by the end of 2005. The re-offending rate is only 7%, bringing in a significant saving to taxpayers compared with the national average re-offending rate of over 70%. From 2006, 1,300 offenders will be trained and employed by five industrial sectors offering the potential to reduce the cost of re-offending across the UK still further. As well as providing motivated, skilled gas network operatives, the programme is meeting a business need and delivering shareholder value.

Amongst a number of business drivers for promoting CSR, I would like to highlight corporate reputation as one of a business's key assets and one which resonates immensely at the board level.

Corporate reputation is no longer based only on price, quality and brand; there is recognition that a business's ethical reputation, which it achieves through engagement with the community, contributes to a company's wider image. A strong reputation, which can be achieved through demonstrating that the company is behaving responsibly, translates into hard economic gains. This is one business driver where boardroom directors are starting to see that CSR can make a valuable contribution to economic performance and increased competitive advantage.

The consumer response to the products of a company is integral to that company's reputation. It follows therefore that care for stakeholders and consumers should be seen as valuable in its own right and central to building the trust on which corporate reputation depends. For example the growth in FairTrade products in recent years (Fair-Trade is now recognised by one third of the UK population!) demonstrates that consumers are increasingly discerning about the processes involved in production. FairTrade is now one of the Co-op's major selling points. This reflects the value consumers place on ethical business. Surveys consistently show that consumers care about ethical production and are influenced by the media and campaigning organisations. As there is evidence that consumers will trust those sources more than they will trust information from the business itself it is vital that business works to build relationships with those civil society groups.

Companies are recognising the value their employees place on a company's contribution to society as well. For example, a MORI survey showed that 82% of employees involved in a company's CSR activities would recommend that company as an employer. A survey commissioned by the Chartered Institute of Personnel and Development showed that 2 out of 3 graduates said a company's ethical reputation would influence their decision to apply.

Whilst consumer trends are very important to business, employees also care about a company's reputation; both as a good employer and as a responsible company within the market place.

Therefore, attracting and retaining the best employees is a key tangible benefit. High performance work places depend on the motivation and skills of employees. The way business directly rewards and values its employees as well as the way it behaves towards its suppliers and wider stakeholders in the community can have a powerful effect on those working within the business.[5]

PARTNERING

As part of the Government's role is to raise awareness and promote the business case, we work with a number of partners such as Business in the Community (BitC) and the Small Business Consortium. So, DTI has endorsed BitC's highly successful Corporate Responsibility Index – which enables companies to assess the extent to which their corporate responsibility strategy is translated into responsible business practice throughout the organisation. The Index has been running since 2002 and in 2006 over 130 companies took part. The DTI also sponsors Business in the Community's annual Awards for Excellence. The awards are an opportunity for both large and small companies to receive nationwide recognition for their commitment to responsible business practice. They also recognise their achievements in integrating responsible business into their mainstream operations resulting in a positive impact in the workplace, the marketplace, the environment or the community. The awards are independently assured and have become a powerful benchmark of good corporate practice.

While BitC focus on larger companies, the Small Business Consortium (SBC) supports small and medium sized enterprises. Formed by small business and CSR organisations including the

---

[5] More information on High Performance Workplaces can be found at: http://www.dti.gov.uk/employment/europe-dti/high-performance/page26171.html

Institute of Directors, the British Chambers of Commerce and the Federation of Small Businesses, SBC aims to raise the competitiveness of small businesses by improving their social, environmental and community impact. In 2004, with financial support from this Government, the Small Business Consortium launched the Small Business Journey, a toolkit for small firms and their advisers, which highlights ways in which small businesses can work towards taking up the CSR journey.[6]

CSR AT THE INTERNATIONAL LEVEL

CSR transcends national boundaries. Internationally, major conferences such as the World Summit on Sustainable Development in Johannesburg and the World Summit on the Information Society in Geneva have recognised the part CSR can play in tackling the many social and environmental challenges we face. In response to this, DTI commissioned Chatham House to undertake a study assessing the options for action at the international level. This followed up outcomes on CSR from the World Summit on Sustainable Development and in March 2005, DTI published an International Strategic Framework on CSR. This sets out our objectives for promoting continuous improvement in the business contribution to each of the economic, social and environmental pillars of sustainable development.

In December 2005, the UK Government hosted a conference, as part of the UK Presidency of the EU. Supported by the European Commission, the event explored how we can stimulate the finance industry, in Europe and internationally, to think long-term about environmental, social and governance issues in their day-to-day operations. Climate change and poverty, exclusion and

---

[6] More information on the Small Business Journey can be found at www.smallbusinessjourney. com

development were assessed in order to identify risks and potential opportunities these issues pose for the finance sector. Actions arising from the conference include building partnerships to develop new products and services, evaluating and scaling up fiscal and trading regimes and incentives for building financial literacy and improving Socially Responsible Investment (SRI) in emerging markets.[7]

OECD GUIDELINES FOR MULTINATIONAL ENTERPRISES

The UK Government is a strong advocate of the OECD Guidelines for Multinational Enterprises, which are an important part of a broader, balanced package of non-binding principles and standards addressed both to governments and to enterprises in the form of the OECD Declaration on International Investment and Multinational Enterprises (MNEs). The Guidelines themselves are recommendations on responsible business conduct addressed by governments to MNEs operating in or from the 39 adhering countries. While many businesses have developed their own codes of conduct in recent years, the Guidelines are the only multilaterally endorsed and comprehensive code that governments are committed to promoting. The Guidelines express the shared values of the governments of countries that are the source of most of the world's direct investment flows and home to most MNEs. They apply to business operations worldwide. The Guidelines are voluntary for business, but National Contact Points (NCPs) are responsible for helping to resolve issues that arise in specific instances.

In July this year, the Government published its response to a consultation on possible improvements to the UK NCP's promotion and implementation of the Guidelines, increasing the

---

[7] More information on the UK Presidency conference on the finance sector can be found at: http://www.csr.gov.uk/UKPresidencyCSRConference.shtml

effectiveness of the NCP in encouraging responsible business activity overseas. As well as refocusing the NCP to include the Department for International Development and the Foreign and Commonwealth Office as well as the DTI, the Government will further enhance the effectiveness of the NCP by establishing a Steering Board, including independent members as well as representatives of all Government Departments with an interest in the Guidelines, to oversee the operation of the NCP; ensuring that complaints are dealt with more rigorously by tightening timescales and procedures and improving transparency; and clearly identifying firms which breach the Guidelines and providing specific guidance in respect of their future conduct. These changes will mean more expertise, greater transparency and swifter action against those who fail to follow the Guidelines, helping to deter irresponsible business conduct overseas and maintaining the Government's approach of encouraging a culture of corporate social responsibility.

OTHER INTERNATIONAL INITIATIVES

This Government is also a strong supporter of the UN Global Compact and we hosted the Global Compact's conference in 2005. The initiative brings companies together with UN agencies, labour and civil society to support universal environmental and social principles. It advances 10 universal principles in the areas of human rights, labour, the environment and anti-corruption. Launched in July 2000, the Compact is now one of the largest corporate responsibility initiatives in the world with a membership of over 1700 companies and the active involvement of over 20 NGOs and 45 local networks spanning Europe, the Americas, Asia and Africa. The UK Government is very keen for corporates operating abroad to sign up to initiatives such as this as they are a tool for understanding and employing CSR principles.

More specifically, we are committed to encouraging companies to observe labours standards during their production processes. This is central to the Ethical Trading Initiative which is an alliance of companies, non-governmental organisations (NGOs), and trade union organisations committed to working together to identify and promote ethical trade, i.e. good practices in the implementation of codes of conduct for decent labour standards. This includes the monitoring and independent verification of the observance of ethical codes and standards for ethical sourcing.

Members, which have a combined annual turnover of over £100 billion pa, including multinational companies or transnational companies are committed to business ethics and corporate responsibility, the promotion of worker rights and human rights in general. In employment, ethical business includes working towards the ending of child labour, forced labour, and sweatshops, looking at health and safety, labour conditions and labour rights.

The employment standards adopted by ETI members are international standards that come from the Core Conventions of the International Labour Organisation (ILO), to which over 170 nations belong. ETI members visit their suppliers, identify conditions that do not meet the ETI base Code, and then plan improvements in agreement with their supplier.[8]

MAINSTREAMING

I believe that CSR is simply part of the way we do business. As part of our efforts to achieve this, we are committed to raising awareness of the benefits of CSR and encourage their adoption. From the Chief Executive in the Boardroom to the worker in the front-line, CSR should be ingrained into the ethos of the business.

---

[8] More information on the Ethical Trading Initiative can be found at http://www. ethicaltrade.org/

Ensuring that responsible behaviour becomes part and parcel of an organisation's operations and is widely understood and practiced is a key focus of our activity.

As part of our strategy to encourage mainstreaming we launched the CSR Academy in July 2004. The Academy aims to help promote CSR by developing and spreading businesses' skills and understanding of the subject. The Academy, working through its programme partners, tailors its activities to fit its three target audiences: SMEs, large businesses and the professional training and development sector. As a new web based resource for organisations of any size and any sector, the Academy provides a central source of information for training and development with the aim of integrating CSR into day-to-day business practice.

Research undertaken among over 400 individuals and organisations already active in CSR identified that there was a lack of tools to enable organisations to achieve a greater level of CSR integration. In response to this the Academy has provided the first ever dedicated CSR Competency Framework, a template designed to help managers integrate CSR within their organisations, principally by feeding CSR into the recruitment, appraisal and professional development of employees. The framework sets out various levels of attainment for a number of core CSR characteristics, together with detailed behaviour patterns and case study examples. The framework is also achieving its principle aims of promoting and mainstreaming CSR with just over 200 new companies asking for the Framework each month. 30 business and management schools are using the Framework as part of their CSR teaching programme. In partnership with the Chartered Institute of Personnel and Development, the Academy has published a set of case studies regarding the integration of CSR through people management processes. DTI has currently negotiated licensing rights with training providers to use the Framework overseas, as part of in house training sessions and as an e-learning management tool. DTI with the Stationary Office, has this year published a How To Use the Framework resource. The Academy has been very successful. Over 5,000 businesses have registered for the Competency Framework; over 1,200 companies have attended Academy events, including masterclasses. Academy events tailored to the SME market have also increased. Other products have been developed including a case studies publication 'Making CSR Happen' and a Competency Framework Resource Pack.[9]

CONCLUSION

As CSR Minister, I believe CSR brings together two themes – improving business performance and helping to combat social injustice. It moves away from the old idea that economic, social and environmental goals are mutually exclusive. The significance of different elements of responsible business practice and the identity of relevant stakeholders will vary depending on the context, whether this is local, global, European or developing country. CSR is relevant to all companies, whether large companies with global reach or complex supply chains or SMEs with very local operations.

The UK Government supports continuous development and application of CSR best practice and we will continue to direct our support to those areas where, with help from our partners, we can have the greatest impact. This Government aims to transform CSR from being seen as an 'add-on' to being a core part of business practice for more and more organisations. This is becoming a reality and our policy of mainstreaming CSR is central to encouraging employees and boardroom staff to recognise the importance of CSR to the holistic development of their business.

---

[9] More information on the work of the Academy can be found at www.csracademy.org.uk

PART II
....

SHARING GOOD PRACTICES AND LESSONS LEARNED

CHAPTER 6

Transnational Corporations and the Global Mindset

Walther Ch. Zimmerli and Markus Holzinger

INTRODUCTION: TRANSCULTURAL COMPETENCE AS A RESPONSE TO GLOBALISATION

The last decade of the twentieth century was marked by the dynamic globalisation of markets. The territorially bound economic sovereignty of states is playing a smaller and smaller role in globalised world trade. Industry has taken leave of the nation–state. Corporations can organise the spatial distribution of manufacturing of their products so that borders are no longer obstacles. The old assumption that political space coincides with economic space has become obsolete.

As a consequence, industrial corporations are playing an active role in political events, thanks to the gaps in regulation left by nation–state political institutions. Now that these companies have

The ICCA Handbook on Corporate Social Responsibility   Edited by J. Hennigfeld, M. Pohl and N. Tolhurst
© 2006 John Wiley & Sons, Ltd

become players crossing territorial borders, they must enter the politics in the countries where they invest. As global political players, industries also bear moral responsibility and cannot limit themselves to short-term economic goals alone. They should contribute as 'citizens' to the foundations of the community. 'Big firms nowadays are called upon to be good corporate citizens, and they all want to show that they are' (*The Economist*, 2005).

Multinational corporations must develop a standpoint and acquire a rational orientation for their strategies in line with these socioeconomic developments. This chapter claims that transnational corporations can tackle the most important challenges successfully only if they understand that management today is management in a transcultural arena. Achieving economic goals is tied to the development of transcultural skills. 'Transcultural competence means a concern with differences. This ability presupposes a deep understanding of both foreign and native cultural requirements' (Zimmerli and Palazzo, 1999: 141). Even if economic processes have always involved cultural exchanges of some form and of varying intensity, the ability to deal with cultural diversity has become a crucial factor for success in the present age of increasing internationalisation and globalisation.

Given these developments, we will first of all reconsider the significance of transcultural management under globalised conditions. In the second section, we explain the extent to which the idea of transcultural management is already integrated into corporate practice. As an example, we will discuss how the relevant factors influencing 'transcultural competence' can be operationalised and dealt with in the Volkswagen Group.

MULTINATIONAL CORPORATIONS IN THE GLOBALISATION PROCESS

A number of assumptions are commonly made about the nature of globalisation. We shall focus on four of these beliefs

(Zimmerli, 1999). (i) The first may be described as the assumption that globalisation is an economic fact. Economists tend to see globalisation as an economic process. While much of the emphasis is on changes caused by economic trends, such as trade and international capital flows, other forces are also involved. (ii) Globalisation is also a technological event, as Daniel Bell (1973), Manuel Castells (1996) and Nico Stehr (2003) have argued. The rise of the Internet is not just the emergence of a useful new communication technology. It is also the basis of a new, non-hierarchical form of organisation uniquely adapted to the demands of an information-intensive economic world. (iii) Another dimension of globalisation is ecological globalisation. The threat to the earth's ecosystems posed by economic activity is placing the market under pressure to produce and operate in a more sustainable way. (iv) Finally, politics plays a key role in the process of globalisation. The notion of globalisation breaks with the idea of the nation-state as the ultimate sovereign actor of politics (Holzinger, 2006: 79). Globalisation reduces the capability of the nation-state to control its own economic and political affairs. The nation-states have lost some of their partial monopoly.

Globalisation in general can be defined as 'the compression of space and time' (Menzel, 2004: 31). Capital has emancipated itself from space. Deregulation has led to the emergence of relatively autonomous financial markets. Nevertheless, globalisation is not the same as homogenisation, as is often claimed. The phenomenon of globalisation does also imply a 'glocalisation' phenomenon (Robertson, 1992). Global corporations adapt their product ranges to local conditions. The prevailing trend is to link global development, production and marketing strategies to local adaptive processes. One could characterise this trend as exemplifying the 'dialectics of globalisation': 'While globalisation shrinks the world to the dimensions of a village, regionalisation and localisation seem to expand the world to an incredible extent as far as plurality is concerned' (Zimmerli, 2000).

It has become increasingly clear that in our society people live together in manifold and complex sociocultural contexts. Internal corporate culture (Schmidt, 2004) is not the only issue to become more variegated, as tomorrow's workforces form a practically unlimited mixture of peer groups, ethnic groups, nationalities, religions, origins, experiences, etc. Multinational corporations may no longer assume that the same cultural identity and homogeneous values prevail between corporate headquarters and foreign subsidiaries. Instead, on the international level the stock of shared values reaches its culturally defined limits. Nowadays, an international corporation operates in a net of different players, forms of rationality, rules and institutions. To mention just a few examples, Volkswagen AG has to deal with US and Japanese suppliers, with the workforces of Volkswagen plants in Germany, Brazil, Mexico, South Africa and the Czech Republic, with Chinese, Brazilian and Mexican governmental agencies, with the trade unions in all of those countries, with the International Labour Organisation (ILO) and with both the United Nations' Global Compact programme and the ICCA Code of Conduct.

Three different cultural levels must be integrated: level 1 concerns an awareness of the organically developed culture of the corporation itself. Level 2 represents the underlying national cultural starting point. Finally, level 3 must be kept in mind, consisting of the different cultures into which the transcultural network of the corporation is extending (Zimmerli and Palazzo, 1999: 142).

It comes as no surprise that these new developments also affect relationships between headquarters and foreign subsidiaries. Traditional multinational companies are based regionally on certain parent companies according to the principle of centre versus periphery. The relationship between headquarters and foreign subsidiaries has, however, tended in recent years towards the reduction of hierarchies on the corporate level, and towards the transformation of roles among the subsidiaries 'away from that of auxiliaries' (to headquarters) and towards 'partners on an equal footing' (Riedl, 1999: 101).

Markets and customer requirements have also become increasingly segmented in ever smaller subgroups. Products are to be geared to the issues of why customers need them and how they are to be used. At the same time, these external contexts represent an important lever for innovations and 'fountainheads for valuable resources and skills that headquarters must protect and promote' (Bartlett and Ghoshal, 2003: 97). It then becomes obvious that the ability to understand other cultures has taken on crucial importance for companies. Their central concern is not to lose sight of the plurality and contrariness of the heterogeneous contexts, but to utilise them in a positive way: diversity matters. The rule industrial companies should follow is: if the extent of a company's strategic alternatives is less than the complexity of its environment, the company will succumb to turbulence. W.R. Ashby (1956) has formulated the imperative of diversity as follows: 'Only variety can absorb variety.'

MANAGING DIVERSITY: THE VOLKSWAGEN FINANCIAL SERVICES AG

As a company engaged in global competition, Volkswagen has to deal with very heterogeneous business segments and customers. This diversity should also be reflected by the workforce and is an important success factor. Diversity in personnel is first of all essential to satisfy the manifold requirements of a complex environment. For Volkswagen 'managing diversity' means utilising and promoting the diversity of its employees: unleashing the creative potential of diversity.

The 'Diversity Management' department of Volkswagen Financial Services AG is dedicated to providing ideas and proposals and to develop concepts for appreciating diversity. For Volkswagen Financial Services AG 'diversity' means above all a climate of openness, ensuring plurality and equal opportunities for all. An interculturally open workforce will also be better in acquiring diverse customers. A separate mentoring project promotes equal opportunities within the company. Other projects, such as equal treatment audits and assertiveness training, increase awareness of diversity. For some years now Volkswagen Financial Services AG has supported Christopher Street Day at the head office in Braunschweig. Employer/Works Council agreements also concern conduct befitting partnership in the workplace. Events take place with the following themes:

- Intercultural competence as a key qualification.
- Working in international teams.
- Gender competence.
- Information events on diversity.

THE MANAGING DIVERSITY MODULE AT VOLKSWAGEN AUTOUNI

Appreciating diversity as a source of added value for the company (team performance, innovation, marketing, etc.) is also the purpose of the Managing Diversity module, a specially designed course at Volkswagen AutoUni.[1] The module teaches skills to managers who in the future will increasingly often have to adapt to rapidly changing planning contexts and perspectives and act effectively within different cultures. The module aims at building both an awareness

---

[1] On Volkswagen AutoUni, cf. the article by M. Holzinger, K. Richter and D. Thomsen in this volume.

of the diversity of global identities and management skills to utilise diversity effectively. 'Managing Diversity' means appreciating the value of diversity, creating a professional environment to use utmost the workforce's potential to the full ('an environment that works for all ...') and in which employees of various backgrounds and orientations feel at home ('...and everybody wants to work in').

Based on a combination of face-to-face and online teaching, the structure of the module utilises a wide range of different educational tools (chat rooms, essays, motivational talks and group presentations). Besides professional skills, the module also teaches social skills, such as acceptance and the constructive development of group cohesion through cooperativeness and communicativeness, coping with conflicts and persuasion.

The module begins with a six-week online phase followed by a one-week face-to-face teaching phase with participants meeting in South Africa, and is concluded by a second online phase. While the face-to-face teaching phase focuses on social and personal skills, the two online instruction phases concentrate in particular on teaching methodological skills and academic knowledge. Both the applied tools and the perspectives to be developed are geared towards dealing with diversity (and complexity) as well as with the different forms of knowledge. Diversity should express itself in both the learning processes and the learning methods, to ensure a high measure of self-reliance and freedom of choice. Besides lectures, fixed components of the seminar include films, group work, cultural and simulation games, role-playing, readings and discussion forums. Postgraduate instruction at Volkswagen AutoUni is organised in a strictly transdisciplinary way, for sound corporate decision making requires access to different stocks of knowledge and methods from a range of disciplines.

The principle of holistic, transdisciplinary learning is supported by regional topics wherever possible: these should be treated and worked on locally, where they have maximum authenticity. That is why 'Managing Diversity' was taught in South Africa for the first time in autumn 2004, where managers experienced the problems of coping with diverse cultures in their everyday work. There is no other location in the whole of the Volkswagen Group where ethnic diversity is so great and the linguistic and cultural differences are so abundant as in the – still young – democracy of South Africa. On-site learning processes on location hold much greater potential than classroom simulations. Learning is no longer reduced to the conceptual processing of taught content. Given the premise of a structural identity between abstract forms of human thinking and goal-directed conduct, an active approach to the subject matter in a concrete context is by far more effective.

'Managing Diversity' employs systems theory, cultural theories, organisational culture and self-reflection methods to analyse and discuss stereotypes, as well as the political and legal frameworks. These topics in particular reveal how an organisation with ongoing specialisation and channelling of fields may increasingly shut itself off from the outside and fend off diversity. Each formation of a system draws boundaries and entails the exclusion of dimensions, which, once excluded, can no longer be grasped from within the system. System boundaries act as 'highly selective constrictions of contact' (Niklas Luhmann). Many elements of the module on 'Managing Diversity' are aimed at making us aware of how we constantly exclude diversity and plurality. Self-reflective thinking can also uncover the restrictions imposed on the observed system by its own modes of operation.

The module also offers approaches to enhancing and utilising diversity. The risks and opportunities generated by everyday business are treated systematically and in depth. The module demonstrates how diversity can exert a positive influence on team performance, motivation, managerial conduct, innovativeness and a company's marketing. The goal here is to appreciate diversity among employees as enriching the company but also to prepare for possible conflict scenarios. Systems are outlined to operationalise diversity as a managerial approach and to introduce the idea of diversity into the company's management. The ultimate issue is how to use diversity as a source of added value and to unleash the creativity of difference.

GLOBAL EXCHANGES AS A PERSONNEL MATTER AT VOLKSWAGEN

While companies have increasingly defined their strategies beyond national borders and now have to deal appropriately with local conditions pertaining to culture and markets, employees accordingly have to gear themselves to the labour market of a 'global village'. The organisational culture must thus be stimulated to esteem diversity.

At Volkswagen the 'Global Assignment' department is responsible for international exchanges of managers. Here as much professional expertise as possible is to be made available worldwide. Work abroad helps managers understand cultural differences and deal with them appropriately. The focus is not only on the development of employees, but also on their contribution to adding value where they will be going. Companies deploy their workers worldwide to ensure success in international competition. Distributing employees among all locations has a major impact on the diversity of perspectives within the company. Bridges are built between cultures and regions in different countries. Promoting diversity among employees therefore also enables companies to react more flexibly to their diverse customer groups. Cognitive diversity could improve team and organisational performance, especially in innovative decision making and in situations requiring a high level of (cognitive) flexibility. Teams with a balanced make up can profit from the diversity of their members, as this generally allows matters to be analysed from thoroughly different perspectives. A large stock of cognitive resources usually leads to greater adaptability in innovative competitive fields. The organisation can thus have recourse to a plethora of skills and knowledge. Creative organisations search for the best pathways and new solutions, and create the corresponding infrastructures for this purpose both internally and externally. One HR director at Toyota has put it this way: 'Toyota regards global diversity as the most important challenge for future growth and securing capable human resources.'

The 'Global Assignment' department plans the entire organisational cycle of assignments abroad, starting in the home town and encompassing all related tasks. The most important tool for Volkswagen HR managers in planning the best possible employee transfers is a pool of candidates (GET=Global Exchange of Talents) eligible for such an assignment.

A parallel process matches the candidates with the positions to be filled. First, the individual companies of the Group designate suitable candidates interested in a given assignment abroad. These candidates are then entered into the pool of GET candidates. Secondly, the departments of the individual regions responsible for transfers abroad provide this pool and the respective HR departments with a list of the vacant positions. If a position seems to be suitable for a prospective transferee, he or she notifies the local HR department. The employee's CV is then sent to 'Global Assignment' headquarters, which initiates the placement process for the candidate and the respective department. The challenge, of course, is to fill the vacant position with just the right candidate. If the candidate is interested, the approval process begins. The entire personnel administration process must now be launched, transferring the candidate to the foreign country and subsequently reintegrating him or her back into the parent company in a suitable position after a certain period of time.

On the global level, this process leads to increasing incorporation of heterogeneous cultures, nations, ethnic groups and status groups, and thereby undermines the traditional relationships between centre and periphery. 'Hybridisations' between cultures, such as those deliberately accelerated here, indicate the 'fading, destabilisation or subversion of these hierarchical relationships' (Nederveen Pieterse, 1998: 105).

CONCLUSION

By way of conclusion, we can say that the individual's willingness to grapple with new challenges and not to limit oneself to business as usual has become crucial for the survival of companies. Creativity and innovations have their roots in diversity, the diversity of people, their personalities, ideas and perceptions.

Volkswagen Group is engaged in promoting diversity at various points in the company. The global exchange of people from different cultures, promoted by the global character of the Group, and new forms of learning that enhance the value of diversity in the company, indicate an increasingly broad spectrum of possible organisational structure and forms of cultural hybridisation. Doors are being opened in cultural terms to formerly segregated geographical spaces, a sign of an 'age of crossing boundaries' (Nederveen Pieterse, 1998: 118). In this age of globalisation we must deal with emerging cultural dissonances and tackle the issues of 'intercultural communication' (Schein, 1998).

It is true, however, that the potential for a diversity-motivated corporate culture at Volkswagen – especially at corporate headquarters in Wolfsburg – has not yet by any manner of means been fully unleashed. To date, top management's attempts to thoroughly change the corporate and management culture at Volkswagen have not yet fully succeeded. A strictly hierarchical managerial style is presently being transformed into a somewhat more decentralised process, resulting in a company where expertise counts more than hierarchical status. The micro-political power struggles (Ortmann, 1995; Mohr, 1999) that also govern careers and vocational plans remain too heavily focused on headquarters and exclude diversity. However, the tools outlined above are an initial step towards re-equipping the Group for globalisation, a more cosmopolitan stance (Beck, 2004) and a truly global mindset.

References

Ashby, R. (1956). *An Introduction to Cybernetics.* London: Chapman & Hall.

Bartlett, C. and Ghoshal, S. (2003). Mythos global manager. *Harvard Business Manager,* November, 84–101.

Beck, U. (2004). *Der kosmopolitische Blick oder: Krieg ist Frieden.* Frankfurt/M: Suhrkamp Verlag AG.

Bell, D. (1973). *The Coming of Post-Industrial Society: A Venture in Social Forecasting.* New York: Basic Books.

Castells, M. (1996). *The Rise of the Network Society.* Oxford: Blackwell.

Economist, The (2005). 22 January.

Holzinger, M. (2006). Der Raum des Politischen. Politische Theorie im Zeichen der Kontingenz. Munich.

Menzel, U. (2004). Paradoxien der Weltordnung. Frankfurt/M: Suhrkamp.

Mohr, M. (1999). *Mikropolitik und Moral. Die Bedeutung persönlicher Macht für eine Ethik in Unternehmen.* Frankfurt: Campus Verlag.

Nederveen Pieterse, J. (1998). Der Melange Effekt, in U. Beck (Ed.), *Perspektiven der Weltgesellschaft,* pp. 87–124. Frankfurt/M: Suhrkamp.

Ortmann, G. (1995). *Formen der Produktion.* Opladen.

Riedl, C. (1999). *Organisatorischer Wandel durch Globalisierung,* p. 101. Berlin: Springer-Verlag.

Robertson, R. (1992). *Globalization.* London: Sage.

Schein, E.H. (1998). Organisationsentwicklung und die Organisation der Zukunft, *Organisationsentwicklung,* **17**(3): 37–9.

Schmidt, S.J. (2004). *Unternehmenskultur,* p. 39. Weilerswist: Velbrück.

Stehr, N. (2003). *Wissenspolitik.* Frankfurt/M: Suhrkamp.

Zimmerli, W. Ch. (1999). Einleitung: Kulturelle Werte und die Zukunft der Ökonomie, in J. Rüsen, u.a. (Hg.), *Zukunftsentwürfe. Ideen für eine Kultur der Veränderung,* pp. 132–41. Frankfurt/New York.

Zimmerli, W. Ch. (2000). In globale Netzwerke verstrickt. Zur Neubestimmung der Aufgabe von Hochschulen, in *Neue Zürcher Zeitung,* 7 November. Studium und Beruf.

Zimmerli, W. Ch. and Palazzo, G. (1999). Transkulturelles management, in A. Grosz and D. Delhaes (Eds.), *Die Kultur AG. Neue Allianzen zwischen Wirtschaft und Kultur,* pp. 139–44. Munich: Hanser Fachbuch.

CHAPTER 7

Corporate Social Responsibility: Past and Present Practice at National Bank of Greece

Takis Arapoglou

INTRODUCTION

The concept of corporate social responsibility generally applies to large companies that decide to contribute to economic development while voluntarily integrating social and environmental concerns in their business, thereby enhancing the quality of life of the workforce and their families, as well as of society at large. Companies should thus treat corporate social responsibility as a long-term investment. Furthermore, corporate social responsibility implies that a company takes social actions on its own initiative and of its own free will, according to an ethical code of conduct that extends beyond purely legal requirements.

It is in this perspective that the Lisbon European Council in March 2000 made a special appeal to companies' sense of

The ICCA Handbook on Corporate Social Responsibility   Edited by J. Hennigfeld, M. Pohl and N. Tolhurst
© 2006 John Wiley & Sons, Ltd

social responsibility with regard to best practices for lifelong learning, work organisation, equal opportunities, social inclusion and sustainable development. According to the European Council, the factors driving this move towards corporate social responsibility are the new concerns and expectations of citizens, consumers, public authorities and investors within the context of globalisation and large-scale industrial change, the social criteria that are increasingly influencing the investment decisions of individuals and institutions both as consumers and as investors, together with increased concerns *vis-à-vis* the damage economic activity causes to the environment and the transparency of business activities brought about by the media and by modern information and communication technologies (European Commission, 2001).

CORPORATE SOCIAL RESPONSIBILITY AT NBG: THE PAST

Corporate social responsibility practices at National Bank of Greece (NBG) have a long tradition, going back to the time of its establishment in 1841. Of course, these practices have changed over time. In its first decades, from the foundation of the bank in 1841 until 1928, these practices were dominated and influenced by the bank's role as both a commercial and a central bank, as well as by the Greek state's prolonged struggle for national integration and independence, which continued until 1950. The close ties between NBG and the Greek state gave the bank a special sense of increased responsibility towards the Greek state and society, even if the concept of corporate social responsibility had not yet been explicitly set out.

Corporate social responsibility activities for the benefit of the community were first established at the initiative of the first governor of National Bank, Georgios Stavros. In line with nineteenth-century social sensitivities, the bank's corporate social responsibility activities tended to focus on charitable organisations, providing them with loans and donations. Yet even at this early stage it gave smaller amounts for artistic and cultural ends (Stasinopoulos, 1966: 67–8). Notably, in 1904 the bank contributed towards the settlement of the debts of the Church of the Holy Sepulchre in Jerusalem; in 1907 it donated a church and its surrounding land (Saint Panteleimon in Athens) to assist the municipality of Athens; while in 1910 it donated a large piece of land in the Ilia region of the Peloponnese to the Agricultural Association in order to set up a pilot crop cultivation project.

The bank also channelled aid to Greek refugees who settled in Greece after being evicted from Turkish territories, provided financial support to national causes, relief for war victims and aid to the families of soldiers fighting in the Balkan War of 1912–13. At the outbreak of World War I the government asked National Bank to assist with the importation of food into the country. The chairman of the first food aid committee, Spyridon Loverdos, managing director of National Bank, reported at the last meeting of the committee (16 February 1916): 'Now that the work of the committee, which has had to deal with considerable difficulties but nevertheless succeeded in organising the food supplies, has reached completion, it is a pleasant duty to acknowledge the services rendered by the officers of the bank, and by the committee members, who were entrusted with this onerous task ... which they undertook in addition to their regular work at the bank. These employees carried out their duties very admirably, as regards both quantity and quality, and with commendable zeal. Without any extra remuneration, they enabled the bank and the committee to carry out their task, without incurring any losses to the business, and even, thanks to careful administration and improvements in organisation, generating savings' (Evlambio, 1924: 199).

During World War II, the bank donated money to support the military effort and also donated a mobile operating theatre for the needs of the Red Cross. In recognition of the staff's dedication to the bank's business objectives, the bank has always cared for their welfare and supported employees on both an individual and family basis through a wide range of facilities and benefits. In 1910, the bank founded and donated money to a mutual benefit fund for employees. In 1931, it undertook to finance the cooperative set up to develop a residential district for its employees in the suburb of Filothei near Athens. In 1941, with the blockade of Athens following the Nazi occupation of the country, the bank provided desperately needed food to its 4000 employees, who were threatened by starvation or death.

CORPORATE SOCIAL RESPONSIBILITY AT NBG: THE PRESENT

In recent decades the bank has stepped up its corporate social responsibility actions; this is reflected in the special annual report published by the bank on its cultural and community-oriented activities, which are much more extensive than demanded by mandatory requirements. In this way the bank is able to convey the message about its corporate social responsibility work to its staff, shareholders and the public. The bank also applies international standards, for example the ISO14000 standard on environmental issues. National Bank of Greece sees it as a duty to extend the corporate social responsibility practices applied in the bank to the other companies of its group and its branches abroad.

Human resources development. Health and safety in the workplace

The bank has stepped up its role in the provision of welfare to its staff and society at large. These activities have their roots in the history of the bank and the specific corporate culture it has developed.

The bank today attaches great importance to the advancement of its staff and this is very much part of its new corporate culture. General and specific staff selection and staff training programmes have been designed and set up to underpin this strategy. Through its diverse professional staff training programmes, which include seminars, distance learning, foreign language learning, postgraduate studies and so on, the bank offers its clerks and officers an opportunity to develop and improve their professional expertise and personal skills. Besides issues related to banking procedures, professional training and development programmes also aim to provide guidance and familiarise staff with the bank's sales and best customer service policies, in order to promote the bank's customer-oriented focus and enhance bank–customer relations. Staff training focusing on new computer platforms and electronic communication and information capabilities (i.e. Internet, Intranet and email) aims to use the advantages of these new systems and tools to the full. Special staff selection and training programmes are implemented for staff at the bank's units in neighbouring Balkan countries, with a view to boosting the bank's profile in Southeast Europe.

In the sphere of alternative training methods, a distance-learning programme has been launched in the context of basic training for new recruits. The bank also provides a wide range of assistance to staff members who wish to pursue postgraduate studies and accredited courses in specialist professional fields or to enhance their foreign language skills.

In 2004, the bank's human resources development programmes included:

- Staff participation in in-house training programmes: 11 113 participants in 889 courses.
- Staff participation in external training programmes in Greece and abroad, and in postgraduate and foreign language courses: 2465 participants.

- Training for regular staff at NBG branches and NBG subsidiary companies, and for contracted associates: 503 participants in 37 courses and training events.
- Cooperating with higher education institutions on student trainee experience at bank units: 35 participants, 1085 days.

Furthermore, with a view to promoting the bank's image and operations, the bank's staff training unit engaged in the following activities:

- We once again took part in the Youth Entrepreneurship Programme, which was implemented at a number of schools in Athens and in regional schools, in conjunction with the Teacher Training Institute of the Ministry of Education and the Federation of Greek Industries. The programme seeks to enhance student awareness of how markets and businesses operate. The staff training unit also ran presentations at six schools in cooperation with the teaching staff of these schools.
- In response to a request by the 47th Middle School of Athens we ran a presentation at the school on the Greek banking system as part of the school's career orientation course.
- In response to a request from the Directorate of European and International Relations, Department of European Programmes, within the Organisation for Vocational Training, we undertook to run an information seminar for 12 representatives and experts on vocational training from various European banks pertaining to the training carried out at National Bank of Greece; this was organised as part of the EU's Leonardo da Vinci vocational training action programme, specifically under the aegis of the study visits measure.
- We gave university students an opportunity to acquire practical experience at the bank.
- We promoted academic research by helping students to carry out research projects. Through its active collaboration with

universities, the bank enhances its social role and provides essential assistance to the emerging generation of scientists and academics.

Support to staff today includes allowances for family housing, maternity leave, nursery schools and home help, child benefits (paid until completion of military service for boys) and children's summer camps.

The bank is highly conscious of its social role. As a result, it supplements its employees' and retired employees' income by means of low-rate personal loans, social benefits, financial aid to seriously ill employees and benefits to spouses and children of employees who die while employed by the bank. Furthermore, the bank continues to insure its entire staff with Ethniki Hellenic General Insurance in a group life and total/partial disability scheme. It also awards prizes to employees' children who excel in high school, university or postgraduate studies, and supports staff unions and associations in their activities, including cultural events, sports, career guidance and Christmas gifts to employees' children.

National Bank of Greece shows particular sensitivity to issues of health and safety and maintains sound protection standards and policies to ensure a safe and healthy working environment throughout the organisation. Within the framework of the operation of NBG's Internal Protection and Prevention Service, safety experts and workplace doctors visit various units of the bank to identify potential occupational hazards and offer recommendations to make their health, safety and accident prevention practices more effective. Furthermore, the bank provides staff training on how to react in the case of robbery, as well as on fire protection and prevention issues.

The NBG Staff Health Fund provides direct health care and hospital services in the event of staff illness or accident via clinics operating at various locations around the country. All health-related matters fall within the responsibility of NBG's health committee.

Environmental policy

National Bank's deep concern for environmental issues is reflected in its belief that implementing a corporate environmental policy constitutes a cornerstone of proper corporate behaviour and contributes to sustainable growth. Today NBG's longstanding initiatives are organised under an integrated and documented environmental management system based on ISO14001 standards. The bank's environmental policy reflects its commitment to conform to the relevant legislation and to implement and constantly improve the system itself. The system seeks to mitigate the effects of the bank's operations and its business activities on the environment, thereby enhancing its environmental performance. The bank's programmes aim to save energy and reduce air pollution, rationalise work-related travel and commuting, manage paper and waste effectively, adopt environmental standards in procurements, while also analysing and assessing the environmental risks involved in our financing operations. The bank renovates its buildings in order to improve their operation and appearance and to ensure they are compatible with their surroundings. The bank has also supported the work of various environmental bodies and has stepped up recycling of large quantities of waste paper and metal generated by the group's network, as well as recycling of obsolete computer equipment.

As part of our environment policy, we assess potential environmental impacts deriving from borrowers' activities. When evaluating a customer's credit rating in the context of our credit policy, we also consider the environmental risks that may derive from the customer's activities and take any risk affecting our corporate image and reputation into account. Since the beginning of 2004, the credit rating of medium-sized and large enterprises (with over €2.5 million turnover) is performed as per Moody's Risk Advisor model, which includes indices related to the environmental effects and risks of the businesses' activities in line with EIRIS ratings.

NBG actively supports the developing market of renewable energy sources, and currently holds over 60% of the Greek market in related credit. Furthermore, since 1997 a special task force has been working to handle processing and approval of financing related to such investments. In 2004, our disbursements to renewable energy projects totalled €30.8 million. These projects included wind farms, small hydroelectric plants and a biogas power station.

Last year we also financed private investments related to the Regional Business Programmes of CSF III for SMEs, taking steps to protect the environment, including energy sources, environment-friendly waste management and a number of other issues.

The bank actively participates in funding large or small-scale privately financed development projects in Greece and abroad. These projects aim to upgrade infrastructure (mainly roads, bridges and energy projects) and improve conditions in urban areas (for example, by creating parking lots); the schemes make a substantial contribution to protecting and preserving the environment, mainly by saving energy and reducing pollution. We have also been involved in funding some privately financed projects in Greece, including the Athens ring road, the new international Athens Airport and the Rio-Antirio Bridge.

In response to the general need to renew the world's shipping fleet, we are also keen to make effective investments in Greek shipping. We invest in the building of new ocean-going tankers in line with international treaties and regulations on environmental protection and preventive pollution measures for ocean-going tankers.

We continued our sponsoring of organisations working for viable growth and environmental protection for a further year. These included:

- The Gaia Centre-Goulandri Natural History Museum, involving implementation of a special environmental programme to raise young people's awareness of critical environmental problems.

- The Hellenic Society for the Protection of Nature, which implemented environmental education programmes entitled 'New reporters for the environment' and 'The school playground: like being at home'.
- The Renewable Energy Unit of the Athens Polytechnic School, with the organisation of the third National Convention on 'Application of Renewable Energy Sources – Prospects and Priorities for the Target Year of 2010'.

Moreover, as a corporate member of the Hellenic Association for the Protection of the Marine Environment, we promote initiatives aimed at instilling and nurturing environmental awareness throughout the shipping industry to help it comply with statutory requirements on safety and pollution at sea.

The bank and the community

During the 164 years of its operations, the bank has always stood by cultural and social institutions through a broad range of activities, including assistance to the arts, science, research, sports, environmental protection and humanitarian causes. It has given substantial support to cultural and artistic expression in Greece, sponsoring performances, musical and operatic events, the visual arts, exhibitions and dance festivals. At the same time the bank has played a significant role in preserving the Greek cultural heritage by facilitating architectural studies, monument restoration and conservation projects and publication of specialist books.

Responding to the concerns of the community and keen to foster social cohesion, National Bank has provided assistance to well-regarded social organisations and bodies, supporting health-related projects and care for the disabled, culture and arts, history and the cultural heritage, science, research and education. The bank has consistently facilitated access to knowledge by sponsoring conferences and research, as well as by awarding prizes and scholarships to various educational bodies. Moreover, we support the publication of books and other printed materials, enriching the libraries at educational and other social institutions, and help to provide computer equipment to schools and other bodies. The bank sponsors various sports associations and provides assistance to organise international sports meetings. Our activities to promote sports were particularly evident in 2004 on the occasion of the Athens Olympics, when we were the official sponsors of the Greek weightlifting team and the ensemble gymnastics team, as well as providing material and moral support to handicapped athletes participating in the Athens 2004 Paralympics. In 2004, the bank's overall sponsorship in favour of third parties amounted to approximately €4.8 million, while the total contribution to similar causes by the rest of the NBG Group was €626 000.

The National Bank Cultural Foundation (MIET)

The bank created the National Bank Cultural Foundation (MIET) in 1966, the year in which it celebrated its 125th anniversary. At the opening ceremony the governor of the bank, George Mavros, noted that 'during its long history, National Bank has always stood by the world of letters, the sciences and the arts. To better organise our activities in these spheres, we are pleased to announce the launch of the National Bank Cultural Foundation. This non–profit foundation will be provided with initial capital of five million drachmas, plus an annual contribution of one million drachmas. Thus, National Bank will be able to fulfil its mission in the cultural sphere more effectively' (Stasinopoulos, 1966: 179–80).

Since 1966, the National Bank Cultural Foundation has made a substantial contribution to the country's artistic and cultural life, notably with an extensive and impressive presence in publishing. The Foundation also organises art exhibitions in Greece and abroad, as well as literary events where eminent writers are invited to speak. The Historical and Palaeographical Archive of the Foundation is constantly extending its microfilm collection with manuscripts from private collections, has acquired seventeenth-, eighteenth- and nineteenth-century manuscripts, co-organises scientific programmes in conjunction with various research institutes, holds a series of Greek palaeography seminars and facilitates research in its reading room. The Paper Conservation Laboratory of the Foundation carries out conservation work on manuscripts and printed books, archives, architectural plans and engravings from the collections of the Foundation and other bodies, participates in exhibitions and other events and provides advice on paper conservation to other institutions. In 2004, the National Bank Cultural Foundation received no less than €1.1 million from the bank to fund its activities.

NBG's historical archive

National Bank also considers it important to preserve all documents relating to its activities. Many of these documents contain valuable historical information about economic, social and political developments in Greece. To this end, the bank has set up a historical archive, which has grown into one of the most important archive institutions in our country. The work of NBG's historical archive involves archive management and preservation, economic history and publishing activities. The historical archive serves as one of the richest sources for the economic history of modern Greece and highlights the bank's diverse contributions to the development of the modern Greek state, as well as to society in general.

In order to upgrade the archival services provided, the bank decided to move its collections to a renovated, specially adapted building. The renovation aimed to achieve top-class functionality, archive safekeeping and smooth workflow, and also involved installing state-of-the-art technological infrastructure and facilities. The new premises thus provide optimum conditions for the safekeeping and preservation of the historical archive's invaluable material, which spans 160 years, together with direct and full access to the archival material for its numerous visitors/researchers, a first-class research environment and exhibition spaces where the public can view the bank's permanent and temporary exhibitions.

CONCLUSION

National Bank of Greece is committed to maintaining the strong social profile it has built up during its 164 years of business, and is keen to promote and uphold long-standing social values. At NBG we are fully aware that economic growth only acquires real meaning when the community as a whole benefits from the fruits of that growth.

References

European Commission Green Paper (2001). *Promoting a European Framework for Corporate Social Responsibility.*

Evlambio, M.S. (1924). *The National Bank of Greece. A History of the Financial and Economic Evolution of Greece.* Athens.

Stasinopoulos, E. (1966). *History of National Bank of Greece, 1841-1966.* Athens.

CHAPTER 8

The Reinhard Mohn Fellowship: Not-For-Profit and Business Learning from Each Other

Liz Mohn

*T*he entrepreneur's contribution to society has always been a topic of fundamental importance for both my husband and me. Fundamental, because it not only sets high standards for corporate management, but also points to the deep anchoring of these companies in their community. Business ventures are an integral element of our society, not a separate, foreign body. Like the political or scientific sector, the business sector and especially businesspeople and those that make the decisions in business have a responsibility to ensure the well-being of the whole, the 'commonwealth'. This is how we understand the dictum that ownership comes with obligations.

In the early 1970s, my husband began publishing his numerous essays and books on the social responsibility of entrepreneurs.

The ICCA Handbook on Corporate Social Responsibility   Edited by J. Hennigfeld, M. Pohl and N. Tolhurst
© 2006 John Wiley & Sons, Ltd

At the time, the now-popular term 'corporate responsibility' was virtually unknown. His writings, and especially his business actions, make it clear how important the topic is to Reinhard Mohn. In 1974, Bertelsmann became one of the first companies in Germany to publish a *Sozialbilanz*, or social report. Responsibility toward employees and society at large has become an integral part of Bertelsmann's thriving and motivating corporate culture, which has brought forth a number of forward-looking initiatives over the course of the years. Our employees enjoy our trust. The principle of delegating responsibility creates entrepreneurial freedom. Certainly one key element in this model is employee participation in the company's economic success. But other factors contribute to the model's success as well, including the in-house pension scheme, opportunities for personal growth and development, a culture that emphasises information, communication and participation, and regular employee surveys on work climate and the leadership conduct of supervisors.

My husband put his experience as an entrepreneur at the service of society as well. In his efforts to be a good citizen and make a contribution to society, he founded a non-profit organisation called the Bertelsmann Stiftung in 1977. In 1993, he transferred most of his assets to it. The Bertelsmann Stiftung is thus Germany's largest private corporate foundation. It plans, carries out and evaluates a number of projects that address fundamental questions in our society. Politics, business, education, health and culture are the main fields of action for the Bertelsmann Stiftung, which has already sparked many processes of progressive reform in the public sector and society. The foundation's work has shown my husband and myself, again and again, that taking entrepreneurial criteria and applying them to other areas of society can provide a considerable boost to efficiency. For instance, the introduction of the performance principle and of competition to municipal and state administrations has tangibly improved the situation of the citizens while also lowering costs.

But politicians and government institutions cannot shoulder all the responsibility for a society's well-being. In the end, citizens themselves play the crucial role in the positive evolution of a community. Individual initiative is a precondition for an active civil society whose citizenry shows a pronounced sense of self-responsibility, a strong sense of identification with the community and a high level of community involvement.

The 'Reinhard Mohn Fellowship' was set up to actively promote civic involvement in the community and contribute to corporate responsibility. The Fellowship honours the lifetime achievement of Reinhard Mohn, entrepreneur and philanthropist, by promoting entrepreneurial drive in all social sectors on the one hand, and communicating Bertelsmann's corporate culture and philosophy of leadership to other social sectors on the other. Bertelsmann AG's fellowship programme is designed for leaders and entrepreneurs from all over the world, who have already become involved and made a contribution to their communities with innovative projects. We promote 'social entrepreneurs', people who tackle social problems with entrepreneurial spirit and tools.

Projects initiated by our Reinhard Mohn fellows include the establishment of a youth orchestra in Calcutta, which gave rise to new jobs and outlooks on life for disadvantaged young people. Thanks to its marketing ideas and international attention, the orchestra became a developmental motor for the local community in Calcutta. Another project involved setting up a training programme for a community of approximately 1600 coffee growers in the primeval forest areas of Mexico's Chiapas region. The small farmers were given training and advice on basic agricultural and business knowledge that helps them to improve their situation under their own steam. The fellows also include the CEO and co-founder of LUMBU, a foundation that represents the interests of the rapidly dwindling aboriginal population of Australia, of which currently about 400 000 remain. Its particular emphasis is the promotion of economic independence for the aborigine community.

By setting up the Reinhard Mohn Fellowship, Bertelsmann AG has chosen a quite unique approach to endorsing social entrepreneurs. The programme systematically promotes the people behind socially relevant projects, not the projects they apply with. Every one-and-a-half years, five people from all over the world are given the chance to go through an elaborate 12-month Fellowship programme at Bertelsmann AG. The fellows acquire valuable knowledge and skills through systematic training and a wide range of project work in a global media company, and can also build far-reaching networks. The programme centres not on the transmission of theoretical knowledge, but on the opportunity to gain first-hand, hands-on entrepreneurial experience. The Reinhard Mohn Fellowship offers deep insights into Bertelsmann AG as a global media company, close collaboration with inspiring personalities, the communication of profound professional and specialist knowledge about business and the media and many opportunities for personal and professional advancement.

During their fellowship year, the fellows work intensely on up to three different projects, in various companies and cultural areas throughout Bertelsmann. Mentors from the executive floors are assigned to them as contacts and advisers. These mentors help the fellows to find suitable projects, get them started on their respective projects, point up important contacts and finally give them expert feedback. In addition, the fellows participate in professional training, seminars and skills enhancement events at Bertelsmann University, which help them to sort the many different hands-on experiences into a larger picture. Another invaluable aspect for the fellows' future development is that during their time at Bertelsmann they will come into contact with a wide range of inspiring personalities. They thus have the opportunity to build their own personal network both inside and outside the company and to cultivate it using the Reinhard Mohn Fellowship network.

Nor is this network reserved for only the actual fellows. Beyond powerfully promoting the Reinhard Mohn fellows, our programme also offers a broader network for selection conference participants who didn't quite make the limited Fellowship programme. The 30 finalists of each selection conference were outstanding among hundreds of applicants and thus constitute a highly talented group of social entrepreneurs with whom we make a point of staying in touch. The Internet-based Reinhard Mohn Fellowship Network provides a platform for the international exchange of ideas, contacts and information. The network helps, for example, to arrange contacts with the Reinhard Mohn Fellowship's collaboration partners or to identify best-practice approaches in entrepreneurial problem solving. The network serves to build an international community of social entrepreneurs that links the isolated and discrete projects of individuals in different social sectors and cultural regions. This sharing of ideas and experiences in a network is designed to boost and lastingly strengthen its members' self-confidence, motivation and shared identity as social entrepreneurs.

The aim of the programme is for the fellows to augment their existing potential as social entrepreneurs during their time at Bertelsmann, in order to advance other projects in their social field of activity with their new-found knowledge and know-how. The programme seeks to help professionalise community involvement, which is frequently rooted in volunteer activities. It does so by conveying transferable business insights and skills on topics such as leadership, project management and communication. Sustainable financing for organisations and projects is becoming more and more of an issue as well. Tight governmental budgets and increasing competition in the donations market have made the influx of public and private sponsorship funds ever more unsteady. This increasingly threatens the survival of many socially important organisations and projects. To offset this, the introduction of entrepreneurial principles to not-for-profit organisations can help to ensure the continued existence of initiatives valuable to society.

We can successfully master the challenges of the future only through a continual process of learning and change. Against this backdrop, profit- and efficiency-oriented businesses and socially committed people and organisations can benefit from each other in many ways.

And so, the Reinhard Mohn Fellowship also serves as a bridge between Bertelsmann AG and other social sectors and cultures. It helps us to look beyond our own noses and learn from each other. The Reinhard Mohn Fellowship not only serves to transmit our knowledge and our experience at Bertelsmann to other areas of society – we get something back as well. Within our global company, the Reinhard Mohn fellows function as catalysts for a wide range of discussions about social responsibility and purposeful change. The fellows' unique experiences and ideas, their creativity and out-of-the-box thinking help Bertelsmann to gain new perspectives and harness them in an entrepreneurial spirit. The programme allows for a powerful exchange about values and leadership philosophy between the fellows and Bertelsmann AG's employees. The fellows' suggestions and questions help us to keep our corporate culture dynamic and put it to the test.

All these impulses feed into our being able to meet the challenges of a globalised world. Our mutual exchange helps us to better live up to our responsibility toward society and to see it as a chance for evolving our own corporate culture. Our employees, too, can feel a greater sense of identification with a socially committed company. The exchange also causes us to be perceived by other social sectors as a company that takes responsibility. The result is a classic 'win–win situation' that allows us to pass along to other companies a conclusion we have arrived at through this learning experience: it pays for companies to shoulder social responsibility.

CHAPTER 9

CSR Implementation – How the Bertelsmann Foundation Supports the Implementation of Corporate Responsibility in Companies

Birgit Riess

For the Bertelsmann Foundation, its mission and its understanding of 'corporate social responsibility' rank among the most important policy issues facing society at present and for some time in the future. The ongoing pressure for reform in Germany, the limited options for political action and a general sense of unease regarding the phenomenon of economisation have led to paradigmatic upheavals in many areas of society. The consequences of this new perception, which is capable of transforming society, are already evident in many areas, e.g. in the increasing vitality of civil society. This is also particularly true because it is the onus of the business community, as the primary agent of economism, which is increasingly perceived as omnipresent, to view social

The ICCA Handbook on Corporate Social Responsibility   Edited by J. Hennigfeld, M. Pohl and N. Tolhurst
© 2006 John Wiley & Sons, Ltd

responsibility as part of its mission and task. With its 'corporate social responsibility' project, the Bertelsmann Foundation carries on the tradition of social and entrepreneurial commitment established by its founder Reinhard Mohn. Its primary concern is to promote the implementation of social responsibility *in the business community* and to instigate a public discussion of social responsibility involving all segments of civil society.

THE 'CORPORATE SOCIAL RESPONSIBILITY' PROJECT

The Bertelsmann Foundation initiated the 'corporate social responsibility' (CSR) project in 2004 to help companies put into economic practice current scientific realisations regarding CSR. The project comprises three modules with the following objectives:

- Promote awareness of CSR: with a view toward establishing corporate social involvement as a natural task of companies – particularly as perceived by the political community and society at large – studies and public events are carried out to emphasise the potential of CSR for society and for companies themselves. The goal is to establish a German standard for CSR that takes into consideration the specific situation, e.g. with regard to the existing legal stipulations in this area, but which also includes the challenges arising from changing expectations about what companies should deliver.
- Develop management competence for CSR: the Bertelsmann Foundation will offer practical support by compiling good examples and models, by conducting studies and compiling European benchmarks, as well as by publishing guidelines for successful cooperation between the business community and the service sector.

• Involve members of civil society: to learn how social capital can be acquired and strengthened, the Bertelsmann Foundation will catalogue and evaluate excellent projects and business models and adapt them for a large audience. With the help of field trips for representatives of the service sector, positive examples for cooperation with the business community will be publicised and recommended for imitation.

An example of what the project has already achieved is the *Analysis of Existing Instruments for Measuring CSR*, the results of which are presented here. They reflect the central demands made by stakeholders on CSR within companies. These demands, presented to companies by investors and the capital market, are reflected in a management approach the Bertelsmann Foundation is currently developing on the basis of 15 comprehensive case studies. This management approach, along with the case studies, will be made available in midyear 2006 in the form of a practical *CSR Handbook*. The insights gained during the course of the project will be used to create a *CSR tool* designed to enable companies to carry out a *self-assessment* and subsequently plan and implement appropriate measures. Sustainability will be ensured through *thematic workshops* conducted over the course of the project, in which experienced experts will be available to provide advice and assistance for CSR novices.

The project, which will continue until 2007, has already produced two widely discussed findings – the transparency study commissioned by the Bertelsmann Foundation and conducted in 2004 by Professor Henry Schäfer,[1] and the results of the 2005 corporate survey of 500 top managers on the subject of corporate responsibility.[2] The corporate survey clearly showed that German

---

[1] http://www.bertelsmann-stiftung.de/cps/rde/xbcr/SID-0A000F0A-D8C6F85A/stiftung/Executive_Summary.pdf or entire text available under http://www.bertelsmann-stiftung.de/cps/rde/xbcr/SID-0A000F0A-F19121F9/stiftung/ Studie_CorporateSocialResponsibility.pdf.
[2] http://www.bertelsmann-stiftung.de/cps/rde/xbcr/SID-0A000F0A-89DFCAB6/stiftung/Unternehmensbefragung_CSR_200705.pdf.

managers are convinced that addressing social problems is essential to profits. It confirmed that CSR activities are not being forced on companies through external pressure, but that they are an integral part of the way companies view themselves in Germany.

The following report will present the findings of these two studies, beginning not chronologically but with the results of the company survey, since these findings support the motives and convictions of the Bertelsmann Foundation and also point up the areas in which the foundation sees the need for further action and for improved professionalism in the implementation of CSR.

FINDINGS OF THE DECISION-MAKER STUDY

The survey results were compiled in multi-subject telephone interviews with 500 randomly selected decision makers in the German economy[3] – CEOs, managing directors, board members and division managers – conducted by the opinion research institute TNS Emnid on behalf of the Bertelsmann Foundation in May and June of 2005. Only companies with 200 or more employees or with a sales volume of more than 20 million euros in 2004 were contacted.[4]

The sample comprised representatives of various industries: 41.6% of respondents were in manufacturing, 23.6% in service industries (excluding financial services), 13.4% in the retail industry, 11.8% in the financial services industry and 6.8% from the primary sector. The sample was representative of the German economy in terms of both number of employees and annual sales volume.

The spontaneous statements made by the managers indicate that they perceive corporate responsibility as a matter of accepting

---

[3] From a group of 4726 companies.
[4] As its source, TNS Emnid relied on the Hoppenstedt Systematics for Large Companies.

responsibility for their employees first and foremost, e.g. by providing secure employment (38% each). A slightly smaller number, namely 26%, whereby particularly large companies took this view, consider overall responsibility for society to lie with the business community. In general, large companies were more apt to emphasise their responsibility than small ones were. See Figure 9.1.

A policy of 'shareholder value' is but a tertiary aspect; managers primarily feel responsible for their customers and employees. See Figure 9.2.

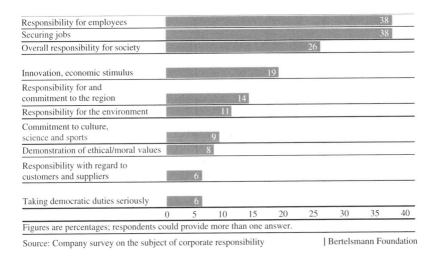

Figures are percentages; respondents could provide more than one answer.

Source: Company survey on the subject of corporate responsibility | Bertelsmann Foundation

Figure 9.1   Statements associated with 'corporate social responsibility'

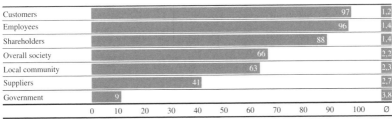

Figures are percentages; summarised representation of top two values (great responsibility/responsibility) on a scale of 1 to 5.

Source: Company survey on the subject of corporate responsibility | Bertelsmann Foundation

Figure 9.2   Responsibility toward selected players

The *social tasks of the business and political communities* are subject to changing perspectives: the idea that a company's tasks should include social and ecological as well as economical issues was supported by a high percentage of decision makers.[5]

There is strong agreement for the view that besides maximising profits, companies should make financial contributions to social issues.[6] On the other hand, respondents believe accumulation of profits alone should not be the exclusive objective of entrepreneurial activity.[7] A majority of decision makers is of the opinion that pursuit of profits and commitment to social issues need not be mutually exclusive per se. Commitment to society involves more than sponsorships and charity donations, and is seen – particularly when it comes to social and ecological issues – as an integral component of business activity. Large companies above all are of the opinion that entrepreneurial management must include social and ecological aspects (93 %).

At the same time, the business community calls on the political establishment to do its part. In this regard, it is predominantly the smaller companies who welcome governmental support of their social commitment and involvement.[8] This finding goes hand in hand with the opinion of the majority of respondents that the distribution of tasks between the government and the business community needs to change – 82 % believe many activities now carried out by the government could be privatised; only 15 % are satisfied with the current distribution of responsibilities.

And yet companies are not merely responding to increasing external pressure. Factors influencing corporate responsibility primarily arise within the companies themselves. For an

---

[5] A value of 1.8 on a scale of 1 to 5, where 1 = total agreement and 5 = total disagreement.
[6] A value of 2.6.
[7] A value of 3.6.
[8] The statement 'The government should support this kind of social commitment' received an agreement rating of 2.3, the statement 'The government should (…) not become involved' was for the most part rejected: value 2.8.

overwhelming majority of respondents (87 %), corporate culture is a decisive factor for their social involvement. A company's economic situation (83 %) and ownership structure (71 %) comprise additional, decisive parameters for social involvement.

Companies become involved first and foremost in order to motivate their own employees (84 %); carrying on the traditions of the corporate culture and protecting company reputation are the primary factors for two-thirds of companies surveyed. Just over half of respondents justify their companies' social involvement as a means to win new customers and meet the demands of shareholders (!). Avoidance of risk (36 %) and pressure from NGOs (11 %) play a lesser role.

Regardless of the industry in which they are active, decision makers are for the most part satisfied with their implementation of their commitment to social involvement – the values range from 60 to 70 %. More than two-thirds say that spending on social issues has increased over the past two years. But there are also obstacles to social involvement: in addition to costs, time constraints were the primary hindrances (Figure 9.3).

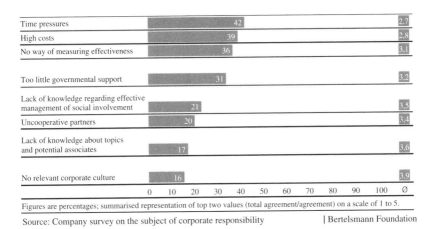

Figures are percentages; summarised representation of top two values (total agreement/agreement) on a scale of 1 to 5.

Source: Company survey on the subject of corporate responsibility | Bertelsmann Foundation

Figure 9.3 Obstacles to corporate social involvement

Support for education and training, along with customer management and handling of complaints (83 % each) and promotion of equal opportunities for employees (with 78 %) are the most common implementations of CSR. However, compared with other management topics such as recruitment of qualified employees (98 %), reduction of costs (87 %), growth (79 %) and R&D (59 %), CSR plays an important role for only one half of the managers surveyed. On the other hand, two-thirds (67 %) expect CSR to play a more important role in their companies in the future.

More than half of those surveyed primarily work together with associations or other companies (56 %) or with not-for-profit or charity organisations (54 %) to implement their social involvement. A third cooperation partner is the scientific community (42 %). Cooperation with citizens' groups, environmental organisations and non-governmental agencies, on the other hand, plays only a subordinate role. See Figure 9.4.

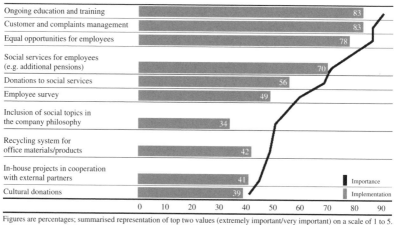

Figures are percentages; summarised representation of top two values (extremely important/very important) on a scale of 1 to 5.

Source: Company survey on the subject of corporate responsibility | Bertelsmann Foundation

Figure 9.4   Areas of corporate involvement

In the companies surveyed, responsibility for the subject of corporate social responsibility lies primarily with top management.[9] 57% of the companies have a CSR budget (on average 800 000 euros), whereby the larger the company, the greater the probability that funds are budgeted for CSR. More than half (62%) do not use a management system, preferring to rely on their own methods. The traditional media mix is used to communicate CSR themes.

In response to the final question regarding expectations for the future, more than half of decision makers responded optimistically. Especially those companies that see themselves as proactive, along with the large companies, take a positive view of the future.

CONCLUSIONS OF THE DECISION-MAKER STUDY

The survey conducted by the Bertelsmann Foundation is an impressive indication that managers decisively reject the role of companies as exclusively profit-making entities. A clear majority do not believe in the repeatedly proposed thesis that companies exist primarily to maximise profits. Rather, they seem to share a more integrated understanding of entrepreneurship that also includes social and ecological issues. More than 60% of companies surveyed see themselves as taking an active role when it comes to accepting responsibility for society. Indeed, one-fifth of managers view themselves as pioneers in this regard. German companies feel responsible for their employees and customers first and foremost. Motivating employees is the primary driving force for social involvement. For large companies, as may be expected, capital shareholders also play an important role.

A majority of corporate representatives desire collaboration with the political community, with whom they believe they share overall

---

[9] Either the managing director (47%) or the board of directors (35%).

responsibility for society. Just under two-thirds of companies desire more governmental support for their social activities. Only 4 out of 10 managers surveyed stated that government should keep out of the matter of social involvement. Still, they do not believe the political community can solve the urgent problems alone, a view reflected in the fact that a large majority advocates the privatisation of governmental tasks. More than half of respondents see a larger degree of social responsibility falling to the business community as a result of such privatisation.

Fundamentally, there is potential for improvement:

- In the increased application of standards (62% do not use a management system).
- In cooperation with citizens' groups, NGOs and environmental organisations, since such cooperative efforts are not yet prevalent (only 35% of companies already cooperate with one or more of these groups).
- In more governmental support, which is desired by two-thirds of respondents.
- More budgets and coordination offices within companies themselves would also be conducive to making good CSR more prevalent.
- 37% of retail and manufacturing companies surveyed do not yet consider their own CSR goals to have been achieved.

MAKING MEASURABLE SUCCESS VISIBLE

A total of nearly 40% of companies surveyed are not yet satisfied with the quality of CSR implementation in their own companies. How can quality and progress be measured? In which areas are companies implementing CSR satisfactorily; in which areas unsatisfactorily; what progress is being made, and where? How can these questions be answered? How can we measure whether companies are living up to the responsibility they accept for themselves?

There is currently one industry above all that concerns itself with quantifying concepts of this kind: the institutes and rating agencies of the financial markets possess the methodological know-how to compare goals with reality.

For the business community, these ratings are important orientation values; they create transparency, enable strategic orientation and targeted communication (in the area of investor relations as well as with the general public) and identify weaknesses within the company. As a result, more and more companies are themselves customers of the ratings institutes. These ratings play an important role for funds managers, who use them to support their investment decisions, but also for the other players on the financial market, for cognisant consumers, for their employees and for the public at large, who want to know how companies are living up to their social responsibilities. Precise knowledge of the objectives and procedures of ratings and rating methods is therefore an important foundation for actions by social stakeholders and companies themselves.

For the further development of CSR, the proper definition of the initial situation is an urgent prerequisite for improvement and for ongoing developments. This is why the Bertelsmann Foundation commissioned a major meta-study in 2004.

FINDINGS OF THE TRANSPARENCY STUDY

The most comprehensive analysis to date, the 'transparency study',[10] examines various evaluation concepts in Europe and North America, and reveals shared attributes that can be considered a 'lowest common denominator'. However, it also reveals that *there is no real consensus on the criteria of what constitutes 'good CSR'*. In terms

---

[10] http://www.bertelsmann-stiftung.de/cps/rde/xbcr/SID-0A000F0A-67B68E02/stiftung/ Studie_CorporateSocialResponcibility.pdf.

of content, the paradigms upon which the evaluation procedures are based are themselves very diverse.

Professor Henry Schäfer[1] examined both evaluation systems developed for players on capital markets as well as for consumer organisations or the companies themselves. The ratings providers operate on a continuum ranging from non-profit to clear orientation toward private maximisation of profits. Primarily, these evaluation methods are used:

- *By banks* (e.g. the Swiss private bank Sarasin & Cie, the Swiss bank UBS AG and the Dutch ING-BHF Bank).
- *By asset managers* (e.g. Allianz Dresdner Asset Management, one of the world's largest asset managers, and Sustainable Asset Management Group Holding AG, the world's first sustainable asset manager).
- *By independent (rating) agencies* such as Oekom Research AG, the association Institut für Markt – Umwelt – Gesellschaft, IMUG (Institute for Markets – Environment – Society), the Ethical Consumer Research Association, a not-for-profit organisation and the CoreRatings Agency.
- *By operators of indexes* such as the FTSE4Good (in cooperation with EIRIS, an independent researcher) and the non-profit agency Ethibel.

COMMONALITIES

The large majority of evaluation systems examined are based on an Anglo-Saxon *stakeholder model* that maps the interests of employees, customers, suppliers, the local community and society at large. European evaluation systems, on the other hand, are influenced more by the tradition of *ecologically* focused sustainability analysis. The enhancement since the 1990s of these evaluation systems to include the *social* dimension has resulted in the stakeholder approach becoming more widespread in Europe as well.

Sustainability analyses are generally applied on the level of companies and industries. The so-called *best-of-class approaches* measure the sustainability of a company on the basis of its relative position to the industry average, with the result that e.g. petroleum producers and energy suppliers are not generally classified as 'non-sustainable'. Only in a few cases are absolute criteria (negative, exclusive or positive criteria) used to determine a sustainability rating.

In most procedures used to rate sustainability, the companies to be evaluated are classified as 'Leaders' (mature companies with a high degree of market capitalisation, a broad range of products and a global approach) or 'Pioneers' or 'Innovators' (young, growing companies with recognisable ecological and/or social innovations) with regard to their sustainability activities.

The investigation procedures demonstrate the following shared indicators in terms of analytic method:

- The entire value-added chain is investigated.
- The entire product lifecycle is analysed.
- All social, ecological and economic effects to stakeholders induced by the company are observed.
- The tremendous significance of a mission statement, a sustainable strategy and the degree of entrepreneurial transparency are taken into consideration.
- Economic, social (to some extent cultural) and ecological macro- and micro-trends are tracked in the entire scope of the company's activities.
- The entire management process from strategy development and implementation to practical steering and actual results, reporting and dialogue are all analysed.

DIFFERENCES

Schäfer distinguishes between approaches that are primarily *economically oriented* than those that are primarily *normatively oriented*, whereby in practical terms, the transition between the two is a fluid one:

- The most common economically oriented concepts concentrate on those ethical, ecological and social criteria that are most likely to have economic effects on the company to be evaluated. Here, the focus on the 'CSR-business case'. They are more often found on the capital market and among business-oriented concepts. Among these approaches, however, there are different methods:

  - *Risk assessment*: the focus is on the analysis of how a company deals with environmental and social risks. Fundamental is the idea that reducing these risks with a view toward avoiding potential damage will result in improved financial success for the company. The sustainable development of a company is therefore seen as avoiding non-sustainability.
  - Approaches based on *enhancement of company value*: these include the management strategies of companies oriented toward the postulate of sustainability. Through early recognition and implementation of economic, ecological and social trends, management aims to proactively generate competitive advantages. In this way, stakeholders in sustainable companies can profit from increasing company value, responsible product technologies and 'good' products. From the point of view of entrepreneurial policy, enhancement of company value is achieved through measures to improve eco-efficiency, i.e. investments in ecological measures that at the same time reduce costs or raise profits, and investment in intangible assets, particularly human resources, which influence the motivation and innovative spirit of employees.
  - Approaches involving above-average growth through *'Innovators'* or *'Pioneers'*: the focus is on ecological and economic opportunities arising from ecologically innovative products or production processes. The examination of the

relevant stakeholders of the company is neglected. Innovator models are particularly prevalent in continental European sustainability ratings.

– *Management models* differentiate themselves from the above-mentioned models to the extent that they place more emphasis on what may be considered the best practices with regard to management of CSR issues. These models are closely related to the models of quality management (EFQM) and the AA1000 accountability standard developed in Great Britain. Process elements such as strategy and planning, operative implementation, evaluation and reporting as well as the design of stakeholder dialogues are of central importance here.

- For *normative*-oriented concepts (e.g. the Frankfurt–Hohenheimer guidelines), the CSR evaluation criteria represent a value in themselves. Management adherence to these criteria may have direct economic consequences. However, this influences neither the choice nor the weighting of criteria. Normative approaches are particularly prevalent in the area of consumer-oriented concepts.

The capital market-oriented evaluation procedures produce a rating or ranking, while the consumer- and company-oriented procedures produce a rough graduation.

CONCLUSIONS OF THE TRANSPARENCY STUDY

The ratings do not conform to common standards. Schäfer comes to the conclusion that the further development of CSR will be influenced more by markets than by political decisions, since the most highly developed approaches have been created by market players whose understanding of CSR in turn influences the markets themselves, e.g. because companies modify their behaviour in order to improve weaknesses revealed by a particular rating. In the future, markets will concentrate on a few providers of ratings whose view of CSR will dominate the markets. This results in a loop in which market players tend to confirm their own view of CSR. Schäfer refers to an *ethical bias*.

ADDITIONAL PROJECT STEPS SUPPORTING THE IMPLEMENTATION OF CSR IN COMPANIES

The findings of the sophisticated meta-analysis described in the *Catalogue of Requirements* for CSR in companies will be incorporated into a management approach that can serve as a model for companies. The *CSR Handbook* to be published in the next project step in midyear 2006 provides practical implementation assistance. It promotes management competence by presenting case studies suitable for implementation, best-practice tips and guidelines for action, and further differentiates the model.

The Bertelsmann Foundation aims to instigate a public discussion of the CSR project with a view toward promoting awareness for CSR. It represents a targeted intervention in the discussion process and stimulates cooperation, joint approaches and shared solutions. A CSR Congress in May 2006 gave an important impetus in this debate. In particular, the Foundation will endeavour to place CSR on the political agenda, for the findings of the two studies demonstrate anew how important it is to involve the forces of civil society (project model 'involving civilian players') in the further development of CSR. They also strengthen the conviction of the Bertelsmann Foundation that the political community should play a more passive, moderating role in ongoing developments. Responsibility structures for CSR in Germany are complex. A coordinating department in a federal ministry should therefore supervise the subject. Its tasks could include the establishment of an information exchange platform for companies, particularly for medium-sized companies, with the goal of improving public awareness for the subject in a long-lasting manner. Additional tasks could include federal/state coordination (special focus: strengthening the local level) and the involvement of associations and stakeholders. In addition, emphasis should be placed on promoting mediatory structures between the business community and not-for-profit organisations, so that entrepreneurial commitment can be more efficiently harmonised with the needs of society, particularly in the area of social services.

CHAPTER 10

Social Responsibility – a Sustainable Strategy for Business Success or Making a Profit with Non-profit

Peter Walter

*V*isions are strategies for actions, that is what distinguishes them from utopia. Visions require courage, strength and the willingness to achieve them.

Roman Herzog (1934, Professor Dr, German constitutional law expert, member of the Christian Democratic Union (CDU), 6th Federal President of the Federal Republic of Germany)

betapharm was incorporated in 1993. At the same time, I took up my position as the company's managing director. And I did so with a vision: I wanted to show that a company could be successful and profitable when led in a humane and responsible fashion. That it is possible to manage an enterprise in such a way that its employees

The ICCA Handbook on Corporate Social Responsibility   Edited by J. Hennigfeld, M. Pohl and N. Tolhurst
© 2006 John Wiley & Sons, Ltd

enjoy working there, while at the same time ensuring the interests of the people in the company's environment will be respected.

Twelve years have passed, and today I can claim that my vision has become reality: betapharm is a successful enterprise, *because* its conduct is based on social responsibility and *because* its focus is on the human being.

BETAPHARM ARZNEIMITTEL GMBH

betapharm Arzneimittel GmbH is a healthcare company selling generics (patent-free drugs). With a range of 148 active ingredients in 897 different commercial sizes, betapharm covers all important medical conditions from the simple cold to severe cardiovascular diseases. The company currently has approximately 390 employees and according to Insight Health (NPI) achieved a turnover of 186 million euro in 2005. Since 2006, betapharm has been owned by the Indian pharmaceutical company – Dr. Reddy's Laboratories Ltd.

The company is based in Augsburg, a small city situated roughly 60 kilometres west of Munich. Although the location of its headquarters is, in itself, of minor importance to a nationally operating healthcare company, this fact may well have constituted an advantage for betapharm's social commitment, which has developed over the years. With approximately 400 000 inhabitants, Augsburg is still small enough to allow people in leading positions to remain down to earth, which makes it much easier to win their personal support for innovative developments.

ON BEER GARDENS AND ESPRESSO BARS

From the outside, the modern office building housing betapharm's headquarters does not look much different from other offices.

However, our visitors agree that the building has an extraordinary atmosphere. On the one hand, this is certainly due to our interior design concept, which is at the same time a communications concept. The walls are decorated with large-format paintings by the artist Mára (Erlangen). These paintings spread positive energy and some were even commissioned for specific locations. Many offices open straight onto the corridors and glass walls make it possible to gaze through from one space to the next. Meeting places such as kitchens, a cafeteria, an espresso bar and a beer garden were also deliberately included in the design. However, the crucial point is that our concept does not stop at the interior design level but is actually lived and used by our employees. It is not unusual to find betapharm employees intently talking business at beer garden tables under the shade of trees. If you need a few words with a busy head of department, you have a good chance of getting hold of him or her after lunch in good spirits at the espresso bar.

This may sound as if we were spending our time idly, which is, of course, not true. At betapharm, we do in fact do a lot of work, yet while we work very hard and with great concentration, there is an open, positive mood. That is the second element that contributes to the special atmosphere at betapharm. Our employees like to work with us. They assume responsibility willingly, they feel good in their workplace, they are fully committed to the enterprise, and we feel it.

This is not by chance, but is instead the result of our fundamental attitude of 'putting the human being at the centre' of our activities. This is a motto many companies promise to act upon in their corporate philosophy, although in fact only numbers count for them and the human being easily turns into 'human capital'. At betapharm, however, we all try to make human beings the measure of all things. We have introduced flexible working hours and many employees have individually adapted their working hours to match their schedules as parents. At the same time, we also remain true to our motto in dealing with clients and business partners alike. We are fair, reliable and open. These are important criteria, because in the generics sector products alone do not allow you to stand out from your competitors.

TOP GROWTH RATES

A few words on generics: generics are 'copies' of drugs no longer protected by patents. After the patent has expired, anybody may reproduce the active ingredients a drug is composed of, apply for a marketing authorisation and sell the new generic drug. As generics incur no research and development costs, they are far cheaper than the original products. They are all more or less the same, too, which is why it is essential for generics companies to establish their individual brand name in order to stand out from other generics manufacturers.

In terms of turnover, betapharm is currently no. 4 on the German generics market. The company has grown continually over the last few years and since 1998 has not only become one of the 10 biggest companies, but is also among those showing the strongest growth rates. The obvious questions to ask are: What is it that betapharm does differently? And why has the company been able to develop so well in recent years?

We are convinced that the top growth rates are a result of our corporate culture and management. To support this statement, we should first explain betapharm's corporate policy: our aim is to encourage physicians to prescribe betapharm products and to ensure that pharmacists stock and sell the prescribed betapharm drugs. There are a number of prerequisites if we are to achieve this aim. betapharm must offer a wide range of top-quality prescription drugs. The generic versions must be available as soon as the patents expire. And the market must be willing to prescribe and sell generics instead of the original products. So far, this may be true for many other manufacturers of generic drugs. Our challenge is to stand out in a market of homogeneous products, to be different from all the others. And we have found ways to do just that. One is the strength and efficiency of our sales representatives, the people who present betapharm products to physicians and pharmacists; they promote the image of the brand name or rather the additional benefits our brand can offer in comparison to others. betapharm had to break some rules here, because to stand out in a market of homogeneous products, one must offer a competitive advantage in competition that is difficult to copy.

BREAKING THE RULES. PART 1: PERSONAL RESPONSIBILITY

Sales representatives in the pharmaceuticals sector usually receive very strict instructions: when to visit which client, what to present in which order and using which wording etc.

betapharm has a different philosophy: our employees are to a large extent personally responsible for how they structure their work. On the part of the company, this requires a high degree of confidence in its employees, while the employees need to be highly motivated and able to identify with the objectives of the company.

This mutual trust and responsibility are grounded in the company's corporate guidelines. With a few amendments, this mission statement has been in force at betapharm ever since the company was set up:

Corporate guidelines
Working with betapharm
each individual should feel part of a community
and find meaning and pleasure in his or her work.
We are open with each other, reliable and treat our colleagues and
clients as partners.

Social responsibility is an issue we take seriously.
Thus, we also address psychosocial healthcare issues and sponsor
socio-medical projects.

We develop our values on the basis of our economic success.
In doing this, we trust in the creativity, performance and
responsibility of our employees.

Success based on trust is our aim.

Many companies have similar guidelines. In most cases they are
hardly ever read and certainly not lived. betapharm is different. We
take these words seriously and endeavour to act on them – at all
levels and with everyone we deal with. This is what distinguishes
us from others and this is the secret of our success.

LEADERSHIP AS A CENTRAL TASK

This corporate culture is the result of hard work. It cannot be
prescribed – rather it must be lived out. This is a management task.
In a study on successful companies and the secrets of their success,
Professor Sonja Sackmann of the University of the Federal Armed
Forces in Munich found that leadership functioning as a role model
is an important key to success.

Applied to betapharm, this means that all employees will
identify with the company and its aims only if I, as the managing
director, as well as all my colleagues in the company's management,
live up to and consistently apply the principles of our corporate
culture by demonstrating fairness, motivation and openness to
dialogue. When people realise and experience what is important
for us they, too, will behave accordingly and spread our corporate
culture.

BREAKING THE RULES. PART II: TRANSPARENT PRICES

When betapharm broke the rules for a second time, it was also due to its corporate philosophy: openness and fairness with regard to pricing. When betapharm was launched in 1993, most generics manufacturers followed a mixed-price strategy: low-priced drugs were advertised while higher priced ones secured profits.

betapharm had a permanent low-price policy for all its products – a strategy that proved very successful in the market. Physicians appreciated betapharm's open and simple pricing system and made betapharm a high-flyer in its sector.

This permanent low-price strategy was successful for years – until our competitors caught on to this concept and copied our approach. The rule we had broken was no longer a rule and in 1998 our growth ground to a halt.

BREAKING THE RULES. PART III: SOCIAL RESPONSIBILITY, RESEARCH AND INNOVATION

As a consequence of this slowdown in growth, betapharm looked for a way to stand out from our competitors that would, on the one hand, comply with the company's ideals and on the other hand, be a little harder to imitate than the pricing strategy. The company's socially responsible approach was the key feature that distinguished betapharm from others. This inspired the decision to demonstrate this fundamental attitude openly and launch betapharm's social sponsoring initiatives.

We consciously abstained from intensifying traditional advertising efforts, especially as marketing strategies of the pharmaceutical industry have a particularly negative image in

Germany. betapharm did not distribute any giveaways – there is not even a ball-pen with our logo – it produced no expensive TV commercials, but instead invested in social projects.

It all began in 1998 with the *Bunter Kreis*. This aftercare organisation helps families in and around Augsburg with chronically and critically ill children to cope better with the specific problems caused by the illness, in particular with the transition from high-tech care in the hospital to the family home. betapharm has been supporting this *Bunter Kreis* since 1998 with donations and volunteer work.

Inspired by this cooperation with the people in charge at *Bunter Kreis*, we came up with the idea of establishing *Bunte Kreise* all over Germany. For this purpose, in 1998 betapharm set up the betapharm *Nachsorgestiftung* (betapharm Aftercare Foundation), an incorporated foundation. The foundation promotes the development of the Augsburg aftercare model and endeavours to introduce the idea in other regions. We quickly realised, however, that the nationwide introduction of a new patient care model would require more extensive efforts, e.g. a scientific cost-benefit analysis. In order to provide a platform for such efforts, in October 1999 betapharm and *Bunter Kreis* founded the *beta Institut für sozialmedizinische Forschung und Entwicklung* (beta Institute for Socio-medical Research and Development), a non-profit company.

What began as 'social sponsoring' quickly developed into full-fledged corporate social responsibility. However, to ensure that this commitment could contribute to the entrepreneurial success of betapharm, two key conditions had to be met.

1. Our commitment focused on the healthcare sector, the environment in which betapharm engages in commercial activities. This facilitates communication on the activities and makes it easier for employees to identify with the company's commitment.
2. *Bunter Kreis*, beta Institut and betapharm share a key concern: the human being. The exemplary work of the

Bunter Kreis highlighted a general problem in the healthcare system: although they receive state-of-the-art medical and pharmaceutical treatment, patients and their families are often left alone to cope with the many problems and strains that arise as byproducts of critical and chronic illnesses.

betapharm's holistic approach to the human being was perfectly suited to fill this 'social gap' in the healthcare system. For this reason, the company initiates, supports and works as a partner with innovative social healthcare projects that encourage holistic patient care and psychosocial health. This commitment combines well with our strategic marketing aim, namely to stand out from our competitors as a socially responsible enterprise and to ensure that betapharm's customers associate our brand name with attributes such as social awareness, capability, reliability and a humane approach.

RESEARCH AND DEVELOPMENT, KNOWLEDGE AND EDUCATION

We seek to close the social gap at various levels. beta Institut serves as a hub for various R&D projects on patient assistance. It distributes expert information and offers further education and training, as well as advisory services.

Our *development* efforts are focused on finding and implementing solutions and care concepts to ensure that patients and their families receive effective assistance. The *Bunter Kreis* key care model for families with critically and chronically ill children is based on method case management. With the help of this complex method both the individual needs of the patient on the one hand and the complex economic requirements in the healthcare sector on the other hand can be taken into consideration and optimised. A care concept for breast cancer patients has now been developed and implemented successfully, as well as assistance concepts for patients in pharmacies. There are also training programmes for children with chronic illnesses, together with Papilio, a prevention programme to combat substance use and aggressive behaviour, which starts at nursery age.

Any developments will be backed by *scientific research* in order to analyse and prove the feasibility and the benefit of the respective models both for the patients concerned and for the healthcare system.

In order to enable professionals in the healthcare sector to offer competent advice to their patients on social issues too, we created the information service 'Informationsservice betaCare' in German. This service includes the social lexicon 'betaListe', the telephone information service 'betafon' and the Internet search engine 'betanet'.

We pass on the results of our R&D activities by means of *training and consulting*. We concentrate on accredited case management training programmes and consulting for social and healthcare institutions that wish to introduce holistic patient management.

RESULTS AND SUCCESSES

By now all these activities have had an impact on the healthcare sector. In 2005, Augsburg hosted the fourth Augsburg Aftercare Symposium (4. Augsburger Nachsorgesymposium), an interdisciplinary platform for aftercare research and practice. There are already 15 aftercare institutions in Germany that assist critically and chronically ill patients and their families based on the *Bunter Kreis* approach. Socio-medical aftercare was included in health insurance legislation due to an initiative by beta Institut, *Bunter Kreis* and betapharm, and has recently helped to facilitate the financing of such institutions.

Several breast cancer assistance centres inspired by the mammaNetz approach were launched in Germany in 2005 and we have already received enquiries from interested parties in Austria. The Papilio prevention programme is expanding and will become a standard in all nurseries in the Federal State of Hesse. More and more pharmacies stand out from the crowd by offering socio-pharmaceutical advice and assistance to their customers.

In most cases, the financing of such activities is not undertaken by betapharm alone. The beta Institut secures the financial and scientific support of other partners: government ministries, foundations, other enterprises, associations, universities and medical centres. betapharm benefits in many ways from these partnerships and contacts. The company obtains information, makes friends and gains recognition and acceptance. The company received its highest accolade in 2002, when betapharm won the *Freiheit und Verantwortung* ('Freedom and Responsibility') contest and received the top award from former German Federal President Johannes Rau. The prize is awarded to companies for outstanding corporate citizenship. All in all, these contacts and the award considerably boosted the company's reputation and it has become much easier for us to establish new contacts and find new business partners.

betapharm has made the classic journey from sponsoring to partnerships to corporate citizenship. This was neither planned nor controlled but a completely natural development resulting from our beliefs and the situation we found ourselves in. Looking back, it is evident that parallel to this successful social 'evolution' the development of our business took a positive turn, too. The slump in 1998 was followed by a period of constant growth, even though the economic environment grew increasingly hostile for healthcare companies. Since its incorporation in 1993, betapharm has climbed to rank 29th on the healthcare market in general and is number 4 among generics suppliers.

SOCIAL RESPONSIBILITY IN TIMES OF ECONOMIC CRISIS

The reform of the German healthcare system implemented in 2004 had a negative impact on the sales of almost all healthcare companies, including betapharm. The constant upward trend was interrupted by a stagnation of sales – and the tantalising question: Would social commitment be sustainable as a corporate strategy for the future? As far as drug prices are concerned, the healthcare reform is only the first step towards a governmental shake-out of the healthcare market. Companies will be under considerable pressure to keep costs low and past experience shows that the first budget cuts generally affect social responsibility activities.

Not so at betapharm. We have maintained our investment in social responsibility at the same high level, convinced that it is above all this investment that makes our company stand out in a market of interchangeable products. This has repercussions in two sectors.

The first sector is 'reputation, corporate branding, culture'. betapharm's dedication to social issues created its reputation both with the general public and in the eyes of its customers. This gave the brand 'betapharm' a much more clearly defined positive profile. Our corporate culture and reputation made our employees much more motivated than one would normally expect. Employees at betapharm are proud of and passionate about every aspect of their company. This lends them credibility in their dealings with customers and is the key to our success.

The second sector in which betapharm stands out is 'service, research, innovation'. Our performance in the socio-medical sector is unique and even offers additional benefits to betapharm's customers. betaCare, for example, represents a singular instrument to win and keep customers' loyalty. Physicians and pharmacists who have access to this comprehensive top-quality information service are able to assist their patients in a more holistic way. In the light of increasingly tough market conditions for the medical profession, and considering that the 'product' they offer is, after all, interchangeable, it becomes more and more important for physicians and pharmacists to retain their patients' loyalty. betaCare helps physicians and pharmacists to establish strong relations with customers (i.e. patients). As a result, betaCare eventually helps betapharm to enhance loyalty among its own customers (i.e. physicians and pharmacists).

With the help of its corporate citizenship, betapharm managed to stand out in an otherwise homogeneous market. The company trusts that this will help it sustain its market position and is looking to further growth. betapharm's corporate citizenship policy became in 2005 even more important in generating good profits in the light of the bad market situation faced by pharmaceutical firms following the recent law changes in the sector. As well as betapharm's corporate citizenship policy, one can say that the company's size will be a decisive criterion for its survival, as the number of players on the generics market is predicted to drop, leaving just a small number of suppliers.

NEW PARTNERS THANKS TO SOCIAL COMMITMENT

There is a new challenge ahead. As a result of cost pressure in the healthcare sector, new customer relationships are emerging, i.e. between drug manufacturers and health insurance companies. betapharm has managed to secure an excellent position here, because health insurance companies are also facing increasing competition and betapharm has more to offer than simply drugs. Thanks to its partnership with beta Institut, betapharm can offer solutions for the crucial question faced by the German health system: How does one provide ongoing support and assistance to patients in an increasingly complex system, while keeping an eye on quality, costs and human needs?

Patient management schemes, such as the *Bunter Kreis* for critically ill children or mammaNetz for breast cancer patients, enable health insurance companies to make special offers to their customers (i.e. patients) and thus retain existing members while winning over new customers. Furthermore, some partners in the negotiations on prices and discounts appreciate betapharm's negotiating culture: open, reliable, humane – betapharm's corporate culture ensures that the company remains true to itself – and that makes an impression.

I believe that this culture not only impresses others but is an element of success in its own right. Significant changes have been set in motion in the German healthcare sector, and networking and cooperation are in high demand: for the first time ever, networks are being created between various healthcare providers: physicians, pharmacists, medical centres and health insurance companies. The key players of the future will turn their attention to structuring entire healthcare processes instead of merely aiming to maximise performance in specific areas. Central management companies will coordinate and develop healthcare networks. This will call for a pioneering spirit, creative unrest, an ability to handle conflicts and work in a team, as well as communication skills to get the message across. All these characteristics have always been among betapharm's strengths and have informed our corporate culture.

Are ethics and social responsibility a basis for success? Our sales figures for the first six months of 2005 demonstrate that corporate citizenship can help a company to achieve long-term and sustained success even in times of crisis. In contrast to conventional marketing activities, however, corporate citizenship requires patience and stamina and the courage to stick to one's visions.

PAPILIO: A STEP INTO THE FUTURE

By sponsoring Papilio, betapharm has already made the next step in this direction. Papilio is a prevention programme developed by beta Institut in cooperation with several universities. Starting at nursery age, its aim is to give children a better grounding to help avoid addictions and aggressive or violent behaviour later in life. The first results of the accompanying scientific research study are encouraging: the children who took part in the Papilio programme display fewer behavioural disorders and behave in a more socially aware manner.

betapharm's primary motivation in supporting the development of this programme is as a response to certain aberrations in our society that cannot be overlooked (betapharm seeks to counteract these negative trends with the help of the Papilio prevention programme). As a socially responsible enterprise, betapharm sees itself as part of society and therefore assumes responsibility for an idea that, in a broader sense, is also concerned with psycho-social health. 'Healthy people', in betapharm's holistic definition of the term, are not violent or prone to become addicts when confronted with a difficult situation.

Only time will tell whether a commitment that serves society for its own sake without creating a specific competitive advantage for betapharm's clients will be able to enhance the company's business success sustainably.

I am convinced that it will do so.

CHAPTER 11

The Body Shop: Living the Dream

Jan Oosterwijk

*D*reaming of a better world where people live in peace, prosperity and are carefree is a way of how people visualise the world's future. Like human beings, companies also visualise how they want to be and how they can contribute to a more sustainable development. Increasingly, companies aim to be more socially responsible in their operations, implementing their values across economic, social and environmental dimensions. However, just like humans, corporations also need to take a long walk to translate their values into practice.

This case presents the unique insight story of Jan Oosterwijk, former director of the executive board of The Body Shop International, who shares his views on the company's early steps in what is known as the corporate social responsibility (CSR) arena today. The Body Shop is a high-quality skin and hair care retailer operating in 50 countries with over 1900 outlets. It is famous for

The ICCA Handbook on Corporate Social Responsibility   Edited by J. Hennigfeld, M. Pohl and N. Tolhurst
© 2006 John Wiley & Sons, Ltd

the introduction of the first naturally inspired skin and hair care products with which the company unintentionally created a niche market with inspiring growth and success. The case of The Body Shop remains interesting today because of its value-oriented (rather than compliance-oriented) approach concerning corporate social responsibility and its efforts to apply its values to business contexts throughout the world. During its establishment and tremendous growth phases The Body Shop has always been guided by the core values of its founders; the implementation and adaptation of these values in times of progress and change have been influenced by the people at The Body Shop and their approach to living the underlying corporate culture. Jan Oosterwijk presents his personal journey of over 25 years of experience with The Body Shop and shares his exceptional story in two interviews with ICCA and Alberic and Lambert Pater on which this chapter is based.

SETTING THE SCENE

The career of Jan Oosterwijk is characterised by serendipity. As a 17-year-old high school graduate, he left for the United States as an exchange student to participate in a programme of the American Field Service aimed at promoting understanding between people of different countries and diverse backgrounds. 'In retrospect, I know that this year has set the course of my life', says Oosterwijk. Leaving Rotterdam behind, on a boat with 800 young people of different countries, opened the world for him. 'I learned to value cultural diversity and became a global citizen.' A desire to engage in activities that went beyond his self-interest and the will to create something good that outlives himself, has followed him ever since. Due to family ties, Jan Oosterwijk was offered the chance to go to Brazil for the Dutch confectionery producer Van Melle and after he returned became CEO of the company in the UK until the beginning of the 1980s. While working at the company he went to Harvard Business School to deepen his business insight. This newly gained knowledge coupled with the high value Oosterwijk places on nature would ultimately lead him to leave Van Melle.

In his interview Oosterwijk shares his personal story behind the break-up with Van Melle. He was hiking in the forests close to his home, when scattered litter, among it wrappers of his own company's sweets, caught his eye. As nature, and its protection, had always been very important to him he suggested to Van Melle to print a request on the wrappers to throw the paper in litter bins instead of polluting the environment; thereby spreading the message: 'Keep your country tidy'. Printing these new wrappers would not even have incurred additional costs but Van Melle did not consider his suggestion and so Jan Oosterwijk decided to leave the safety of this family-run business to return to the Netherlands. Although corporate social responsibility was still uncharted territory back then, and there was no official term for environmentally friendly behaviour, under today's definitions, one can say that Jan Oosterwijk left the company over a CSR issue. For him environmental concern and entrepreneurial goals were not in contradiction, and so, this apparently trivial issue ultimately stimulated his desire to become an entrepreneur himself, thus allowing him to more freely express his personal values and interests by means of commerce.

A few years earlier, in 1976, Anita Roddick had founded 'The Body Shop' in the UK. Initially, she started a small shop to generate her own income while her husband was travelling in South America. To give her assortment of just 15 natural cosmetic products a boost, she presented them in five different sizes, using refillable bottles and minimal packaging to keep start-up costs low. This approach was to become one of the unique selling points of The Body Shop in its success years, combining business sense with environmental friendliness. At this stage, however, environmentalism was not intentionally at the core of Roddick's business concept; there were no words or theories describing the behaviour to protect the environment; instead she just followed her instincts and did what she thought was right and good, states Oosterwijk.

From the beginning, the enterprise clearly positioned itself as an alternative to the traditional cosmetics business. As opposed to spending big budgets on advertising, playing on the fears of women and creating a demand for everlasting beauty, The Body Shop concentrated on promoting the use of unheard of natural ingredients such as aloe vera, jojoba oil and cocoa butter, which was quite revolutionary at the time. As a result The Body Shop started its own, unconventional campaign against animal cruelty by using its stores as billboards. Instead of using whale oil in products, they promoted the use of plant-based ingredients and demanded a halt to whaling. Because of its interesting concept The Body Shop was also very accessible. Enthusiastic shoppers were attracted by its products and the family atmosphere conveyed in the stores; additionally, no other company sold cosmetics in small or sample sizes. Publicity for this new shop experience increased and some people even asked if they could open a shop like that for themselves.

The first franchise store was opened in 1977, based on a self-financing concept that provided The Body Shop with the opportunity to expand without having to make substantial investments. The opening of a shop in Covent Garden, London, in 1981, marked the start of a rapid growth phase. Customers were increasingly turning towards small, innovative, original stores and tourists from all over the world visiting the Covent Garden shop stimulated expansion in the European market. At that time Jan Oosterwijk was introduced to the Roddicks and The Body Shop by reading an article about the company. Even though he did not have a particular affinity with cosmetics, he was inspired by the company's attempt to use the business as a platform for spreading values, a very unconventional approach to business. Especially, the aim of promoting animal welfare resonated with his personal values.

'They were even a bit militant in their approach', says Oosterwijk. His joining the company seems unbelievably easy when he says: 'I spoke to Anita for 20 minutes and afterwards I had the rights for five countries, for free.' According to Oosterwijk, increasing interest in the concept at that time led them to the conclusion: if so many people were inspired by the approach, the concept should also appeal to many more. Oosterwijk opened the first shop in Leiden, the Netherlands, in 1982. It was run by his wife and his sister-in-law. Soon, Oosterwijk rolled out more Body Shops in the Benelux, Germany, France and Austria.

THE GROWTH PHASE

With its accelerating expansion throughout the UK and internationally, headquarters started exercising more control over the design of the shops and how they ought to be run, thereby also influencing the assortment of The Body Shop products by gradually decreasing 'third-party' products in its stores.

Because of the company's growth the roles of the Roddicks changed substantially. Anita was responsible for PR communication and product development, Gordon managed the finances, production and suppliers, while Oosterwijk opened up new markets in Spain, Portugal, Italy and other countries. The three were primarily busy running the day-to-day operations, opening shops and managing their supplies. As business development and marketing issues were largely demand led they did not represent the main focus of their energies. With the stock-market flotation of the company in 1984, this all changed. The organisation had decided to go public in order to attract investment for additional production facilities – and this decision turned out to be very effective, as well as an unintended bonanza for marketing and PR. This was due to a large extent by the image of Anita Roddick as a young, passionate and eloquent woman of migrant origin, challenging traditional business, causing commotion and turmoil among the more traditional profit-oriented companies. This led to enormous publicity and marked the start of an explosive growth phase. Oosterwijk remembers that from then on the company became known internationally. Anita Roddick wrote her first book and became Business Woman of the Year further accelerating the company's success. Rapid growth did not, according to Oosterwijk, necessarily run counter to the core values of The Body Shop. On the contrary, in order to achieve the mission's objective to achieve social change, a wide audience had to be reached.

At that time Oosterwijk was asked by the Roddicks to join them as co-director of The Body Shop because of his background. Especially his affinity with different cultures and speaking various languages having lived in Brazil, the USA and the UK were greatly appreciated by them. His insight reveals the Roddicks' personal influence on management. Oosterwijk compares entrepreneurs with artists: their soul takes a central position in their work. The Roddick's soul not only influenced the organisation's core values, it also influenced the way the company was managed. Oosterwijk remembers that no formal notes were taken and formal documents were not yet developed. The core organisational values had not yet crystallised fully and had not been written down in a mission statement until the company went public. This step, however, had serious effects for the internal organisation. Whereas the company was previously characterised by an informal management style, a publicly listed company requires a mission statement, a well-defined strategy and thorough planning. In addition, The Body Shop gradually started to employ more professional staff such as financial and production directors, auditors and law firms requiring formal integration.

In order to be able to live up to its mission of being a force for social change the 'company's DNA' had to be put in writing by means of a mission statement, which enabled the core values to live beyond the founders, says Oosterwijk. In fact, formalising a mission statement might have been an early sign of a more professional management style. As a co-founder of the Social Venture Network Europe (an international non-profit network that aims to promote corporate social responsibility), The Body Shop, along with Oosterwijk, were inspired by their ideas. Indeed, one can say that the Social Venture Network's goal of 'Transforming the way the world does business' has therefore shaped The Body Shop mission: 'We want to be a force for social change'.

Core values of The Body Shop

Although Anita Roddick had started The Body Shop as a means to survive economically, it soon became known as a company living and communicating its core values. According to Oosterwijk, the then most prominent core value was 'promoting animal welfare' and one way of communicating this to the public was to include labels stating 'This product has been produced without cruelty to animals'. As a result of the Roddicks' anti-big business orientation other core values had been established such as to 'purchase as close to the source as possible' and to do business with people they could identify with or people they knew. Oosterwijk also refers to activities emphasising The Body Shop's values such as refilling, the concentration on plant-based ingredients or fair trade and recycling in which he himself played an important role. Despite this emphasis on social and ecological values, the company should not be considered as a charitable organisation. On the contrary, it intended to blend social and environmental goals through entrepreneurship. By running a financially, socially and ecologically sustainable enterprise, the Roddicks as well as Jan Oosterwijk wanted to make a point to traditional business that social responsibility makes business sense. These core values did not appear out of the blue. They are closely related to the personal values of the Roddicks and country franchisees such as Oosterwijk, as well as the interaction with the public, which contributed to the development and communication of these values.

Maintaining values by franchising

In the quest for expansion, The Body Shop still heavily relied on a master franchising strategy per country. This strategy allowed rapid expansion without large capital investments as master franchises and individual store subfranchises had to do their own financing. At that time, however, the expansion was not only driven by financial terms, but rather by the company's desire to spread their mission and values, explains Oosterwijk. However, for a value-oriented organisation the degree of control of a franchise provider may cause difficulties in the implementation of its values. Generally accepted rules and regulations are enforceable through contracts and governments. Values, on the other hand, are shaped by different experiences, insights and cultures and are therefore more difficult to implement with the same meaning throughout the world.

According to Oosterwijk, franchisees' adherence to the organisation's core values was ensured through self-selection processes, contracts and board engagement. The self-selection process was based on the fact that mostly potential franchisees, whose personal values matched the organisation's values, were attracted to the concept. Additionally, the board would control the allocation of franchise rights through personal interviews ensuring that the values would match. Finally the organisation included important topics – such as anti-animal testing, fair trade, environmentalism – in the franchise contracts.

Franchisees did not merely have to adhere to The Body Shop's core values, but were encouraged to actively contribute to the defining and redefining processes through discussions and interaction. This way there was no static definition of values, rather their interpretation was kept dynamic and supported the establishment of a corporate identity. Discussions were taking place between headquarters and franchisees and continued among employees at headquarters and among franchisees. Oosterwijk recalls a particularly comic discussion about whether selling natural sponges matched with the company's animal-friendliness values. Eventually, the board reached a consensus; the ultimate question to be asked was: ' "Can you train a sponge?" The answer was no, so a sponge was a plant, not an animal', recalls Oosterwijk.

Oosterwijk started to contribute actively to the further development of the organisation's core values. Whereas the Roddicks were primarily focused on animal welfare and the fair trade approach, Oosterwijk was inspired by his knowledge about early environmental problems as well as his personal love for nature. He explains that the refilling idea had not been inspired by environmental protection ideals but was the result of logistic problems. When Anita ran out of a specific bottle size she would simply ask customers to bring an old bottle from home and have it refilled. Later on, Oosterwijk transformed this existing refill idea into a more innovative environmental protection concept introducing a pioneering recycling system in 1989.

Until the beginning of the 1990s, the organisation's values had been defined and redefined to shape a set of unique values inherent to The Body Shop. Looking back to that decade, Oosterwijk considers The Body Shop as a happy family. Oosterwijk: 'It felt that we were busy with something heroic.' The company's DNA was created and explicitly communicated. According to Oosterwijk, The Body Shop as a relatively small organisation allowed processes of 'co-creation'. However, with the expansion of the company throughout the world it became increasingly difficult to integrate the multitude of opinions and views of the franchisees from so many different generations and places of origin.

GROWING PAINS

During the 1980s, the company had grown rapidly from a humble UK-based cosmetics chain to a multinational corporation with thousands of shops and a global presence. However, during the last decade of the twentieth century, The Body Shop started to face serious challenges. These originated from internal aspects as well as from external pressures.

Internal factors

Although the organisation expanded the number of its shops and finetuned its assortment, its internal management capacity did not quite keep pace with this evolution. The organisation was still managed in an informal and personal leadership style. According to Oosterwijk, during the growth phase, the organisation had primarily focused on enabling growth led by demand. This focus on growth is not surprising, since it is consistent with the organisation's mission to be a global force for social change. The Body Shop had become a large multinational enterprise by the 1990s, which required clear structures. However, the company was still based on a management designed for a smaller, informal entrepreneurial enterprise. The informal management style, aimed at two-way communication and regular value discussions, could not be sustained in its current form. Oosterwijk stated that by the middle of the 1990s, the internal discussions about the core DNA gradually decreased. Whereas previously, franchisees were encouraged to actively contribute to the development and interpretation of the organisation's core values, new franchisees were required to more and more concentrate on adhering to the codified values covered in their contracts.

At that time, many new shops were opened in countries with very distinct cultures. The customer base of The Body Shop was rapidly becoming more heterogeneous. This cultural diversity posed another challenge to The Body Shop. Since (the interpretation of) values are quite culturally specific, the company's DNA was put to a serious test. The organisation's core values resonated in a different way with the new customers. For example, to be an environmental company in Western Europe might imply engaging in efforts to maintain biodiversity whereas in Asia it might prefer to focus on recycling.

Abandoning these value discussions also impacted the firm's marketing capabilities. Since frequent contact between headquarters and franchisees could not be sustained, the head office lost its feeling for the end-customers' needs. The shops – an essential interface between headquarters and the consumers – were less stimulated to communicate market trends to the headquarters at a regular basis. As a consequence, headquarters did not sufficiently recognise the danger of other companies copying The Body Shop formula and selling animal and environmentally friendly cosmetics, too. For a company that wants to be 'a force for social change', leadership ought to be a goal in itself fencing off serious derivative efforts. However, The Body Shop had become complacent and found itself in the middle field instead of leading the market. Oosterwijk believes that the company served as an example for competitors showing them a better way to do business; imitating The Body Shop concept was a compliment, but the company had neglected to reinvent itself and its culture in order to maintain its leadership position.

In addition to emerging competition, societal changes, especially in Western Europe, also challenged the organisation. During the 1980s, the Body Shop pioneered in refilling and later recycling their own bottles and containers and in using plant-based ingredients. However, during the 1990s, governments increasingly implemented environmental policies directed towards reducing excess packaging and stimulating recycling. These societal developments made The Body Shop's environmental ambitions less unique in the market. The progressive environmental norms that The Body

Shop embraced had become the standard, which in fact is what the organisation wanted as it represents social change. Yet, the management remained too wedded to the company's traditional values. Oosterwijk believes the organisation 'forgot' to redefine what it meant to be socially responsible with a new millennium approaching and thus lost some of its innovative capability and competitive edge.

External pressure

In 1994, an article written by John Entine, appeared in the *Business Ethics* magazine, claiming that The Body Shop used petrochemical substances in its products. Furthermore, it stated that only 1% of the raw materials were purchased from fair-trade producers. Finally, the article suggested that The Body Shop headquarters did not treat its US franchisees fairly. This story came as a shock and hit the company very hard. In particular, the organisation's ethical reputation received an ugly blow as the story spread quickly around the globe. As a result of this story, a substantial institutional investor dumped its Body Shop shares and the stock price plummeted.

Looking back, Oosterwijk still feels agitated by this incident; 'I felt emotionally raped'. First of all, like The Body Shop the *Business Ethics* magazine was a member of the Social Venture Network in the USA. Thus, the attack on The Body Shop came from within 'its own ranks', which made the incident even more agonising. Moreover, both Oosterwijk and the Roddicks assumed that self-interest was the main reason for the magazine to publish this story. Nevertheless, Oosterwijk also acknowledges that The Body Shop itself was partly to blame. Firstly, The Body Shop had started to suffer from a slight sense of arrogance. 'We thought that, as an honest, innovative and progressive company, we could not do wrong', says Oosterwijk. 'It was a time when we thought we could defy gravity', he adds. This overconfident stance made the company very vulnerable to attacks. Secondly, according to Oosterwijk, not everyone in the traditional business world was charmed by Anita Roddick's management style. In her activist role she had become popular in broad circles. This had allowed her to build a strong brand reputation for The Body Shop. However, by fulminating against big businesses or particular industries, she frequently stepped on people's toes. 'When you become too much of a superstar, you create friends, but enemies as well', says Oosterwijk.

The Roddicks took it very personally and responded to the public criticism. They took legal action against the press that published or broadcasted – in their eyes unfair – stories. According to Oosterwijk, the Roddicks understandably were busy with protecting the organisation's (and also their personal) reputation and were occupied with defending themselves rather than reacting to the emerging management challenges of the time.

A NEW MANAGEMENT

In 1998 Anita Roddick stepped down and took a role of non-executive director of The Body Shop. A North American-style management was installed to take responsibility for the company's strategy and the management of daily operations. Headquarters became more involved in the day-to-day operations of the franchisees and strict compliance to core operations and core values was enforced by contract. In order to facilitate the management of culturally specific values, the company was divided into five regional blocks. Whereas the core values were still considered to be universal, the regional blocks allowed, to a degree, particular interpretations of these values. The new management turned away from charity and oppositional activism – Roddick's main activity – and focused on solution-led approaches in terms of the company's core values. Offering solutions and being proactive, from a business perspective, became more important.

Today the anti-animal testing standpoint is still at the heart of the organisation. Environmentalism and community trade remained as two other core values of The Body Shop. Nevertheless, the interpretation of environmentalism has, for example, changed somewhat according to Oosterwijk. Refilling was replaced by recycling and other environmental goals have overtaken such as the use of green energy. However, in many developing countries environmental issues are hardly addressed by local governments. Oosterwijk believes that refilling and recycling would still make a tremendous difference in these countries. Furthermore, he is convinced that fair community trade could be extended and intensified across all levels and all products. The old values are still relevant; however, a fresh interpretation of these values might be required of The Body Shop in order to maintain socially responsible leadership in the new millennium as was the case in the past.

MISSIONS ACHIEVED AND LESSONS LEARNED

Thirty years ago, Anita Roddick founded The Body Shop as a small entrepreneurial venture to generate some extra income. Today, the company has grown into a multinational organisation. More importantly, The Body Shop is one of the success stories of corporate social responsibility. In fact, its success has shown that corporate social responsibility is not a fad, nor the exclusive domain of PR. It proved that, by 'doing business as unusual', healthy financial results can be combined with social and ecological sustainability. As the case of The Body Shop is told over and over again, the company has set an important example for many businesses and may have initiated change in the way the world does business in the twenty-first century.

Although the company grew very rapidly creating a niche for natural cosmetics, the success did not come easily. It seems that The Body Shop's rapid growth has somehow surprised the entrepreneurs themselves. As a result, and in hindsight, they spent too little resources to create internal mechanisms to the needs of a multinational organisation. The development of The Body Shop provides interesting insights into the dynamics of a value-based growth strategy. The remainder of this section intends to identify important lessons that can be learned from this overview.

Value-based growth requires formal management

The Body Shop's development emerged from two crucial characteristics. Firstly, strong social and environmental values were at the basis. Secondly, in order to achieve the desired social change, The Body Shop adopted a franchising strategy. Although franchising allowed the organisation to spread its message quickly across the globe, this strategy might have hindered the implementation of redefined, up-to-date core values.

During the first years, it was relatively easy to exercise control over, and communicate with, its very motivated franchisees. Being relatively small, personal supervision was a feasible control mechanism. The board personally interviewed potential franchisees and orchestrated frequent values discussions. However, following the decision to go public, the company, by the mid-1990s, started to outgrow its management's span of control. There were simply too many franchisees to be personally supervised by relatively few board members and managers.

Whereas rapid growth rendered personalised control at The Body Shop less effective, the organisation hardly experienced a transition towards more bureaucratic control mechanisms. This, however, is not to say that management should have formalised and imposed the organisational values upon their franchisees. In fact, it can be argued that no management can exercise total control over the salient organisational values. Instead, to a great extent, the formulation and interpretation of organisational values develops spontaneously in interaction. Oosterwijk claims that one cannot leave the company to its devices. 'For values to take root, a lot of energy must be put in nursing and nurturing the values and the energy in people.' As a result of relying on personal control, the company's internal management did not keep pace with its challenges. Formal communicative structures supporting the development and implementation of organisational values were not jointly undertaken. Looking back, Oosterwijk also casts doubts at the effectiveness of the franchising strategy. He claims that, in changing times, headquarters should get more control over its franchisees, not just forcing rules and regulations on them, but more gently introducing new approaches and adjustments. Procedures and regulations remain useful instruments, also in a value-based organisation: 'These allow one to practice what one preaches', says Oosterwijk.

Values must be developed

It is often suggested that an organisation's core, primordial values are everlasting and unchangeable. The Body Shop underlines this rationale by referring to the company's DNA. However, is it realistic to expect core values to be permanent? In the case of The Body Shop, environmentalism has been an important (and enduring) core value. However, what it means to be a frontrunner as an environmental company is subject to change. In the 1980s, the environmental ambitions were understood as refilling and recycling packaging material. However, these environmental efforts have been surpassed by societal changes that have occurred in Western Europe and North America during the last decades. Today, according to Oosterwijk, being an environmental company might for example be expressed by a strong emphasis on efforts to maintain intact ecosystems and thus also biodiversity. Moreover, the interpretation of the core values also depends on the geographic context. Whereas the private recycling initiatives seem to be outmoded in Western Europe, it might still be relevant in countries with underdeveloped ecological policies. Thus, organisations that operate in various cultural and economic contexts need plural interpretations of the organisation's core values adapting them where necessary.

Oosterwijk's experience leads him to the conclusion that The Body Shop's DNA has not yet adapted to the multicultural reality of the organisation. Whereas the company operates in over 50 countries, characterised by various socioeconomic contexts, Western values still dominate the organisation's core. Moreover, Oosterwijk contends that, due to the success of its present values, the organisation forgot to match the interpretation of its core values to different contexts and recent developments in society. For example, a shift from anti-animal testing towards a more wider ranging focus on the ecosystem, preventing the demise of unique animal species and generic animal welfare would be more appropriate in the new millennium. 'One can never be satisfied. Instead, one needs to aim for perfection. An organisation continuously needs to reformulate challenging goals in order to sustain the momentum', states Oosterwijk. Since, generating financial value has become increasingly important to the organisation, the social and ecological oriented values did turn a bit rusty, according to him. Despite, or maybe because of, its commercial success, the organisation gradually seemed to have become part of the establishment it once fought against.

Value-based organisations need leadership and counter forces

Leadership has always played a key role in The Body Shop. The influence of Anita Roddick as a charismatic and energetic leader can hardly be underestimated. As the founder, the organisation's early core values bear the stamp of her personality. But also during the growth phase, she remained personally responsible for the development and implementation of the company's core values and strategy. As the company grew, Anita Roddick started to pursue a more activist role. As a result of her appearance in the media, she became an important symbol for The Body Shop and a global icon. Oosterwijk recognises the double effects of Roddick's media performance. On the one hand, as an outspoken activist she generated immense free publicity for the organisation. On the other hand, her outspokenness sometimes offended sensibilities.

Oosterwijk's personal insight of The Body Shop story demonstrates that leadership remains important; it directs the organisation towards certain goals, it inspires and generates commitment. But the company should not become too dependent on one particular person. For one, human beings are not perfect and make mistakes creating a possible state of unbalance. Secondly, an organisation being too dependent on a charismatic leader might become inward looking and lose contact with reality. Oosterwijk thinks that an organisation must try to remain open and accountable. Therefore, it needs to open itself to outside scrutiny to prevent this sense of group-think. Finally, the company will always be linked to the image of its leader as Roddick's activities have become inseparable from the reputation of The Body Shop. Thus, on the one hand clear and passionate leadership seems to be indispensable for value-based organisations inspiring people within and outside the organisation. On the other hand, leadership might be most effective when it is flanked by counter-forces such as procedures, devil's advocates and media departments.

Oosterwijk concludes: the good news is that in the last two years an effective new management appears to have found the right balance again between traditional professional leadership, a greater assortment with an up-to-date shop appearance and the absorption of new values and ideas such as the attempt to become carbon neutral, integrating nature conservation activities or becoming even more organic.

EPILOGUE

Jan Oosterwijk is no longer associated with The Body Shop, apart from an advisory position. Currently, he dedicates his time to various small entrepreneurial ventures that aim to change the world. Looking back, Oosterwijk experienced his journey with The Body Shop as an interesting interaction between personal and organisational values. Oosterwijk is convinced that personal conviction is important in managing a value-based organisation. 'What moves me?' is a central question for him. He is convinced that, what moves him might move others as well. For Oosterwijk, personal convictions and being open to new avenues form the basis for a living vision, which forms the heart of a value-based organisation. 'People within an organisation need to live their dream', says Oosterwijk.

The success and victories of The Body Shop are anything but a dream. The contribution the organisation made to internationally sustainable development and its part as a role model for the concept of corporate social responsibility has been very real. At the beginning of the twenty-first century, 30 years after its creation, The Body Shop – a living company – appears to have refound its capability to contribute to a better world.

References

Böhmer, Katja, Hennigfeld, Judith and Tolhurst, Nick (2006). Personal interviews with Jan Oosterwijk, 17 February, ICCA, Frankfurt am Main, Germany.
Entine, John (1994). Shattered image, *Business Ethics* magazine.
Hennigfeld, Judith, Pater, Alberic and Pater, Lambert (2005). Personal interviews with Jan Oosterwijk, 29 August, Utrecht, The Netherlands.

ICCA, personal interviews with Jan Oosterwijk.

Pater, L. and Pater, A. (2005). The Body Shop: Living the Dream. Written for ICCA and Jan Oosterwijk.

Pater, L. and Roest, S. (2005). *Implementing Change*. Utrecht: Lemma Publishers.

http://www.anitaroddick.com/ accessed 1 November 2005.

http://www.svn.org accessed 19 February 2006.

www.jonentine.com/articles/bodyflop.htm.

CHAPTER 12

Translating Corporate Social Responsibility Policy into Practice in BT

Ben Verwaayen

*T*oday, corporations face complex and sometimes competing expectations from different stakeholders – employees, shareholders, customers, suppliers, communities and governments. Business ethics, working conditions in the supply chain, health and safety, human rights, environmental management, diversity, employee relations and community investment are all the responsibility of corporations wanting to conduct good business.

CSR is a fascinating subject, as it requires a company to make a choice – whether to make it a 'tick in the box' issue or to see it as something that can contribute to the bottom line if practised

The ICCA Handbook on Corporate Social Responsibility   Edited by J. Hennigfeld, M. Pohl and N. Tolhurst
© 2006 John Wiley & Sons, Ltd

on a day-to-day basis, at the heart of a company. I am sceptical of the 'tick in the box' approach. I believe that living our values (for BT that means being trustworthy, helpful, inspiring, straightforward and warm) helps make us a responsible business and contributes to shareholder value.

So, in BT we don't take the 'tick in the box' approach, but try to make CSR a part of how we do business. We do more than live up to the minimum legislation in the markets in which we operate. We go 'beyond compliance', thinking that by making a positive contribution to society, both BT and society will benefit. This is not an easy task!

Our CSR strategy is evolving. With international expansion a key part of our business strategy, CSR is playing a particularly important role as we extend our reach into new countries where there are often different approaches to corporate governance and ethical issues. This expansion is happening through acquisition, through growth in our networked IT business serving our large corporate customers around the world and through the rise in outsourcing and in-sourcing as a key part of our business model.

You may be asking why we put CSR at the heart of BT. Well, like most things, there are a number of factors that explain it.

To start, limiting the exposure of BT to risk is important.

As a part of plc board accountabilities, we have responsibility for BT's risk management systems, which include significant social, environmental and ethical issues relating to BT's business. Recently we started to measure our CSR risks using the same methodology used to measure overall risk within the corporation. We have identified seven key CSR risks (in no particular order) – climate change, diversity, offshoring, working conditions in the supply chain, breach of integrity, health and safety, and privacy. These are now reported in our annual report and accounts. Over time, we will build up a better understanding of trends in the CSR risk profile of our business, which helps us manage our business better and builds trust with our customers.

But I don't want to give the impression that CSR in BT is all about being defensive and managing risk. We see lots of opportunities too. BT is not alone in being interested in CSR. Our current business strategy is about growing our revenue from large multinational corporations and governments. These customers are telling us that CSR is important to them too. More and more, we find that when we tender for large contracts with these clients, they want to know what our CSR credentials are – £2.2 billion worth of contracts in the 2004–5 financial year alone. Am I saying that CSR is definitely winning us business? No. But it is playing a part in getting and keeping us in the running for big contracts and differentiating us in the marketplace.

Being in the technology business means we have a real opportunity to use ICT products and services to help promote sustainability. This works not only for how we run our own business, but for helping our customers benefit too. Let me give some examples. From a social perspective, greater use of home working and video-conferencing could help enable people to find better balance in their lives. And we are working on a number of technological solutions, which, for example, will enable remote diagnosis and a system of sensors to help elderly people remain in their own homes for longer. In October 2004 we joined forces with the CBI, RAC Foundation and Bradford University to call for broadband communications to be seen as part of the solution to tackling congestion problems in the UK.

Good CSR makes sound financial sense too. Within BT we saved millions in the 2005 financial year as a result of our environmental programmes. And with the value of our brand at several billion pounds, it pays to protect it.

Finally, we are passionate about being an employer of choice. This means operating our business on a common set of values, which guide our interactions with our customers and society. In this way we bind together our external brand and how we approach the market with an internal value set inside the company, which determines how we want to operate. CSR is a logical extension of this combination of values and we want to be measured on and transparent about these values.

Every year we find a positive correlation between our CSR work and the motivation of our employees – 63 % of our employees this year said they were more motivated to work for the company knowing about our social and environmental activities; 30 % of graduates said that our reputation for social responsibility had either influenced their initial decision to apply for a graduate placement with BT, or influenced them to accept the placement.

TRANSLATING POLICY INTO PRACTICE

So if this is why CSR is at the heart of BT, what does it mean in practice for us?

Identifying, understanding and improving our business's environmental and social impacts

Our social impacts are becoming increasingly complex with the transformation of our business from a telephony business to one centred on networked IT services. New issues are emerging and as a responsible business we need to address these. Sometimes it is up to us to stand up and be counted and make sure we act and make a difference where we can. For example the accessing of child pornography through the Internet – in 2004 we launched an initiative which blocks all outbound traffic from the UK to addresses on the Internet Watch Foundation's blacklist.

The development and commercialisation of radio frequency identification devices (RFID) is another area that can be controversial. Therefore in June 2005 we published a research paper looking at the trade-offs between advancements in networked technologies, the risk to personal privacy rights and the responsibilities we need to consider as a responsible corporation active in this marketplace.

As one of the largest business consumers of electricity in the UK we have a significant environmental impact. And the roll-out of broadband is increasing our electricity consumption. As a part of our commitment to improving our impacts we were proud to announce in October 2004 that we had become the world's largest purchaser of green energy.

Leading by example

But for us it is not just about improving our impacts. We take an advocacy position to publicly raise awareness of CSR and get involved in moving the agenda forward as part of our contribution to society in the wider sense.

Climate change is a challenge that we all bear some responsibility to take action on. We are delighted that we have been able to negotiate a three-year contract to provide our 6500 telephone exchanges, satellite earth stations and numerous offices and depots with environmentally friendly power – half from sustainable resources, such as wind generation, solar, wave and hydroelectric schemes, and half from CHP, a technology which generates electricity and heat together and typically achieves a 35–40% reduction in primary energy usage.

BT was an active participant in the industry contribution to the preparations for the G8 summit in 2005, sharing our experience and programme of environmental activities. The culmination of this work was a meeting with UK Prime Minister, Tony Blair, at which a number of industry leaders submitted a call for action by G8 governments.

We are also represented on the UK government's Sustainable Procurement Task Force and are members of the Alliance for Digital Inclusion, working to promote the use of ICT for social benefit.

Alongside our active CSR programme we work with external bodies and organisations that are contributing to the development of industry standards and guidelines in the CSR field. For example we:

- Support the United Nations Global Compact, an international commitment to principles on human rights, labour and civil society.
- Supported the Global Reporting Initiative in its development of sustainability reporting guidelines.
- Input into multilateral dialogues via the Global e-Sustainability Initiative (GeSI), an ICT sector initiative promoting technology that fosters sustainable development, and the European Telecommunications Network Operators (ETNO).
- Worked with the UK Centre for Economic and Environmental Development (UK CEED), an independent charitable organisation aiming to raise environmental standards through research and policy development, and Sustain IT.

We work collaboratively with other organisations, as we know that creating change on the scale that needs to be achieved cannot be done by single companies alone. A number of years ago, working conditions in the supply chain became a big issue for the apparel sector, and the spotlight is beginning to turn onto the ICT sector. We have been closely monitoring working conditions in our supply chain for a number of years and are glad to be sharing our experiences across the sector through our involvement in developing a standard for Supply Chain Working Conditions with the Global e-Sustainability Initiative

(GeSI), which will be accessible to all members of GeSI across the industry.

Engaging in the public debate on CSR for us also means producing papers and 'think pieces' publicising the thinking behind our approach. A couple of years ago we published a paper on the importance of corporate values and their role in business decision making, something that is very dear to my heart:

> All decisions are value laden, whether the driving value is respect for the natural world, creating delighted customers, providing a service to society, caring for employees or making a profit. Values are embodied in corporate structures and cultures, in the relationships with other companies and stakeholders and in the business models the company employs.

Being transparent and accountable

It is my belief that being transparent and accountable in what we do is essential.

Since 2001 we have been producing a combined social and environmental report, alongside our annual report and accounts, which discloses our social, environmental and economic impacts. This report is independently verified and assured against the AA1000 assurance standard and is produced in accordance with the GRI guidelines.

Inevitably there are times when as a business we make decisions that are seen as controversial. We are not going to please all our stakeholders all the time; it is as simple as that! A recent example for us was our decision to open call centres in India. In response to the controversy this caused, we commissioned an independent report called 'Good Migrations' on the potential conflicts between CSR and offshoring, including a review of how well BT discharged its responsibilities to its stakeholders when establishing the call centres in India in 2003.

CONCLUSION

So, CSR is not at the periphery of BT; it is at the very heart of what we do for a living, in a society whose requirements of our business seem to change on an almost daily basis. Of course our commitment to CSR costs us money, but it brings us tangible benefits too. In the interactions we have with our customers who see CSR as important too; in motivating our employees and helping us to be an employer of choice; and in protecting and enhancing our brand. In short, it is an integral part of what we think our reputation should be.

CHAPTER 13

The Business of Empowering Women: Innovative Strategies for Promoting Social Change

Barbara Krumsiek and M. Charito Kruvant

*C*reative Associates International, Inc. (www.caii.com) and Calvert (www.calvert.com) are two companies committed to the equality and empowerment of women worldwide. Creative Associates International is a professional services firm promoting a wide range of development endeavours from Africa to the Middle East, Asia and Latin America. Calvert is a mutual fund company and leader in the field of socially responsible investing. While each brings a different perspective, both have come to the same conclusion: equality and empowerment of women leads to more stable societies and provides many opportunities for better business.

There is no question that women have made significant progress towards social and economic equality in recent decades. In the United States today, for example, women account for half of the nation's workforce, and own and run 26 % of America's companies.

The ICCA Handbook on Corporate Social Responsibility   Edited by J. Hennigfeld, M. Pohl and N. Tolhurst
© 2006 John Wiley & Sons, Ltd

They control assets to the tune of $14 trillion and earn more than $1 trillion every year.

As impressive as this progress certainly is, women continue to face many significant economic challenges. Despite their growing role in the workplace, American women earn just 79.7 cents for every dollar earned by a man. Over the course of her career, the average American woman loses $250 000 to the wage gap. According to the Institute for Women's Policy Research, poverty rates in the United States would be cut in half if this wage gap were eliminated.

Women in America also still face significant barriers to career advancement. For example, American women occupy a mere 13.6 % of all board seats and five chief executive positions at Fortune 500 companies. And they hold just 7.1 % of CFO and 1.6 % of CEO positions at the 500 largest companies.

Globally, the economic challenges women face are even greater. Women around the world put in nearly two-thirds of the hours worked and produce half of the world's food. However, they earn only 10 % of the world's income and own less than 1 % of the world's property; 70 % of the more than one billion people in the developing world who live on less than $1 dollar a day are women.

The issue of improving the status of women is often viewed primarily as a matter of ethics and social justice: promoting equality is simply the right thing to do. That is of course true. However, there is also a strong *business* case for promoting women's economic development, entrepreneurship and enterprise.

As a result of gender inequities, women remain – to some degree, in all parts of the globe – an untapped economic resource and an under-utilised economic asset. No nation can achieve its full economic and human potential if half of its population remains marginalised and disempowered, and no corporation can meet the demands of sustainable development while ignoring women's untapped potential.

Indeed, there is a clear relationship between the empowerment of women and the potential for sustainable development. Denying women basic human rights, restricting their access to education and economic resources, and limiting their participation in civic life slows economic growth, exacerbates poverty and contributes to global inequality.

Conversely, women can be a powerful force in promoting development. The UN Millennium Development Goals describe the achievement of gender equality and the empowerment of women as 'effective ways to combat poverty, hunger and disease and to stimulate development that is truly sustainable'. As United Nations Secretary-General Kofi Annan has said:

> Study after study has shown that there is no effective development strategy in which women do *not* play a central role. When women are fully involved, the benefits can be seen immediately; families are healthier and better fed; their income, savings and reinvestments go up. And what is true of families is also true of communities and in the long run, of whole countries.

Quite simply, the empowerment of women is an issue that the world – including the business world – cannot afford to ignore. Indeed, business has a tremendous opportunity to spur social change, create new market opportunities and encourage better operating environments by fostering equity for women.

CREATIVE ASSOCIATES: EMPOWERING WOMEN IN THE MOST CHALLENGING ENVIRONMENTS

Opportunities for businesses to foster the empowerment of women can be found in countries around the globe. For Creative Associates (Creative), founded, owned and managed by women, building a successful business has always gone hand in hand with improving the quality of life in the countries where the organisation works. Founded in 1977, Creative works with the United States Agency for International Development (USAID) and other international donors to reform educational institutions, strengthen civil society and address the needs of societies in conflict all over the world. Creative views these challenges as an opportunity to contribute to profound and sustained societal change.

Based in Washington DC, Creative Associates has field offices in 14 countries, including Afghanistan, Iraq, Guatemala, Uganda and the Philippines. Creative recognises that its approach to business can be influential in transforming attitudes towards women. In its field offices, Creative is committed to setting standards for equitable employment and to creating offices that provide a safe, secure and nurturing environment for women. Almost half of its field offices are run by women and many of its local employees in those field offices are women.

Creative has found that often the most challenging environments present some of the most needed and best opportunities to support and empower women. Frequently those opportunities arise in our standard business practices, such as hiring staff and selecting business partners.

For example, in Afghanistan, where women were banned from public life under the Taliban, Creative has sought to support women's leadership by partnering with organisations run by women. Creative realised that Afghanistan provided a special opportunity to identify and support women leaders at the forefront of the social changes currently under way in their country.

When looking for local business partners for their educational programmes, Creative kept its eyes open for an organisation run by women. It wanted to foster the participation of women in education and in rebuilding their country, especially after the Taliban era, and it needed someone to help develop an accelerated-learning programme for young Afghans who missed out on primary education. Together with its other local partners, Creative discovered the Afghan Women's Educational Center (AWEC), a women's organisation dedicated to promoting the rights of Afghan women and children and fostering self-sufficiency, empowerment and understanding in this group through education, health, peace education and socioeconomic development projects.

AWEC was founded in 1991 to help some of the thousands of Afghan women living in refugee camps near Islamabad, Pakistan, to obtain basic education and learn vocational skills. The Afghan founder, Shinkai Karokhail, is the daughter of a respected regional leader in the Pashtun lands that straddle the Afghanistan–Pakistan border. AWEC was the first resource centre to specifically address women's needs, and their work grew quickly to include health issues, including counselling and other psychological services for women brutalised by two decades of war in their homeland. In 1993, AWEC opened its own high school for women, and five years later added a programme for refugee women living on the streets.

When Creative found AWEC, it realised the organisation could be a great partner and believed in its leadership. It also saw that AWEC would need capacity-building support in order to be successful. Creative and two of our local partners provided AWEC with the financial and other training it required. This combined training effort allowed AWEC to become a better partner on this project and to become a sustainable source of leadership in the region.

To quote AWEC programme manager Jamie Terzi:

> AWEC is a much stronger organisation today, because Creative was willing to take a risk and include us in the partnership. Though we had a good track record with other donors, we had never managed such a large amount of money before. We were forced to learn how to do that.
>
> Creative provided us training in many aspects of financial management. Through that and through interactions with the Creative team, we learned how to create an organisational budget. Now we know where the holes are. We know how to fix them. And we know how to keep the organisation afloat financially if money were suddenly taken away from us.

Perhaps the most important thing that has come from our association with Creative . . . is our increased confidence. Now we know: we can do this.

As a result of the partnership between Creative and AWEC, over 800 teachers have been trained in new methods of accelerated learning and community education committees have been established. This programme has enabled more than 20 000 students in the provinces of Kabul and Paktya, whose schooling was interrupted or denied by two decades of war, to begin their studies again. Many of the students enrolled are girls (76 % in Kabul and 49 % in Paktya), representing the future of women's leadership in the country. Students in the programme are completing six years of education in fewer than three years.

The experience in Afghanistan is typical of Creative's many experiences with business partners around the world. Creative has found that the empowerment of women is a smart business decision even in the most challenging and unlikely places. It has not only provided us with better project results, but has paid enormous lasting dividends by supporting a source of enduring civic leadership in a country undergoing great social and economic transformations.

CALVERT: INVESTING IN WOMEN, INVESTING IN SOCIAL CHANGE

While Creative Associates' work in Afghanistan demonstrates the power of partnerships with local organisations to promote change, Calvert's activities exemplify the tremendous potential of investment capital to shape society.

Calvert was founded in 1976, and today has over $11 billion assets under management in 32 different mutual funds, including money market funds, fixed-income funds and socially screened equity funds investing in US and international companies.

A leader in the field of socially responsible investment (SRI), Calvert's investment approach aims to integrate two disciplines traditionally considered as utterly distinct: economics and ethics. Like a conventional mutual fund, the firm begins by evaluating the financial performance of a company it is considering for investment. However, it also takes a critical second look and evaluates the company's social performance in seven broad categories:

- environment;
- workplace practices;
- product safety and impact;
- community relations;
- corporate governance;
- international operations and human rights;
- the rights of indigenous peoples.

Calvert believes that strong social performance and strong financial performance are linked. One of the firm's guiding principles is that the best long-term investment opportunities are to be found among companies that recognise that today's social and environmental issues are likely to become tomorrow's economic problems. Calvert is committed to meeting the challenges of the future with a broader view of corporate responsibility that includes operating with integrity toward their employees, their community and the environment; this is not just socially responsible – it also makes good business sense.

Recognising the critical role of women in fostering sustainable development, Calvert has a long tradition of supporting and empowering women. The firm's social screening criteria for its investments address a number of issues that impact women's lives and careers. Moreover, the firm is one of the few companies in the financial services industry to be run by a woman, and has been regularly recognised by *Working Mothers* magazine and other organisations for its innovative employee benefits programmes, including benefits for working mothers. It is perhaps not surprising that 60% of Calvert's shareholders are women.

WOMEN IN THE BOARDROOM

In recent years, Calvert has taken a special interest in the composition of corporate boards of directors. The company recognises that diverse boards are good for business, and that advancing the role of women can help to build peaceful bridges across societies and cultures. However, in 2001, when it looked at the representation of women and minorities on corporate boards in the United States, Calvert concluded that the business culture appeared to be stuck. The percentage of women on large corporate boards had reached 13–14% but hadn't moved in many years. There appeared to be a closed loop: there were enough women on the boards to influence the boards to replace them with other women, but there was no breakthrough thinking to achieve higher levels of diverse representation. The question remained: Why is 'one' the right number of women for a board? Why not two or three – or more?

Calvert recognised back in 2001 that there was a tremendous opportunity to promote positive change. It realised that there are roughly 12 000 board seats among Fortune 1000 firms, and that, on average, 15% of those seats turn over annually, creating the need for 1800 new directors each year. Moreover, among all the companies trading on the NYSE, NASDAQ and AMEX, there are more than 60 000 board seats – and 9000 potential vacancies each year. Calvert wondered how many of those vacancies could be filled by women.

To attempt to answer that question, the firm launched the Calvert Board Diversity Initiative, a comprehensive effort designed to increase the representation of women and minorities on corporate boards and in senior management positions. Among the actions Calvert took as part of the Initiative, Nominating Committee Model Charter Language on Board Diversity was formulated as a way for corporate nominating and governance committees to formalise their commitment to creating diverse boards. Calvert urged companies to adopt the model language verbatim for their own charters, or to take it as a basis in formulating their own charter language. The model language has been endorsed by the Connecticut State Treasurer's Office, which recently launched its own statewide board diversity programme.

Calvert also conducted a vigorous shareholder resolution campaign, proposing nine resolutions urging board diversity during the 2003 proxy season. In addition, in 2002 the firm wrote letters to the CEOs of 650 companies, including 154 companies in the Calvert Social Index that did not have any racial or gender diversity on their boards, asking them to add women and minorities to their boards and urging them to adopt the Nominating Committee Model Charter Language on Board Diversity. To date, 48 (31%) of the 154 companies that received this letter have now added at least one woman or minority member to their board. Another 39 (25%) of the companies, which continue to have no board diversity and are still Calvert Social Index members, now include some mention of diversity in their nominating committee charters.

According to a Spenser Stuart study on gender diversity at S&P 500 companies, published in late 2004:

- 24% of new independent directors elected in the prior year are women, the largest increase ever in new female independent directors in one year.
- The percentage of women on boards has increased to 16% (vs. 13% for 2003 and 12% five years ago).
- Overall, 87% of boards have at least one female director.
- 17% have three or more women directors.

A BETTER WORKPLACE FOR WOMEN: THE CALVERT WOMEN'S PRINCIPLES

In 2004, Calvert took its commitment to women to a new level by launching the Calvert Women's Principles, the first code of corporate conduct focused exclusively on empowering, advancing and investing in women worldwide.

Although there are well-established labour and human rights norms and standards pertaining to women, there had been no systematic effort to apply those standards directly and specifically to corporate conduct. The Calvert Women's Principles represent the very first comprehensive attempt to do so. The Principles were launched on 23 June 2004. The co-sponsors included Dell, Starbucks, Pfizer and the United Nations Global Fund for Women (UNIFEM).

What distinguishes the Calvert Women's Principles from other initiatives is their focus on business corporations as key vehicles for addressing gender inequalities and advancing the global empowerment of women. Calvert recognised that corporations are key players in the global economy – often more powerful than national governments and other institutions. For example, two of the world's largest corporations, Exxon Mobil ($210.3 billion) and Wal-Mart ($194.2 billion), each have larger corporate revenues than the *combined* total gross domestic product of Pakistan ($61.6 billion), Peru ($53.8 billion) and New Zealand ($49.9 billion). The tremendous economic power of corporations means that their conduct can significantly affect whether women prosper or continue to fall further and further behind. Calvert believes that promoting responsible corporate conduct could make a real difference in the lives of women around the world.

The real value of the Calvert Women's Principles is their practicality. They are designed to address seven key issues relating to women's empowerment:

1. **Disclosure, implementation and monitoring**
   Corporations will promote and strive to attain gender equality in their operations and in their business and stakeholder relationships by adopting and implementing proactive policies that are publicly disclosed, monitored and enforced.
2. **Employment and income**
   Corporations will promote and strive to attain gender equality by adopting and implementing wage, income, hiring, promotion and other employment policies that eliminate gender discrimination in all its forms.
3. **Health, safety and violence**
   Corporations will promote and strive to attain gender equality by adopting and implementing policies to secure the health, safety and well-being of women workers.
4. **Civic and community engagement**
   Corporations will promote and strive to attain gender equality by adopting and implementing policies to help secure and protect the right of women to fully participate in civic life and to be free from all forms of discrimination and exploitation.
5. **Management and governance**
   Corporations will promote and strive to attain gender equality by adopting and implementing policies to ensure women's participation in corporate management and governance.
6. **Education, training and professional development**
   Corporations will promote and strive to attain gender equality by adopting and implementing education, training and professional development policies benefiting women.
7. **Business, supply chain and marketing practices**
   Corporations will promote and strive to attain gender equality by adopting and implementing proactive, non-discriminatory business, marketing and supply chain policies and practices.

The Principles offer clear, practical standards for each of these seven issues; companies can use these to set goals and measure their performance and progress on a wide range of gender equality and women's empowerment issues. At the same time, the standards provide investors with tools to assess corporate performance on gender equality. (For the complete text of the Calvert Women's Principles, please visit Calvert's web site at www.calvert.com.)

PROMOTING BEST PRACTICE WITH THE CALVERT WOMEN'S PRINCIPLES

Calvert plans to use the Calvert Women's Principles to raise awareness of good business practices, such as supporting equal business opportunities for women-run organisations.

Since the launch in 2004, the Calvert Women's Principles have received a great deal of favourable press. Leading companies, including Dell and Starbucks, have endorsed the Principles, and Calvert is working with partners in the corporate, advocacy, NGO and institutional investor communities to develop action strategies so that more organisations and companies can integrate the Principles into their own code of conduct.

It is important, however, to measure how this support translates into actual business practices. To that end, Verite, a pre-eminent independent social auditing, training and research organisation, has launched a three-year pilot programme that will focus on identifying best practice for translating the Calvert Women's Principles into specific programmes and benchmarks.

Specifically, these initiatives will include:

- Designing audit, disclosure, verification and reporting guidelines to monitor companies' codes of conduct and progress in implementing the Calvert Women's Principles in their business and supply chain operations.
- Developing corporate training programmes for women workers in such areas as literacy, education, civic and community engagement, health and safety and employment skills.

- Promoting the initiative and its goals through model practices, corporate/NGO partnerships and other innovative strategies for promoting gender equality.

For its own part, Calvert intends to integrate the Calvert Women's Principles into its social and environmental research and screening of companies for its investment portfolios. Calvert will also issue ratings of companies based in part upon their commitment to the Principles, both in terms of implementation and aspirations. Finally, as a shareholder, Calvert will engage corporations on gender equity and empowerment issues, asking them to endorse the Principles and to take concrete steps to implement the same.

Calvert realises that the launch of the Calvert Women's Principles is the beginning of a long-term process, and not the end. The firm hopes that the Principles will offer a standard corporations can aspire to, and a measure against which they can assess their performance. They reflect Calvert's view that there is a strong *business case* for gender equity, and its determination that corporations need to be responsive to this imperative.

Calvert recognises that some corporations will be better positioned than others to implement these principles, and that some of the specific principles may be problematic or difficult to implement. The Principles have been designed with these realities in mind. Each section has been structured in a way that generally proceeds from the more elemental to the more difficult. Calvert hopes this approach will allow companies to determine where along the continuum they are most comfortable, and that they will then be induced to build upon their commitments and their successes over time.

The power of a good example is immeasurable. Women who become strong, capable and successful will inspire other women to pursue their own dreams. Corporations can play a vital role in unleashing women's economic capacity, which has the potential to boost economies and transform societies. Calvert hopes that the Calvert Women's Principles may play a small part in hastening that transformation.

The launch of the Calvert Women's Principles has presented the corporate sector with a challenge: rather than condone or maintain or exacerbate gender inequality, be part of the solution. Rather than follow, lead. It is Calvert's conviction that there are business leaders who will rise to this challenge, and that investors, businesses and NGOs, working together, can make a difference.

GOING BEYOND BUSINESS AS USUAL

Many businesspeople are unaccustomed to thinking of their companies as instruments of social change. The conventional wisdom is that the success of a business should be measured solely by its bottom-line profitability.

Profitability is essential. However, many companies today are realising that a successful business is one that not only earns acceptable profits but also helps to build a sustainable future and enhance the quality of life. And they are indeed taking concrete steps to use their financial strength to promote positive social change.

Creative Associates International and Calvert are just two of the many companies demonstrating that business has tremendous potential to promote economic development by empowering women, whether the setting is war-torn Afghanistan or corporate boardrooms in the United States. Such companies are showing all that can be achieved by innovative businesspeople who are committed to going beyond business as usual.

CHAPTER 14

Corporate Philosophy – Seeking Harmony between People, Society and the Global Environment and Creating a Prosperous Society through Making Automobiles

Yoshio Shirai

*E*ver since the company was founded in 1937, Toyota has continuously strived to contribute to the sustainable development of society and the earth by manufacturing and providing high-quality, innovative products and services.

Through such continuous efforts, Toyota has established its own management philosophy, values and methods, which have been passed down from generation to generation throughout the company. Toyota has summarised this management philosophy in what is known as the 'Guiding Principles at Toyota' (originally

The ICCA Handbook on Corporate Social Responsibility Edited by J. Hennigfeld, M. Pohl and N. Tolhurst
© 2006 John Wiley & Sons, Ltd

issued in 1992, revised in 1997), reflecting its idea of what kind of company Toyota would like to be. The Guiding Principles at Toyota were created in the expectation that Toyota would understand and share its fundamental management principles, contributing to society by referring to these principles.

Toyota also expressed its values and methods in writing, in the 'Toyota Way' (issued in 2001). These must be shared globally within the Toyota group to implement the Guiding Principles at Toyota and the company is making efforts to pass them on to future generations.

Recently, as business operations have become more global, society's expectations of a company's contribution towards sustainable development have increased and the scope of such expectations has expanded. Toyota has long engaged in business with the idea of corporate social responsibility in mind, and it has used internal working groups and other bodies to investigate means of responding to societal demands in depth. Toyota strongly believes that by putting the spirit of the Guiding Principles at Toyota into practice, the company is fulfilling society's expectations of Toyota. In January 2005, it prepared and distributed an explanation paper called 'Contribution towards Sustainable Development', which interprets the Guiding Principles at Toyota.

This manual, prepared from the standpoint of how Toyota can contribute to sustainable development, is intended to convey the company's basic policies concerning social responsibility to external stakeholders and to promote a clear and precise understanding of these among all employees, including employees of consolidated subsidiaries and business partners. Toyota also expects its business partners to support this initiative and act in accordance with it.

The resulting Guiding Principles have been embedded in Toyota's day-to-day operations and are presented in Figure 14.1.

Guiding Principles at Toyota
(Adopted January 1992, revised April 1997)

1. Honour the language and spirit of the law of every nation and undertake open and fair corporate activities to be a good corporate citizen of the world.
2. Respect the culture and customs of every nation and contribute to economic and social development through corporate activities in the communities.
3. Dedicate ourselves to providing clean and safe products and to enhancing the quality of life everywhere through all our activities.
4. Create and develop advanced technologies and provide outstanding products and services that fulfill the needs of customers worldwide.
5. Foster a corporate culture that enhances individual creativity and teamwork value, while honouring mutual trust and respect between labour and management.
6. Pursue growth in harmony with the global community through innovative management.
7. Work with business partners in research and creation to achieve stable, long-term growth and mutual benefits, while keeping ourselves open to new partnerships.

Figure 14.1   Guiding Principles at Toyota

TOYOTA'S PRESENT CONTRIBUTION TOWARDS SUSTAINABLE DEVELOPMENT AND IMPLEMENTATION OF GUIDING PRINCIPLES

We, TOYOTA MOTOR CORPORATION and our subsidiaries, take initiatives to contribute to the harmonious and sustainable development of society and the earth, based on our Guiding Principles.

We comply with local, national and international laws and regulations as well as the spirit thereof and conduct our business operations with honesty and integrity.

In order to contribute to sustainable development, we believe that it is particularly important for management to interact with its stakeholders, and we will endeavour to build and maintain sound relationships with our stakeholders through open and fair communication.

Customers

- Based on our philosophy of 'Customer First', we develop and provide innovative, safe and outstanding high-quality products and services that meet a wide variety of customers' needs to enrich the lives of people around the world. (Guiding Principles 3 and 4)

- We will endeavour to protect the personal information of customers in accordance with the letter and spirit of each country's privacy laws. (Guiding Principle 1)

Employees

- We respect our employees and believe that the success of our business is driven by each individual's creativity and good teamwork. We stimulate personal growth for our employees. (Guiding Principle 5)
- We support equal employment opportunities, diversity and inclusion for our employees and do not discriminate against them. (Guiding Principle 5)
- We strive to provide fair working conditions and to maintain a safe and healthy working environment for all our employees. (Guiding Principle 5)
- We respect and honour the human rights of people involved in our business and, in particular, do not use or tolerate any form of forced or child labour. (Guiding Principle 5)
- Through communication and dialogue with our employees, we build and share the value 'Mutual Trust and Mutual Responsibility' and work together for the success of our employees and the company. (Guiding Principle 5)
- Management of each company takes leadership in fostering a corporate culture and implementing policies that promote ethical behaviour. (Guiding Principles 1 and 5)

Business partners

- We respect our business partners such as suppliers and dealers and work with them through long-term relationships to ensure mutual growth based on mutual trust. (Guiding Principle 7)
- Whenever we seek a new business partner, we are open to any and all candidates, regardless of nationality or size, and evaluate them based on their overall strengths. (Guiding Principle 7)
- We maintain fair and free competition in accordance with the letter and spirit of each country's competition laws. (Guiding Principles 1 and 7)

Shareholders

- We strive to enhance corporate value while achieving stable and long-term growth for the benefit of our shareholders. (Guiding Principle 6)
- We provide our shareholders and investors with timely and fair disclosure on our operating results and financial status. (Guiding Principles 1 and 6)

Global society/local communities
Environment

- We aim for growth in harmony with the environment throughout all areas of business activities. We strive to develop, establish and promote technologies enabling the environment and the economy to coexist harmoniously, while also seeking to build close and cooperative relationships with a broad spectrum of individuals and organisations involved in environmental preservation. (Guiding Principle 3)

Community

- We implement our philosophy of 'respect for people' by honouring the culture, customs, history and laws of each country. (Guiding Principle 2)
- We constantly search for safer, cleaner and better technology to develop products that satisfy society's evolving needs for sustainable mobility. (Guiding Principles 3 and 4)
- We do not tolerate bribery of or by any business partner, government agency or public authority and maintain honest and fair relationships with government agencies and public authorities. (Guiding Principle 1)

Philanthropy

- Wherever we do business, we actively promote, engage, both individually and with partners, in philanthropic activities that help strengthen communities and contribute to the enrichment of society. (Guiding Principle 2)

ENVIRONMENTAL MANAGEMENT

To ensure that its products are accepted and well received around the world, Toyota has positioned the environment as a priority management issue and seeks to become a leading company that contributes to the development of a recycling-based society through innovative environmental technologies. In order to achieve this, Toyota has created environmental management systems in all areas and in all regions around the world, and constantly promotes action to this end, with goals set at the highest levels in each country and region.

Basic concepts with regard to the environment

Principles and policies

The Toyota Earth Charter, adopted in 1992 and revised in 2000 (see Figure 14.2), is based on the Guiding Principles at Toyota adopted in 1992 (revised in 1997) and embodies our comprehensive approach to global environmental issues. Based on this Charter, Toyota has made environmental responses a top management priority.

Environmental Action Plan

The Toyota Environmental Action Plan is a medium- to long-term plan that summarises specific activities and goals in order to promote company-wide environmental preservation activities in accordance with the Toyota Earth Charter.

The Third Toyota Environmental Action Plan describes specific action plans for the five years from FY2001 to FY2005. Based on this plan, Toyota also established an Annual Environmental Action Policy in FY2004, to develop and expand environmental preservation activities.

Furthermore, in FY2004 Toyota drew up the Fourth Toyota Environmental Action Plan to run from FY2006 to FY2010, which was made public in May 2005.

Toyota Earth Charter

I. **Basic Policy**
1. **Contribution toward a prosperous 21st century society**
   Contribute toward a prosperous 21st century society.
   Aim for growth that is in harmony with the environment, and set as a challenge the achievement of zero emissions throughout all areas of business activities.

2. **Pursuit of environmental technologies**
   Pursue all possible environmental technologies, developing and establishing new technologies to enable the environment and economy to coexist harmoniously.

3. **Voluntary actions**
   Develop a voluntary improvement plan, based on thorough preventive measures and compliance with laws, that addresses environmental issues on the global, national, and regional level, and promotes continuous implementation.

4. **Working in cooperation with society**
   Build close and cooperative relationships with a wide spectrum of individuals and organisations involved in environmental preservation including governments, local municipalities, related companies and industries.

II. **Action Guidelines**
1. **Always be concerned about the environment**
   Take on the challenge of achieving zero emissions at all stages, i.e., production, utilisation, and disposal.
   (1) Develop and provide products with top-level environmental performance.
   (2) Pursue production activities that do not generate waste.
   (3) Implement thorough preventive measures.
   (4) Promote businesses that contribute to environmental improvement.

2. **Business partners are partners in creating a better environment**
   Cooperate with associated companies.

3. **As a member of society**
   Participate actively in social actions.
   (1) Participate in the creation of a recycling-based society.
   (2) Support government environmental policies.
   (3) Contribute to non-profit activities.

4. **Toward better understanding**
   Actively disclose information and promote environmental awareness.

III. **Organisation in Charge**

   Promotion by the Toyota Environment Committee which consists of top management (chaired by the President)

Figure 14.2 Toyota Earth Charter

To ensure that the goals of the Third Toyota Environmental Action Plan, covering the period from FY2001 to FY2005, are achieved, Toyota conducted a periodic review of the progress in FY2004. Goals were achieved on time or ahead of schedule in almost all areas. Some measures are being accelerated through the end of FY2005; these include research and proposals on transportation systems and development of air conditioning systems with new refrigerants to help prevent global warming. Toyota plans to continue to take action by including these points in the Fourth Toyota Environmental Action Plan.

IMPLEMENTATION STRUCTURE

Three committees were established under the Toyota Environment Committee, which is chaired by the president and meets twice a year to address issues and response policies in each area. The Environmental Affairs Division functions as a secretariat for committee operation. All related departments cooperate to promote company-wide environmental action.

At a Toyota Environment Committee meeting held in FY2004, CO_2 emissions and other issues were discussed, along with the Fourth Toyota Environmental Action Plan.

The organisational framework (Figure 14.3) shows the interrelation between the Toyota Environment Committee and other committees such as the Production Environment Committee or the Recycling Committee.

In FY2000, Toyota introduced consolidated environmental management, which unites Japanese and overseas consolidated companies in concerted environmental action. In addition, Environment Committees were established in Europe in FY2003 and North America in FY2004 to reinforce local environmental activities. In the spring of 2005, full-scale environmental initiatives, overseen by the senior managing director in charge of Asia Operations, were introduced in the Asia region, and Toyota

- **Toyota Environment Committee**
  Chairman: President Katsuaki Watanabe
  Established in 1992
  Directs important environmental programs and promotes environmental preservation company-wide

- **Environmental Product Design Assessment Committee**
  Chairman: Managing Officer Tatehito Ueda
  Established in 1973
  Studies key environmental preservation issues related to development and design of Toyota vehicles

- **Production Environment Committee**
  Chairman: Senior Managing Director Atsushi Niimi
  Vice Chairman: Senior Managing Director Shoji Ikawa
  Established in 1963
  Discusses and determines important issues for environmental preservation in procurement, production and logistics groups, and promotes comprehensive environmental protection measures
  → All-Toyota Production Environment Conference
     All-Toyota Production Environment Meeting
  → Regional Production Environment Conference

- **Recycling Committee**
  Chairman: Senior Managing Director Yoshio Shirai
  Vice Chairman: Managing Director Masamoto Maekawa
  Established in 1990
  Studies easy-to-recycle designs of vehicles, development of recycling/recovery technologies and collection methods

- **Environmental Affairs Division**
  Secretariat of Environmental Committees
  Established in 1998
  Manages action policy and goals. Drafts environmental action plan and annual company-wide environmental policy

  Executives in charge of Environmental Affairs Division Environment Group:
  Executive Vice President Takeshi Uchiyamada
  Senior Managing Director Yoshio Shirai

  Directors:
  Managing Officer Tatehito Ueda
  Managing Officer Tetsuo Agata
  Managing Officer Masayuki Nakai

Figure 14.3 Organisation Framework (positions and areas of responsibility as of March 2006)

is currently working to further strengthen environmental action there. In the future, Toyota will reinforce local environmental management in South America and China, thus promoting environmental management on a global basis.

CONCLUSION

Drafting of the Fourth Toyota Environmental Action Plan on the basis of Toyota's Guiding Principles and environmental management approach

Within Global Vision 2010, Toyota describes what society is expected to be like from 2020 to around 2030 with the 'arrival of a revitalised, recycling-based society'. The Fourth Toyota Environmental Action Plan is a clear statement of the activities Toyota must undertake in order to attain the corporate image it is striving to achieve – to become a leader and driving force in global regeneration by implementing the most advanced environmental technologies. In adopting the plan, Toyota reconfirmed environmental issues that are expected to be on the agenda in the period from 2020 to 2030, and addressed four main topics:

1. Energy/global warming
2. Recycling of resources
3. Substances of concern
4. Atmospheric quality

For each of these four topics, points for action, specific measures and goals have been adopted in Toyota's areas of activity, including development and design, procurement and production, logistics, sales and marketing and recycling. Toyota will also continue to implement and strengthen its environmental management.

Key points of the plan and global implementation

The Fourth Toyota Environmental Action Plan seeks to achieve a balance between Toyota's growth and harmony with society and to contribute to the development of a sustainable society. The following four main points were incorporated into the plan to achieve these objectives.

1. **CO_2 emissions management** – Create medium- to long-term scenarios and start management of CO_2 emissions volumes on a global scale.
2. **Reinforcement of environmental management by business partners** – Reinforce environmental management by business partners globally (consolidated subsidiaries, suppliers, dealers and overseas distributors).
3. **Elimination of substances of concern** – Eliminate substances of concern (lead, mercury, cadmium and hexavalent chromium) globally.
4. **Cooperation with society** – Contribute to the development of a recycling-based society.

Since FY2000, approximately 600 companies around the world subject to consolidated environmental management have jointly adopted the Toyota Earth Charter with TMC. Each company participates in consolidated environmental management including the drafting and implementation of environmental action plans. Based on the Fourth Toyota Environmental Action Plan, each company will draft and implement its next five-year environmental action plan itself in order to further accelerate consolidated environmental management.

CHAPTER 15

The *Kyosei* Philosophy and CSR

Fujio Mitarai

*R*ecently, whenever I meet with journalists, I find that I'm getting asked more and more about the steps that Canon is taking with regard to CSR.

To be honest, I was somewhat puzzled when I first encountered the term 'CSR'. In Japan, whenever something is introduced as an acronym of a concept expressed in English, we tend to view it as an entirely new and novel idea. The moment we translate the term into Japanese, however, we soon realise that, more often than not, it is a concept that we have long been familiar with. This, too, is the case with the term 'corporate social responsibility'.

In my opinion, it is only natural for a corporation to fulfil its social responsibilities. Companies are organs of society and, as such, have an obligation to participate actively in society through making contributions to local communities, and providing support for cultural and humanitarian assistance activities. Furthermore, to ensure that CSR does not merely fade away as simply another

The ICCA Handbook on Corporate Social Responsibility   Edited by J. Hennigfeld, M. Pohl and N. Tolhurst
© 2006 John Wiley & Sons, Ltd

trendy corporate fad, I believe that it is essential that this concept take root with each individual employee. It is with this objective in mind that Canon educates its employees and managers with the aim of fostering a natural consciousness of compliance and a desire to contribute to society as a responsible corporate citizen.

I believe that there are four essential objectives that every corporation must fulfil in order to satisfy its social responsibilities. The first of these is to provide employment and a livelihood for the company's workers. The second is to return profit to the investors who provide the means for the company to carry out its operations. The third objective is to contribute to society. And the fourth is to generate sufficient capital to fund future investment to realise sustainable growth. If a company is not able to satisfy these four objectives, then it has no value as a business enterprise. This is something that I am constantly emphasising to Canon employees.

Over the past few years, CSR has been attracting an increasing amount of attention, as evidenced in the growing number of corporate CSR management rankings appearing in newspapers and other news media. I'm sure that this trend has been keeping a large number of journalists quite busy these days. In 2004, Canon was honoured with a seventh place in the Japan edition of *Newsweek* magazine in the publication's 'Newsweek Global 500' ranking, which rated the world's leading companies based on a combination of business performance and corporate social responsibility. Among Japanese companies, Canon finished in first place. Also, in 2005, *Nikkei Business*, Japan's number one weekly business magazine, awarded Canon first place in its 'CSR Best 100 Company Ranking', which evaluated companies in three areas: CSR activities and reporting, external evaluation and financial performance.

Despite the high acclaim that we have received in the area of CSR, it may come as somewhat of a surprise to hear that Canon does not have a dedicated division that is responsible for the company's CSR activities. What's more, none of our management policies incorporate CSR as a point of focus. Yet, through our day-to-day corporate activities, we continue to fulfil our social responsibilities. I believe that we can credit this to Canon's corporate spirit, which has been alive and well since the company's founding nearly 70 years ago.

Canon was founded in 1937 and one of the themes that has remained constant throughout the company's history is a respect for mankind. In accordance with this theme, Takeshi Mitarai, Canon's first president, introduced three guiding principles during the 1940s aimed to promote the well-being and development of the company's employees while contributing to business growth. These three guiding principles, which are still firmly adhered to today, were: 'Health first', which stresses the importance of healthy and happy employees; 'Familism', to nurture a spirit of harmony between workers based on trust and understanding; and 'Meritocracy', to ensure that employees are evaluated fairly for the abilities and skills that they bring to their jobs. Although such thinking may not sound particularly innovative by today's standards, in 1940s Japan it was virtually unheard of to introduce such ideas in the workplace.

In 1988, the year following the 50th anniversary of the company's founding, Ryuzaburo Kaku, Canon's president at the time, expanded the scope of these concepts beyond the boundaries of the company, outlining a philosophy that could be applied on a global scale. We expressed this philosophy as 'the achievement of corporate growth and development with the aim of contributing to global prosperity and the well-being of humankind'. This is the idea behind Canon's corporate philosophy of *kyosei*.

At Canon, we define *kyosei* as 'living and working together for the common good'. And through *kyosei*, we hope to realise the ideal of 'all people, regardless of race, religion or culture, harmoniously living and working together for many years to come'. Put succinctly, *kyosei* aims for the creation of a sustainable society. It includes the idea that the continued existence and further growth of the company can be achieved through cooperation with and contributions to humankind worldwide.

Consequently, when we talk about CSR today, many of the various concepts that we are referring to were introduced at Canon some 17 years ago, when we first announced our *kyosei* corporate philosophy. The primary reason why any corporation needs to fulfil its corporate social responsibilities is to enable it to achieve sustainable growth. The company that currently audits Canon's Sustainability Report, SustainAbility Limited, based in the United Kingdom, supports the concept of a 'triple bottom line'. The thinking behind this concept is that the term 'bottom line', as a gauge of a company's business performance, should not be limited to just the economic implications of that company's performance. Instead, the term should also be applied to the company's achievements with regard to the environment and society. It is unacceptable for corporations to be economically profitable at the expense of the environment. Also, it goes without saying that a company must not profit from society without offering something in return in the form of meaningful contribution. Without making such efforts, there is no assurance that a company will be capable of maintaining sustainable growth and, as such, risks being viewed by the investment community as carrying high risk.

Furthermore, I believe that each facet of the triple bottom line concept must be given equal importance. As such, these three components must be addressed simultaneously, with companies targeting sound growth while giving full consideration to supporting a sustainable society, which includes focusing on and pursuing solutions to environmental concerns.

For example, at Canon, we do not view our environmental assurance activities as being a cost burden. Rather, we believe that these efforts, which are aimed at maximising the productivity of the resources that we use, are directly tied to the profits that the company generates. Our goal is to align the Canon Group's environmental assurance activities with its economic activities.

We have launched a variety of environmental businesses to share Canon's newest technologies and know-how with society. Canon has also taken the reins into its own hands in respect of standardisation of green procurement and other industry initiatives as we look beyond our own company and strive to reduce the environmental burden on a global scale.

It goes without saying that the ideal of *kyosei*, which Canon continues to pursue, cannot be realised through a company's internal efforts alone. Companies must also strive to achieve cooperative relationships with their various stakeholders, relationships based on mutual trust and understanding. Canon continues to build close relationships with its stakeholders by providing a range of opportunities for open communication. I believe that those companies that fail to realise *kyosei* with their stakeholders will gradually be weeded out.

While participating in social contribution activities is the responsibility of a 'good corporate citizen', it can also serve as a means to improve corporate value and deepen public trust in a company. In 1996, in accordance with our *kyosei* philosophy, Canon announced the Excellent Global Corporation Plan, which embodies our goal of continuing to contribute to society through technological innovation while aiming to be a corporation worthy of admiration and respect worldwide. Over the 10 years since we launched this management plan, comprising two five-year phases thus far, we have promoted management reforms to fulfil our mission of becoming a truly Excellent Global Corporation. And we have watched as these efforts have paid off handsomely in terms of financial performance: our sales and profits have continued to grow and we are currently on track to realising our sixth straight year of record financial gains for the 2005 fiscal year. Additionally, we are eagerly looking forward to Phase III of the Excellent Global Corporation Plan, which begins in 2006. During this third five-year phase, we will pursue a course of sound growth while maintaining our current high-profit structure. Building on the solid trust that we have earned from our stakeholders, we aim to grow into a business group that possesses and makes effective use of the corporate values necessary for sustained development.

From a long-range perspective, the three components comprising the triple bottom line concept in no way conflict with a company's objectives for continued prosperity. Rather, all of these elements go hand in hand with each other. The various activities that we refer to today when we use the term CSR are, in fact, encompassed by the ideal behind our corporate philosophy known as *kyosei*. Accordingly, as we continue to pursue the achievement of *kyosei* in our business activities, we believe that we can fulfil all of our corporate social responsibilities.

CHAPTER 16

A Decade of Environmental and Sustainability Reporting at Credit Suisse Group

H.-U. Doerig[1]

Credit Suisse Group conducts an active, honest dialogue with its employees and the public on environmental and social issues. It provides information to stakeholders in a targeted manner, ensures its actions are transparent and encourages an understanding of different viewpoints. The Group is also involved in various bodies where it can use its expertise and experience to promote environmental protection and sustainable economic development.

CSG Sustainability Report 2001

---

[1] In cooperation with Dr. Bernd Schanzenbaecher.

The ICCA Handbook on Corporate Social Responsibility   Edited by J. Hennigfeld, M. Pohl and N. Tolhurst
© 2006 John Wiley & Sons, Ltd

PROGRESS DRIVEN BY INTERNATIONAL DEVELOPMENTS

In order to safeguard their reputation as well as securing long-term business success, it is essential for global financial services providers to gain broad-based acceptance with a wide variety of stakeholders. At Credit Suisse Group conduct – towards clients, shareholders and employees, as well as society and the environment – is therefore founded on the company's comprehensive understanding of its responsibilities. In concrete terms, this means that Credit Suisse Group actively seeks to establish a dialogue with a broad range of stakeholder groups and engages them in discussions about topics that are as varied as the interests of these groups themselves.

Credit Suisse Group also plays an active role in a number of national and international bodies and networks in order to promote environmental and social progress at various levels. Here, the Group offers its experience and expertise and introduces its own perspective, while gaining new impetus for its own sustainability commitments. Credit Suisse Group considers the following international initiatives to have been the driving force behind the evolution of the concept of sustainability and sustainability reporting:

- **The Brundtland Report: the birth of the concept of sustainability**
  Although the concept of sustainability dates back to the forestry industry of the eighteenth century many in the corporate sector regard 1987 as the year in which the foundations for their subsequent sustainability commitments were laid. That was the year in which the UN World Commission on Environment and Development, chaired by the then Prime Minister of Norway, Gro Harlem Brundtland, published its report 'Our Common Future'. The Brundtland Report, as it became

known, is particularly important because it created a definition of sustainability that can be applied to many different areas of life.

According to the authors of the report, development is sustainable if it meets the needs of the present generation without compromising the ability of future generations to meet their own needs.

This differed from earlier definitions of sustainability by presenting a holistic approach to problems that had previously been viewed in isolation. The report states that the key to sustainable development is to overcome poverty in developing countries and to bring the material wealth of industrialised countries into harmony with nature. In terms of the future, the Commission was of the belief that global economic growth will have to occur within certain ecological limits and that the corporate sector will have an important part to play in this development.

The Brundtland Report remains as important as ever today. This is demonstrated, among other things, by the fact that many companies – including Credit Suisse Group – base their sustainability commitments on this holistic view of the economy, the environment and society, and have implemented this concept in their sustainability reporting systems since the publication of the report.

- **1992 Rio Conference: sustainability becomes an imperative**
  The United Nations Conference on Environment and Development in Rio in 1992 represented a further milestone in sustainable development. The aim of this Earth Summit, which was attended by around 10 000 participants from 178 countries, was to transform the non-binding recommendations of the Brundtland Commission into politically and legally binding imperatives. Despite the many conflicting interests of those

attending the summit, five declarations were agreed upon at the Rio Conference.

- **The Kyoto Protocol: commitments on global climate change**
  The agreements on climate change that had been made in Rio became binding under international law at the third Conference of Parties to the United Nations Framework Convention on Climate Change, which was held in Kyoto, Japan, in 1997. As the main producers of greenhouse gases, the industrialised nations, in particular, pledged to reduce their emissions to below 1990 levels by 2012.

- **Johannesburg 2002: spotlight on global rules for the corporate sector**
  A second Earth Summit took place in Johannesburg 10 years after the Rio Conference. The central theme of the summit was how the model for sustainable development could actually be put into practice in times of globalisation and rapid technological advances. As in the case of previous economic summits, there was an increasing focus on the responsibility of globally active companies as key players in sustainable development.

Credit Suisse Group signed up to a number of environmental and sustainability charters as a direct result of its involvement in various international bodies. In 1992, for example, the Group became one of the first signatories to the United Nations Environment Programme (UNEP) statement for financial institutions, drawn up at the Rio Conference. In 2000, it signed up to the UN Global Compact – an initiative under which it pledged to observe a number of principles relating to human rights, working conditions, environmental protection and the prevention of corruption. Credit Suisse Group's earlier involvement in the Intergovernmental Panel on Climate Change (IPCC) is a further example of its commitment to sustainability at an international level.

MILESTONES IN ENVIRONMENTAL AND SUSTAINABILITY REPORTING

The environmental and social aspects of banking – which is regarded as an essentially 'clean' industry – have only become a subject of broader discussion in recent years. However, Credit Suisse Group addressed these issues at an early stage. This is demonstrated, for example, by its creation of the post of environmental officer in 1989, as well as its efforts in the field of environmental and sustainability reporting. In fact, in 1995, the former Credit Suisse *(Schweizerische Kreditanstalt; SKA)* became one of the first banks in the world to publish an environmental performance evaluation focusing on the energy and material consumption of its internal operations, followed in 1996 by its first environmental report.

Furthermore, by the late 1990s, Credit Suisse Group had already recognised the importance of having a business policy that takes account of both the present and future needs of society, and published its first sustainability report in 2002. This report represented the next stage in the development of its earlier environmental reports and, for the first time, addressed social issues in addition to environmental aspects. Table 16.1 shows the development of Credit Suisse Group's environmental and sustainability reporting.

Between 1994 and 2000, reporting at Credit Suisse Group focused primarily on the status and further development of its environmental commitments, although the topic of sustainability was raised occasionally – especially in the second half of this phase. Environmental reporting was based on the Group-wide environmental policy, which defines the following basic approach to communication on environmental issues:

> Our bank is an environmentally-conscious company. We therefore conduct an open dialogue both inside the company and outside. Our environmental data are accessible. We cooperate actively with external environmental organisations. Meeting our ecological responsibilities forms part of our strategy to secure long-term earnings and sustainable corporate development.

During this first reporting phase, Credit Suisse Group published environmental reports every two years, in which it provided information about its environmental management system and its product and corporate ecology, as well as its dialogue with the general public. Eco-performance reports detailing its principal energy and material flows were published in alternate years to complement these environmental reports.

Table 16.1 Development of Credit Suisse Group's environmental and sustainability reporting

Year of publication	Report
1995	Eco-performance SKA Zurich, 1994
	Eco-performance CS Geneva, 1994
1996	CREDIT SUISSE (SKA) Environmental Report 1995/96
1998	Eco-performance Evaluation Switzerland 1996/97
1999	Environmental Report 1997/98
	MIB AG Energy and Materials Report 1998
2000	Eco-performance Report Switzerland 1998/99
	MIB AG Energy and Materials Report 1999
2001	Environmental Report 1999/2000
	MIB AG Energy and Materials Report 2000
2002	Sustainability Reporting 2001[1]
	MIB AG Energy and Materials Report 2001
	Credit Suisse First Boston Foundation Social Responsibility Report 2001
2003	Sustainability Reporting 2002
	MIB AG Energy and Materials Report 2002
2004	Sustainability Reporting 2003
	MIB AG Energy and Materials Report 2003
	Credit Suisse First Boston Foundation Social Responsibility Report 2003
2005	Sustainability Reporting 2004
	MIB AG Energy and Materials Report 2004

Note: [1] Since 2002, an additional document featuring sustainability indicators and key figures has also been published each year in PDF format on the Internet.

An important milestone on the path towards comprehensive sustainability reporting was the introduction of the Code of Conduct – setting out basic values that apply to all employees worldwide – in 1999. As a guideline for employee conduct, the Code states that Credit Suisse Group is committed to delivering superior value to its clients and shareholders, to being an employer of choice and to acting as a respected member of the community. The way in which Credit Suisse Group implements these objectives, the progress it has achieved towards attaining them and the challenges that remain have been documented in the Group's annual sustainability reporting since 2002.

Looking back, the quantum leap from eco-performance reports for selected locations in Switzerland to comprehensive, validated sustainability reporting was only possible because Credit Suisse Group had continuously and actively participated in the ongoing debate about environmental and social issues. Here the focus was on the opportunities created by a fair dialogue with an ever-increasing number of stakeholder groups. The challenges that this presented in terms of organisation and content – as well as in respect of specific target groups – are outlined below.

SUSTAINABILITY: EASIER SAID THAN DONE

The environmental management system as a basis for sustainability management

The continuing development of Credit Suisse Group's environmental and sustainability-related communication activities is due, in particular, to the early establishment and expansion of its environmental management system. This aimed to consolidate the specialist knowledge that already existed across its wide variety of businesses and locations, and to constantly advance the development of its environmental and sustainability management system. If an environmental management system is to be able to operate, it is essential that it is firmly established at all functional levels and is incorporated into the company's organisational structure.

In 1997, Credit Suisse Group became the first bank worldwide to implement an environmental management system certified according to ISO 14001. This system establishes a framework for the organisational structure, responsibilities, conduct, processes, procedures and requirements involved in implementing the Group's environmental policy and sets out the Group's commitment to continuously improving its environmental performance.

For bodies that closely monitor the environmental and social performance of the corporate sector, environmental management systems certified according to ISO 14001 provide a key indication that companies have a demonstrably high level of commitment to the environment – and that this commitment has been verified independently. The most recent re-certification of Credit Suisse Group's environmental management system in 2003, by the independent SGS International Certification Services AG, as well as the extension of its environmental standards to include its external partners and suppliers, and the integration of locations and organisational units outside Switzerland, provide important evidence that Credit Suisse Group is constantly pursuing efforts to enhance its environmental management system.

An increasingly broad topic: the many facets of sustainability

The topics covered by environmental and sustainability reporting must always be seen in the light of current public discussion. In the early 1980s, when the first finance companies were laying the foundations of their current environmental and sustainability commitments, issues such as ecology were beginning to enter the sphere of public consciousness. Former adherents to the creed of unlimited growth were still in shock following the first two oil crises. Moreover, people grew alarmed as they surveyed growing mountains of waste and saw forests dying as a result of pollution, while also being confronted with global warming.

As a result, companies also became increasingly aware of the need to recognise the direct environmental impact of their actions and to publish the corresponding information on corporate ecology. The former Credit Suisse therefore issued its first eco-performance report in 1995, providing details of energy, water and paper consumption, as well as data on the volume of waste produced and the environmental impact of business travel. Those in charge of the initiative focused particularly on energy consumption, which had by far the greatest direct impact on the environment and was also important in the context of the emerging problem of climate change. In addition to informing employees and raising their awareness of the issues concerned, the eco-performance report was particularly valuable as a management tool to record and quantify all relevant energy and material streams, pinpointing potential savings and enabling realistic targets to be formulated. Just one year later, Credit Suisse extended its reporting to cover the field of product ecology. In addition to the ecological risks initially targeted – such as those to be considered in the credit approval process – attention soon turned to the potential for 'green' products in asset management and investment banking.

At the end of the 1990s, the corporate sector was coming under increasing public pressure to accept responsibility for social issues and to satisfy the need for more comprehensive information. At this time, the focus of interest shifted to issues such as respect for human rights, the prevention of corruption and fairer international trade relations. Moreover, there was growing peer pressure – not to mention calls from non-governmental organisations – for companies to disclose relevant facts and figures.

It is also necessary to consider the fact that information circulates much more rapidly and easily nowadays, meaning that rumours and news about weaknesses and misconduct can soon develop into reputation-related risks, irrespective of whether or not they are true. This highlights how important it is for Credit Suisse Group to establish a dialogue with stakeholders at an early stage in order to promote mutual understanding and to identify the first signs of change.

This presents globally active financial services companies with a host of new issues to consider in respect of their environmental and social commitments. In addition to the environmental aspects referred to above, the key areas of focus at Credit Suisse Group are as shown in Table 16.2.

Parallel to its efforts to expand the content of its reporting, Credit Suisse Group also succeeded in continuously improving its methodology and in refining its environmental and sustainability indicators. These performance indicators are aimed, inter alia, at facilitating cross-comparisons and enabling industry standards for transparent reporting to be created. The below indicator systems

Table 16.2 Stakeholder groups and key areas of focus

Stakeholder group	Key area of focus
Employees	Training and further development
	Equal opportunities and diversity
	Employment conditions
Clients	Availability of and access to needs-based banking services
	Quality management, enhancement of client satisfaction
	Handling of complaints
	Delicate balance between privacy and the prevention of illegal transactions
Society	Economic importance of banks
	Sponsorship and support for cultural, sporting, social and charitable events and organisations
	Compliance with legislation, self-regulation
	Dialogue with political bodies and NGO representatives

are the core models for financial services companies. Credit Suisse Group has reported its performance according to these indicator systems in a separate online report each year since 2002:

- VfU corporate ecology performance indicators.
- EPI-Finance (environmental performance indicators for the financial industry) on environmental management and product ecology.
- SPI-Finance (social performance indicators for the financial industry) on conduct towards employees, suppliers and society, as well as the impact of products and services and commitment to the good of society.

It is interesting to note in this context that the content of the reporting has been expanded in accordance with the interests of internal as well as external target groups. Since the mid-1990s, there has been a growing realisation that good environmental management can ultimately be seen as an indication of good management in general, as demonstrated by the following examples:

- **Cutting costs**: the thoughtful use of resources not only protects the environment but also reduces energy, material and waste disposal costs.
- **More effective risk management**: by taking account of environmental and social issues in the credit approval process, it is possible to ensure an appropriate lending policy and suitable terms and conditions.
- **Exploitation of market opportunities**: sustainable investment funds and loans for groundbreaking projects are examples of how it is possible to enter attractive new markets by incorporating aspects of sustainability into new products.
- **Good image**: companies that fulfil their responsibilities towards the environment and society inspire greater confidence in their employees, clients, shareholders and other stakeholders, and are thus able to secure a better competitive position.

Addressing a broader target group

During the initial phase of the Group's environmental commitment, the authors of its reports were writing primarily for an employee audience – which remains one of its main target groups today. Specific information events, various staff publications and the Intranet are the most important platforms for internal dialogue. For example, the Intranet enables employees to find out about current environmental topics such as the launch of new 'green' products, as well as initiatives concerning environmental and social matters and current issues in this field.

Long before it began its transition from environmental to sustainability reporting, Credit Suisse Group recognised the key importance of establishing contact with relevant stakeholder groups. Hence, cultivating an active dialogue with suppliers, clients and other business partners is also essential. Moreover, it is becoming increasingly important to establish contact with interested sections of the general public. Credit Suisse Group therefore also participates actively in talks with responsible non-governmental organisations in order to listen and respond to their concerns and – wherever possible – to formulate joint solutions. See Figure 16.1.

While it is pleasing that such a wide range of stakeholders are interested in cultivating a dialogue with Credit Suisse Group, this poses a new challenge: as groups with an interest in environmental and, later, sustainability issues grow more diverse, the information they require and their key areas of interest also become more varied. In order to address its different target groups in an appropriate manner and to present the breadth of information in a structured form, Credit Suisse Group has adopted a modular approach to its communication efforts and is constantly expanding the scope of these activities. The Internet and Intranet have formed an integral part of this strategy for several years. For example, the Intranet has its own sustainability web page, which combines data on all the environmental and social issues relevant to Credit Suisse Group on

Figure 16.1 Diverse relationships: interrelationship between the different measures that Credit Suisse Group uses to pursue a sustainable business policy

a single information platform. Meanwhile, the Internet provides the latest information on sustainability for clients, investors and other interested parties. Table 16.3 shows the communication media and modules used by Credit Suisse Group to address its different target groups.

Improving data quality

One of the major challenges facing globally active companies such as Credit Suisse Group is collecting environmental and sustainability-related data on a global scale via a standardised approach and regularly updating key documents required for environmental management. This involves aggregating consumption data for the large number of premises in which Credit Suisse Group operates

Table 16.3   Credit Suisse Group – sustainability-related communication media

Target groups	Internal: Employees	External: Clients	Investors	Others
Environmental reports	X	X	X	X
Eco-performance reports	X	X	X	X
Sustainability reporting	X	X	X	X
Special publications on specific topics (e.g. energy model, environmental standards)	X			
Articles in internal publications/employee magazines and on the Intranet	X			
Articles in external CSG publications, such as the CSG Annual Report or client publications	X	X	X	X
Product information sheets		X	X	
Internet www.credit-suisse.com/ sustainability and www.credit-suisse.com/ sustainable-investments	X	X	X	X

around the world. Although the former Credit Suisse already began to systematically collect energy consumption data for all of its bank premises in Switzerland in the mid-1970s, data collection structures and numerous measures to improve data quality had to be implemented before all of the relevant material flows and energy consumption figures could be recorded in full.

Following on from the Group's banking activities in Switzerland – where these structures were established at an early stage – other locations and subsidiaries have gradually been integrated into the system of data collection. Regional differences in terms of priorities and environmental consciousness, as well as the adaptation of data collection and aggregation processes in line with the many changes in the Credit Suisse organisational structure, mean that this is an ongoing task.

THE BENEFITS OF SUSTAINABILITY REPORTING

Establishing a sustainability management system and the corresponding reporting structures is no small undertaking. However, it is, of course, a reflection of the active role that the Group plays within society and demonstrates that Credit Suisse Group takes its environmental and social responsibilities seriously. This is especially important in the case of a global financial services provider, which is particularly dependent on the confidence and acceptance of a variety of stakeholder groups.

The following issues are of primary importance with regard to the internal audience targeted by sustainability reporting:

- Through its sustainability dialogue with its employees, Credit Suisse Group can motivate its staff to become more aware of sustainability, it can promote trust and understanding, and it can position itself as an attractive employer.
- Sustainability reporting has also gained in importance as a management tool in recent years. In connection with its environmental management system, for example, Credit Suisse Group not only created the necessary management structures but also introduced an environmental controlling strategy as a management tool in 1996. As part of a revolving planning and control process, the data collected for the purposes of sustainability reporting not only serve as a means of monitoring the effectiveness of the measures implemented but also provide a basis for formulating and implementing future targets and initiatives. This makes it possible to identify and exploit the potential to reduce costs through the thoughtful use of resources. In 2004,

for example, more than 6 GWh of energy savings were achieved in Switzerland through rehabilitating and optimising building systems. Furthermore, sustainability reporting can represent a useful starting point in terms of identifying business potential and managing risks.

An example of the external implications of the Group's sustainability reporting is set out below:

• Independent rating agencies perform detailed analyses of companies – particularly those that are traded on the stock market. Companies which communicate their strategies and key corporate data actively and transparently have a clear advantage. This applies not only to traditional but also to sustainability ratings, which are awarded by specialist rating agencies. Particularly in view of its open information policy on environmental and social issues, Credit Suisse Group has repeatedly ranked as one of the leaders in the banking industry in top sustainability ratings.

Credit Suisse Group believes that a good sustainability rating represents much more than an independent confirmation that it is among the 'best in class' in its industry. Far more important is the fact that increasing numbers of investors base their investment decisions on sustainability ratings, placing their money in companies that promise a better stock market performance on the strength of their progressive environmental and social management.

In this context, it is particularly worth mentioning the inclusion of Credit Suisse Group in the FTSE4Good Index (a joint venture between the *Financial Times* and the London Stock Exchange) as well as in the Dow Jones Sustainability World Index. As a result, Credit Suisse Group stock is considered a potential investment by the more than 110 sustainability funds that are offered for sale in German-speaking Europe.

GROWING INTEREST AMONG STAKEHOLDERS

Which characteristics distinguish a good sustainability report in the eyes of a stakeholder? Credit Suisse Group expressly welcomes constructive criticism in order to find out exactly what stakeholders regard as important and to be able to fulfil current information requirements even more effectively. Readers are invited to give their feedback using the questionnaire enclosed with the report or via direct dialogue with Credit Suisse Group. Overall this feedback process has shown that there is considerable interest in Credit Suisse Group's sustainability reporting. In 2004 alone, 8000 copies of the print version of the Sustainability Report were ordered and just as many electronic versions were downloaded. Credit Suisse Group received positive feedback regarding the content of its reports in particular, as well as the clear presentation of its strengths, weaknesses and next steps. However, the process also revealed that many target groups now take such comprehensive reporting for granted and wish to have answers to detailed questions despite the general preference for concise information.

In addition, Credit Suisse is taking part in initiatives aimed at further enhancing and standardising sustainability reports. This has highlighted the following expectations, which are broadly in line with the requirements for financial reporting:

- Comprehensive: coverage of the entire value chain and all aspects of sustainability, i.e. economy, ecology and society, as well as a holistic view of these factors.
- Meaningful: provision of both qualitative and quantitative information (industry standards).
- Relevant: stakeholders want information that allows them to form a reliable picture of a company's sustainability performance.
- Regular: reporting on an annual basis is regarded as standard. It should be possible to make comparisons from year to year as

well as across longer periods; the latest information should also be available on the Internet.

• Verifiable: the report should be based on information that is both reliable and verifiable.

• Truthful: stakeholders want problems to be addressed objectively; window-dressing and advertising-style brochures are seen as counterproductive.

In recent years, around 35 initiatives have dealt with the issue of sustainability reporting guidelines – with many tackling individual aspects of this field. Their work has focused on standards for the formal methodological structure of sustainability reports, the formulation of key performance indicator systems and the drafting of a general content framework. The Global Reporting Initiative (GRI) should be mentioned in particular in this context. This group of companies, accounting experts, investors, unions, NGOs and other stakeholder groups has set itself the objective of formulating globally applicable guidelines for sustainability reporting that are relevant for all sectors. Around 600 companies have adopted the GRI guidelines to date. Credit Suisse Group was also involved in drafting sector supplements for the financial industry and is basing the further development of its own reporting on the GRI guidelines.

OUTLOOK: BROADER PERSPECTIVE – MANY CHALLENGES

Reporting about the environmental and social aspects of business has continued to develop steadily since it began around a decade ago – and not just at Credit Suisse Group. The growing need for information on the part of various stakeholder groups, as well as the integration of sustainability factors into management as a basis for long-term business success, are driving forces which will ensure that the issue loses none of its momentum in the years to come.

There are, however, still a number of challenges to be overcome in order to bring non-financial reporting up to the level of financial reporting. The following trends are of particular importance:

- **Value reporting**: investors, rating agencies and non-governmental organisations, which represent a critical public, are increasingly demanding prompt and precise information on how companies generate added value and integrate the concept of sustainability into their value chains. As the market value of a company is determined not only by conventional financial performance indicators but also by intangible values, further development work is required on systems and standards to capture these values. Specifically, this involves determining the value of brands, reputation, intellectual capital, risk management and the involvement of stakeholder groups or customer loyalty – and then quantifying their impact on a company's value.
- **Social issues**: although a large number of companies now issue a sustainability report, many of these publications still concentrate on environmental factors. In view of the growing interest among stakeholder groups in issues such as human rights or anti-corruption efforts, it is incumbent on Credit Suisse Group – as on other organisations – to address the direct and indirect impact of its business activities on these problem areas, to drive forward the necessary action and to initiate dialogue with the relevant stakeholder groups. Another challenge here is to present the interdependencies of the various aspects of sustainability in a more powerful way.

As the concept of sustainability has expanded to include further topics – particularly in the last five years – it has increasingly been expected that companies should assume responsibility for environmental and social issues. In addition to informing stakeholders and the public about their commitments in key areas, companies must therefore also clearly communicate the limits of their responsibilities.

- **Closer stakeholder involvement**: one of the key success factors with the Global Reporting Initiative was the early involvement of various stakeholder groups in drafting the guidelines. The increased integration of external bodies is also an option worth considering in the corporate sector. It is conceivable, for example, that stakeholder groups may be invited to comment on a sustainability report – especially where it examines challenging issues.

APPENDIX

Milestones in Credit Suisse Group's environmental and social commitment

1976–9	Planning and construction of the Uetlihof complex in Zurich, taking environmental requirements into account
1977	Start of a 10-year energy-saving programme in Switzerland, involving the refurbishment of particularly energy-intensive properties
1986	Launch of the CS Fellowship Fund (UK) – Credit Suisse's first 'green' investment fund
1989	First full-time environmental officer
1990	Environmental protection becomes an integral part of corporate philosophy within the Credit Suisse guiding principles
1991	Establishment of the working group 'Credit Suisse + Environment', headed by a member of senior management
1992	Credit Suisse Group signs the International Chamber of Commerce Charter for Sustainable Development (ICC Charter) and the UN Statement by Financial Institutions on the Environment (UNEP Declaration) Introduction of a Directive requiring that environmental risk be considered in credit decisions
1994	Credit Suisse sets up an environmental risk unit
1995	Publication of the eco-performance report for Zurich and Geneva Signing of the UN Statement of Environmental Commitment by the Insurance Industry (UNEP)
1996	Introduction of an environmental controlling strategy Publication of first Environmental Report by Credit Suisse

1997	Credit Suisse Group is the first major bank in the world to be awarded ISO 14001 certification for its banking locations in Switzerland
1999	Credit Suisse Group is named 'Leading Sustainability Company' in the banking sector in the Dow Jones Sustainability Group Index
2000	Credit Suisse signs up to the UN Global Compact Initiative
2002	Publication of the Group's first Sustainability Report
2003	Adoption of the Equator Principles to take account of ecological and social risks in project finance
2004	Development of a sustainability strategy with short- and medium-term targets
2005	UN Year of Microcredit: Credit Suisse, together with partner banks in the Swiss financial centre, offers its clients a micro-finance fund

CHAPTER 17

Microfinance as Profitable Good Practice

Rolf-E. Breuer

INTRODUCTION

As corporations' economic power and resources grow, there are
increased expectations, in some cases regulated through legislation,
that corporations should take the initiative and become involved
in the development of the communities where they do business.
As a relatively new field, corporate social responsibility (CSR)
departments are struggling to find the optimum means to bring forth
the values of their companies. While the good intentions behind
these efforts are commendable, corporations have traditionally
seen this as an expense of doing business and have mostly acted
alone using their own philanthropic initiatives, without much
accountability for the outcome. This has contributed to the most
common criticism of CSR work: it is oriented towards marketing

The ICCA Handbook on Corporate Social Responsibility Edited by J. Hennigfeld, M. Pohl and N. Tolhurst
© 2006 John Wiley & Sons, Ltd

and is not broad and significant enough to have a meaningful social impact through systematic change.

However, corporations cannot be rightly expected to take on development responsibilities, nor can governments acting alone solve the enormous global challenges putting us all at risk. And yet, the private sector has a significant role to play by contributing its business knowledge and execution efficiencies to create structures in which government and development agencies serve as catalysts to mitigate early risks and attract the scale of the private sector.

At the same time, institutional investors are increasingly demanding structures that have a significant social benefit, are financially viable and meet their fiduciary and prudential obligations. In the US alone, the socially responsible investment industry has nearly US$3 trillion in invested assets, which represents about 12% of the US$20 trillion under professional management. Most of these socially responsible investments are in 'screened' equities of listed companies and liquid securities. However, by its very nature, screening is indirect and focuses on limiting harm rather than proactively seeking capital to change the circumstances of people most in need.

As financial intermediaries, banks have the financial knowledge to structure proactive, innovative and collaborative investment vehicles that permit development agencies, governments and socially responsive institutional investors to invest responsibly, while seeking both a social and financial return. If successful, such vehicles have the potential to reduce the perceived and real investment risks, change perceptions, create liquidity, open up markets and provide the much-needed capital for the development and growth of social enterprises. In short, these investment vehicles and microfinance could serve to bring about systemic change.

Nearly 10 years ago, Deutsche Bank began supporting microfinance institutions as an effective and responsible means of providing the benefits of financial services to low-income people. This approach is actually in line with the bank's core business, i.e. financial intermediation. We saw microfinance as an opportunity to use the financial knowledge and abilities of our employees to effect social change. We soon realised that microfinance institutions have an enormous potential ahead to extend financial services to vast populations of the 'underbanked' poor. As a result, we founded the Deutsche Bank Microcredit Development Fund (DBMDF). Designed with a long-term sustainable approach, DBMDF makes loans to microfinance institutions. The bank sponsored and launched DBMDF in 1997, and it quickly attracted interest from Deutsche Bank's private banking and other clients, who made additional contributions. The fund uses the bank's global resources to hedge currency risks, gain the commitment of local banks and catalyse the establishment of local sources for microfinancing, resulting in a sustainable drive to alleviate global poverty. To date, the fund has invested in 38 microfinance institutions in 24 countries (with one default) and facilitated over US$47 million in local currency financing that has benefited over 240000 micro-entrepreneurs worldwide.

The success of this initial fund led the bank to establish the Global Commercial Microfinance Consortium (the 'Consortium'), an innovative partnership comprising leading development agencies, institutional investors and highly respected global corporations. The Consortium is a US$75 million fund that invests in the development of the microfinance sector. It also fosters relationships between local financial institutions, a fundamental source of capital, and microfinance institutions to create indigenous financial systems that serve the working poor. The Consortium's work is not tied to the business interests of any particular member and each investor has equal status.

Deutsche Bank's approach to CSR includes not only the use of financial resources but also the transfer of knowledge and skills as well as the commitment of our employees to bring about social change. This knowledge and skills transfer as well as our employees' commitment are at the heart of the bank's success in microfinance.

They facilitate the creation of local financial networks and financial systems to serve the working poor and alleviate poverty.

Furthermore, we are convinced that 'downstreaming' financial services through microfinance eventually leads to greater global economic stability. As a global financial institution, Deutsche Bank has an important role to play in helping to establish regional and local business structures that work to reduce the gap between developed and less-developed economies. As the local markets are strengthened as a platform for mainstream business and trade, the development gaps tend to become smaller.

WHAT IS MICROFINANCE? DOWNSTREAMING FINANCIAL SERVICES

Microfinance 'downstreams' financial services to the poor, providing them with access to loans, savings plans, insurance and other services on a sustainable basis. This industry is growing rapidly and over the past 25 years has proven to be commercially viable, in terms of both profitability and risk.

Credit has been a cornerstone in the creation of wealth through the ages. From the de Medicis to the Vanderbilts, the power of credit has been used to leverage resources for people with wealth. In the modern age, the middle class has also had broad access to credit through mortgages, consumer finance and small business loans. Today, microfinance brings the power of credit to the grassroots level – in the form of loans to the self-employed poor – without the usual requirements of existing assets and a previous credit history. While not a panacea, evidence shows that loans to poor entrepreneurs improve household income, education levels, health, self-reliance and community development. A growing body of research indicates that over time, most microfinance borrowers move above the poverty line (Khandker, 2003).

Historically, however, nearly every region and culture of the world has actually had informal credit networks and moneylenders who have recognised the potential profitability of lending to the self-employed poor. And their businesses are extremely varied; they work as street vendors, merchants, cobblers, recyclers, farmers or fishermen, as well as in hundreds of other types of businesses (Ledgerwood, 2000: 13). In the 1970s, Grameen Bank in Bangladesh and others began providing training and loans of US$25 to US$100 to poor entrepreneurs just starting out: typically a poor woman needing working capital for her tiny business. Grameen required these women to group together, participate in pre-loan training and mutually agree to repay each other's loans. Surprisingly, Grameen experienced repayment rates in excess of 98%.

Today, Grameen and other microfinance institutions have demonstrated sustainable methods of providing financial services to the poor. And they all have several aspects in common: small short-term loans, a form of peer review of the applicants, rigorous collection, interest rates set to cover delivery costs and a focus on clients with informal businesses. Some of these organisations are regulated financial institutions with millions of customers, professional staff, financial profitability and a wide range of products and services.

Microfinance provides credible evidence, from regions around the world, which disproves perceptions that the poor are not creditworthy or enterprising and that they cannot be served profitably. Indeed, the track record of microfinance has been one of repeatedly disproving prior assumptions, as shown in Table 17.1.[1]

Microfinance has expanded from credit-based products and methods to include savings, insurance and payment services,

---

[1] The World Bank Institute. A distance learning course in microfinance for non-specialists, Elizabeth Littlefield, CEO Consultative Group to Assist the Poorest. *Microfinance's Evolution: Past, Today, and Future.* http://www.worldbank.org/wbi/banking/eastasiamicro/module06.html and http://www.worldbank.org/wbi/banking/eastasiamicro/pdf/mod06_littlefield.ppt.

Table 17.1 Track record of microfinance

Era	Myth	Fact
Early 1980s	Poor people do not repay their loans	Many microfinance institutions have better repayment rates than banks
Early 1990s	The poor cannot pay the full cost of microfinance	A few microfinance institutions begin covering all their costs
Mid-1990s	MFIs must depend on donor funding rather than commercial sources	Top microfinance institutions begin to attract significant commercial funding
Today	MFIs cannot be profitable and reach the poorest	The microfinance industry is focused on helping MFIs attain these two objectives

all designed to meet the needs of poor customers. Many microfinance institutions (MFIs) retain overall profitability even while linking these products to non-profit services, such as training, literacy and business development skills. A growing number of microfinance institutions have the professionalism, procedures, management and institutional capabilities to deliver these services to the poor in an efficient, customer-friendly and profitable manner (Ledgerwood, 2000: 22).

There is no doubt that microfinance is here to stay. Currently, there are over 70 million microcredit borrowers, with an estimated aggregate loan portfolio of US$7 billion worldwide. The sector is expected to continue its high annual growth rate of 30% per year. Within 10 years, microfinance will potentially reach over 500 million poor people and be a global, profitable industry with microfinance institutions numbering several thousands and assets in the realm of hundreds of billions of euros. Clearly, microfinance will play a major role in the future. The question is: how will we arrive at this future?

THE ROLE OF SOCIAL INVESTMENTS IN MICROFINANCE

One can argue that most investments have a social value in that the economy expands and jobs are created. So, what do we mean by socially responsible investments? The act of investing per se entails foregoing immediate benefits for a later return that hopefully exceeds the present value. When we add the term 'socially responsible', clearly there is an expectation of increased value for the good of society that goes beyond the benefits of economic expansion and higher employment. By adding the dimension of social responsibility, social investing raises the bar from merely a maximisation of profits to a maximisation of profits and of the value for society.

The Deutsche Bank Microcredit Development Fund is representative of the bank's broader approach, not only to microfinance, but also to proactive social investment in general. This is a field where the bank's financial know-how is used to bring capital to communities that do not have traditional access to funding. We are finding that this lack of access often has more to do with perceptions than with reality, and even distressed communities constitute a market in terms of people, capacities, scale and potential profitability. As stated above, microfinance has faced large hurdles in perception, whereby the poor were seen as uncreditworthy, able to benefit from charity; but they were not perceived as entrepreneurs who could leverage the benefits of credit. However, over the past 20 years, microfinance has proven that the latter is true. Data on microfinance institutions shows average portfolio at risk (PAR > 90 days) of $1.5\%^2$ (see Figure 17.1).

---

[2] The Microfinance Information Exchange (the 'MIX') is the global information exchange for the microfinance industry. The MIX strives to facilitate the exchange of information and investments, promote transparency and improve reporting standards in the microfinance industry. See www.mixmarket.org.

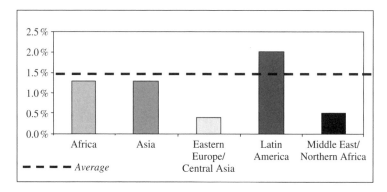

Figure 17.1   MFI average portfolio at risk > 90 days

Figure 17.2 summarises this data by geographic region. Besides having good asset quality and low default rates (using PAR > 90 as a proxy for outright defaults), microfinance institutions have proven to be profitable businesses. 2002 data shows that the microfinance institutions surveyed had an average return on equity after adjustments of 14.6%.

In addition, data shows that many microfinance institutions have accessed commercial debt − 90% of Share Microfin India's gross loan portfolio (US$2 million) in 1990 was financed from subsidised

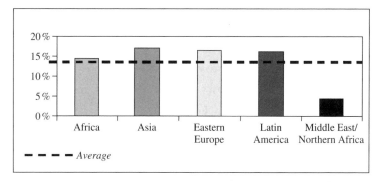

Figure 17.2   Adjusted return on equity for 66 financially self-sufficient MFIs

noncommercial sources. In 2004, 98% of Share Microfin India's US$18.5 million gross loan portfolio was financed from commercial sources.[3]

The development of these microfinance markets presents a potential business opportunity for socially motivated investors willing to consider the 'unbanked' as 'bankable'. Increasingly, commercial banks are providing financing to microfinance institutions directly throughout the world, and some have even established subsidiaries as a business line. And credit-rating agencies such as Fitch and Standard & Poor's have issued ratings on microfinance institutions. Furthermore, in Latin America, Africa and Asia, microfinance institutions have utilised the local capital markets to issue bonds.

The core concept of Deutsche Bank's work in microfinance is to make use of the bank's financial know-how to bring capital to communities that do not have access to traditional capital for various reasons, including preconceptions about the distressed communities and poor people, their limited capacity and scale, the lack of liquidity and, in some cases, constrained profitability. We would argue that the main hurdle is our perceived limitation of the distressed communities and their inhabitants rather than the actual capacity, scale, liquidity or profitability. For one can increase capacity through investment, leading to the scale and volume that necessitate secondary markets and liquidity. Even with small margins, profits are very attractive due to the size of these underserved markets.

Although these markets are underdeveloped, their potential is real and being tapped. Microfinance at the 'bottom of the pyramid' is a leading concept in targeting the largest sector of the population. The poor are now being regarded as a potential business opportunity and the 'unbanked' as 'bankable'. Such shifts in perception are real glimpses of the future. As social investors, we believe our primary

---

[3] Data from Share Microfin Limited, India.

focus should be here, while we continue to provide philanthropic resources for essential projects that are not commercially viable.

For all of their benefits, these proactive social investments are complex, requiring multiple layers of financing between socially motivated investors, philanthropic foundations, development agencies and the private sector. In addition to market potential, financial structuring capabilities are necessary prerequisites for the commitment and development of proactive social investment structures. On the one hand, development agencies face their own challenges and limitations. Because they are outside the private sector, they often find it difficult to bring in the involvement of corporations. It is much easier for them to assume the proxy role of commercial investors rather than to serve as a catalyst by bringing the private sector to the table, especially when most businesses view development issues as the exclusive domain of the development agencies. Corporations have also been historically reluctant to form partnerships with development agencies, which are at times challenged by bureaucracy and inefficiencies. On the other hand, social investors and charitable foundations can often take high-risk positions, but they normally lack the capacity to structure transactions.

This means the private sector has the opportunity to become much more involved, if the hundreds of billions of euros needed to effect change are to be mobilised. What is needed is some innovative thinking to create partnerships and cooperative structures to tackle some of the larger social issues. The scale of global poverty and other social issues is such that they cannot be handled by any one entity. It is going to take all the tools in our toolbox rather than a 'one-size-fits-all' approach. Governments also have a key role to play in making sure that fiduciary concerns and the related regulations are balanced with social needs. There is in fact one area where government regulators could be particularly effective in mobilising resources from the private sector: by allowing responsible microfinance institutions to take deposits from their clients. Although it may be prudent caution, because of fiduciary concerns, to prohibit microfinance institutions from taking deposits, let us keep this in perspective with the issues we are facing, namely that more than 75 % of the population in developing countries have no access to financial services.

THE GLOBAL COMMERCIAL MICROFINANCE CONSORTIUM

As mentioned above, at Deutsche Bank we worked hard to launch a unique US$75 million fund called the Global Commercial Microfinance Consortium, a partnership formed by some of the most innovative global companies and leading development agencies. The governance of the Consortium is through the Board and all partners are invited to join the Board, giving them an equal voice. Ultimately, the Board has the authority to give notice to the present general manager, Deutsche Bank, which was also the Consortium's founder.

The Consortium presents an opportunity for corporations to fulfil their corporate social responsibility through a well-protected, return-based investment, rather than through grants with limited accountability. The Consortium's work is not tied to the business interests of any particular company, but aims at improving the infrastructural environment by addressing poverty and its global issues. The objective of the Consortium is to bring about systemic change by creating indigenous systems for financial support for the working poor by providing risk-reduced financing to local financial institutions. The idea is also to encourage relationships between banks, which are fundamental sources of local capital, and microfinance institutions.

The Consortium has a US$15 million equity base and US$60 million in five-year floating rate debt. In terms of structure, the Consortium is a hybrid of a private equity fund and unsecured bullet revolver. The debt piece, which is targeted for institutional investors, is credit enhanced through a 40 % subordination. Half of this credit enhancement is the US$15 million equity base, provided by DFID (UK development agency) and AFD (French development agency), and the other half is a first-loss US$15 million guarantee from USAID (US development agency). The Consortium also has an embedded cap: debt holders can only lose 75 % of their invested capital. One can question the need for all this protection to bring in the private sector. The 30-year US mortgage market is a good example of why. These days the 30-year mortgage market is one of the most liquid markets, but only 50 years ago banks considered it too risky to make a 30-year loan. It was the full guarantee provided by the US government that propelled this market and created its large capacity, scale and liquidity. Today, within minutes, several offers are obtainable from banks fiercely competing to lend for 30 years. This is how credit enhancement can erode perceived risk.

Even with high levels of risk protection, like that of the Consortium, it is very difficult to bring institutional investors to commit to nontraditional, 'market' or 'close-to-market' investments, even when there are clear social benefits. These investors are looking at social investments with the same benchmarks they use to judge highly developed commercial markets. They want these assets to be rated, and they want them to be liquid with daily price quotes. But you cannot have it all, especially in trying to develop the emerging proactive social investment market. What is important is to develop not only structures and opportunities, but also a track record, and to change the institutional investors' attitudes. The evaluation measurements they use should not only be prudent, but should also take into account the special nature and inherent challenges of socially motivated investing.

The Consortium is taking a pioneering role in the development of microfinance as an asset class, and it is designed to accelerate the development of the microfinance market in general. For example, by attracting and sharing risks with local banks, the Consortium's US$75 million in funding will be leveraged and multiplied, demonstrating the viability of microfinance as a commercial investment at the local level. In addition, by creating new structures that leverage resources and reduce risk, the Consortium forges important new avenues and commercially feasible methods. These vehicles and methods can eventually be replicated and increased in scale to help in the growth of the field. Until now, there has been very little commercial investment in microfinance, but for the first time the Consortium has attracted major global corporations as commercial investors in microfinance, showing others that microfinance is in fact emerging as a viable commercial investment and asset class.

Deutsche Bank is now starting to pursue microfinance as a business. Our asset management business line is, for example, bidding on an opportunity to manage a 200 million euro microfinance portfolio for Eastern Europe. The bank's involvement in microfinance is expected to deepen as the microfinance sector grows and commercialises. The bank's asset advisory business and the Consortium represent a new wave of investment in microfinance, and the bank anticipates a series of investment vehicles will be developed to help meet the rapidly increasing demand. From these small beginnings, the bank hopes to have a role in promoting the growth of what it believes will be an asset class potentially worth hundreds of billions of dollars.

We are at the very early stages of development, not just of microfinance but also of the social investment industry as a whole, and a lot more is still to come. The aerospace industry, the pinnacle of human achievement and innovation, started less than 100 years ago with copper tubes and rockets that looked like firecrackers. Considering its relatively short lifespan of about 120 years, the telephone industry is having a profound effect on developing countries through the growth of the cellular phone business, even in the hands of a poor population. Technology is changing the world right before our very eyes, and the potential of proactive social investment is tremendous. Just imagine what the social investment industry could be like in 100 years' time.

CONCLUSION

Anything that has a potential stream of revenues can be financed. We are not saying that it is always easy – but we can, and we intend to, finance schools, universities, vocational training facilities, healthcare facilities, hospitals, farmers, the development of alternative forms of energy, etc. But before socially responsible investment can take place, it needs to be financed, and thus financial institutions have a special role to play in the development of proactive social investing. As these investments are in their rudimentary stages of growth, development agencies and foundations will have to serve as catalysts by assuming or mitigating early, economic and especially perceived risk, and by helping to create layers of subordinated capital or by taking less in return, to make the investment profitable for private investors.

The good news is that social investors motivated by a desire to achieve social and financial objectives are increasingly calling for public–private partnerships. The corporate social responsibility window can also serve to attract private sector involvement in the development field. It is up to us to take advantage of these opportunities and accelerate these trends.

References

Khandker, Shahidur (2003). *Microfinance and Poverty: Evidence Using Panel Data from Bangladesh*. Washington, DC: World Bank.
Ledgerwood, Joanna (2000). *Microfinance Handbook: An Institutional and Financial Perspective*. Washington, DC: World Bank.

CHAPTER 18

Business Ethics as a Management Instrument – Vision, Values and Code of Conduct at Henkel

Ulrich Lehner

INTRODUCTION

Some time ago, the *Frankfurter Allgemeine Zeitung* headlined a story with the 'return of ethics' to the corporate boardroom. The headline was certainly chosen to attract attention, but at the same time it characterises the recent, increasingly critical discussion about the excesses associated with the principles of the market economy.

Everywhere in today's society we can sense that the world is becoming more pluralistic. In addition to Christianity, Islam and other religions, youth sects and the 'New Age' offer competing visions of the meaning of life. The borders of national economies have become less important, while globalisation accelerates cultural diversification. Changes occur faster, prevail more rapidly and have global dimensions. The collapse of socialist and communist regimes

The ICCA Handbook on Corporate Social Responsibility   Edited by J. Hennigfeld, M. Pohl and N. Tolhurst
© 2006 John Wiley & Sons, Ltd

has led to a sometimes excessive materialism and egoism in business, reflected in the prevalence of individualism and the pursuit of selfish group interests. Political parties, labour unions, business associations and churches complain about falling membership: a drop-out society with autistic traits is arising. Competition over the distribution of economic wealth is intensifying and, in the context of globalisation, is taking on a new social and political dimension that heretofore would have been unimaginable. Loss of values, moral decline and changes in values are all cause and effect at the same time. Television and the electronic media reflect this development and at the same time contribute to an increasingly commercialised consumer culture. The value system of developed countries has fallen into a trap laid by economic prosperity.

Some see the rallying cry of the French revolution 'liberty, equality, fraternity' being corrupted into 'arbitrariness, indifference and apathy'. Nothing counts. Everything is in a constant state of flux; a sense of orientation and grounding is lacking. Values are questioned.

Others turn to a fundamentalism that adheres to traditional values and is in danger of fossilising. Exclusion replaces openness and curiosity. Under such conditions neither the economy nor culture nor society can prosper.

Today, more than ever, we need value systems that are valid across frontiers, cultures and the narrow limits of corporate departments. They must be valid for our own time and in the light of coming developments. The point of departure for the widespread criticism of developments within the business community is to be found precisely in the declining consensus on basic values and the need for a durable frame of reference and orientation. This criticism is articulated not only by anti-globalisation activists or single-interest groups but also by business leaders themselves.

Political leaders have also recognised that an unbridled application of liberal economic principles could endanger the acceptance of the free market economy, in spite of its recognition as the best economic system.

The reservations with respect to uncontrolled liberal economics have their reasons. In its search for the best possible combination of high returns and flexibility in a globalised economy, capital tends to seek locations where it can escape regulation and costly tax or social security levies. From the point of view of nation states, capital is therefore contributing less and less to financing national social security systems. This may be acceptable for market fundamentalists, since global markets contribute to growth and prosperity. At the same time, the workings of global markets tend to limit the contribution of global corporations to financing of social needs.

This criticism applies to the macro-level first of all. Although markets have become global, political decision making is still based on the principle of national sovereignty and limited supranational control of markets.

Comparable arguments and behaviour based on group egoism can be found in the discussion at the meso- and micro-level. The only difference is that business associations, government agencies, corporations or corporate departments strive to achieve their own specific objectives in the local, regional or transnational context.

In the context of the social market economy as conceived by Ludwig Erhardt, the Federal Republic of Germany's first Secretary of Commerce, the decisive question of ethics to be raised is not rooted in our economic system, but in people themselves. The problem lies in the deficiency of society's socio-technical constructs, to the extent that people believe they can manage without a personal ethos. The recent history of our economic theory and practice shows this, since in cases such as Enron and Worldcom – not to mention even more recent developments in Germany – it was not institutions that could be held responsible but individuals and their incapacity or unwillingness to design appropriate processes and structures to manage and control the organisations for which they were responsible. The reason for this widely observed development over the past 10 years is the de-personalisation of business decision making as a result of technological advances and globalisation, which has ultimately caused economic thinking to loosen its bonds with the wider culture. While previously most enterprises identified themselves with the society in which they operated – and this is still the case in many parts of Germany, especially in family enterprises and in medium-sized businesses – in recent years an economic rationality with a strong US influence has come to the fore. But the hopes for greater prosperity and fewer conflicts associated with this approach were not satisfied as fully as expected, which in turn led to a loss of confidence in the market economy, in business, in managers and in government's ability to ensure order and provide social security. For corporations, the objective is therefore to develop confidence once again – and in doing so, to expand the concept of corporate social responsibility over and above a too exclusive focus on short-term economic advantage.

In order to avoid any misunderstandings: corporations are not to be seen as charitable organisations! Nor can they assume government's responsibility for general public welfare or for reducing the unemployment rate.

But the entrepreneur's profit-achieving objective is subject to two considerations, which broaden the purely economic definition of the term corporate responsibility – also in terms of optimising business processes:

- Firstly, frictions resulting from an overemphasised focus on economic objectives can negatively influence the company's image and lead to unwanted reactions on the part of its stakeholders, thus damaging the company's global positioning, which in turn can lead to a lower market valuation of the company, as well as a reduction in employees' effectiveness and efficiency.
- Secondly, business ethics can be used as a management instrument to help achieve an internal, functioning order, which in this pluralistic world does not rely on a rigid code of behaviour, the details of which can never be sufficiently defined.

For this reason Henkel does not regard business ethics or related issues like corporate governance or corporate social responsibility, including corporate citizenship, as cost centres, but as value-creating (at least value-conserving) regulative instruments of modern enterprises.

BUSINESS ETHICS – A DEFINITION

In the *Encyclopaedia of Applied Ethics* published in 1993, Professor Georges Enderle defined ethics as '(…) the teaching of right or good behaviour. (…) The subject of ethics is people's behaviour (i.e., the manner in which they lead their lives) and actions. (…) Relevant topics in the context of ethics are questions of differentiating good and evil, defining the purpose and the meaning of life, the good life, and happiness.' On this basis, ethics is to be defined as a conceptual frame of reference for action, fully consistent with Kant's dictum: act only in accordance with a maxim that could serve at any time as a universal law.

Business ethics involves conveying this definition into corporations; it therefore focuses on morals or morality in the field of business.

In doing so, business ethics do not only focus on the 'company', but on the individuals that form the company as a socio-technical system and advance it – and thereby have to act in a context which is not always free of conflicts of interests given the multifarious objectives of individuals, the company and its various departments, not to mention the general public. The philosopher Jeremy Bentham (1748–1832) captured this reality very accurately by defining ethics as nothing but the regulation of egoism through values.

The concept of 'values' is to be understood in an interdisciplinary manner. On the one hand it must reflect the practical value of business activity and on the other hand the moral principles mirroring the specific ethos of individuals, cultures or corporations.

While 'practical value' can be captured rather simply with the help of economic metrics, moral values undergo certain changes over time and in their specific context, which explains why a static definition and a one-dimensional anchorage across cultures appear to be false. Simultaneously the moral values associated with ethical approaches are so 'profound' that a desired change of values takes a long time.

In the context of corporate management, for many corporations ethics is an effective instrument, but one that works over the long term and which serves as a constant frame of reference for other management instruments (for example, incentive systems or general guidelines for corporate behaviour).

Used effectively, business ethics can be considered a regulating and control system for corporations, and one which ultimately – in the ideal situation – actually leads the corporation through its contribution to corporate identity and the definition of corporate objectives. Yet reality is characterised by a high degree of heterogeneity and complexity, which, like most unstable factors, challenge the ideal type of regulating and control system.

BUSINESS ETHICS AND SOCIAL JUSTICE

The growth of international business has fostered criticism by anti-globalisation activists, but this criticism has no foundation either in ethics or catholic social teaching. On the contrary: social solidarity is only possible to the extent that liberty, responsibility and associated self-interest have the opportunity to unfold their benefits. This is because there cannot be any economic dynamism unless one accepts responsibility for oneself. But no one will assume the responsibility necessary for economic development unless there is a reward for accepting entrepreneurial risk, i.e. unless it is possible to achieve a risk premium.

Those who seek to halt this process on the basis of an erroneous understanding of social justice and who willingly confuse the objectives of the social insurance system with politically enacted egalitarianism will achieve exactly the opposite of what they intend. Viable jobs will be lost, or at best relocated, the entrepreneurial spirit so vital to economic development and indispensable structural change will be discouraged and standards of living will decline.

Social justice therefore does not mean ensuring a particular distribution of goods and wealth among different social groups, but rather implies ensuring equality of opportunity and requiring individuals to assume responsibility for their own lives. This applies as much to the (re-)integration of the unemployed into the labour market as it does to acquiring knowledge and education. Ethical values and social responsibility thus have nothing to do with the allocation or distribution of material goods, whether at the level of the corporation or the overall economy. The question is not which projects a company spends its money on; the question is how a company earns its money.

THE HENKEL GROUP

Henkel is an international provider of branded articles and systems solutions. Within its chosen business sectors, the Henkel Group is a leading participant in the global market. In order to further strengthen this position, Henkel repositioned itself strategically in 2001 – its 125th anniversary. The former 'Specialist for Applied Chemistry' is now a corporation focusing on high-quality branded articles and cutting-edge technologies. As part of this strategic reorganisation, Henkel disposed of its chemicals unit, Cognis, and its stake in the Henkel-Ecolab joint venture. In addition, certain business units were regrouped into new, globally operating business sectors.

Today, the Henkel Group has three strategic areas of competence: home care; personal care; and adhesives, sealants and surface treatment. For the latter strategic area it makes sense to differentiate between consumer and industrial businesses so that Henkel's strategic areas of competence are covered by four globally operating business sectors:

- Laundry and Home Care;
- Cosmetics/Toiletries;
- Consumer and Craftsmen Adhesives; and
- Henkel Technologies.

People in more than 125 countries put their trust in Henkel brands and technologies. Of Henkel's approximately 52000 employees worldwide, some 80% work outside Germany. With its world headquarters in Düsseldorf, Henkel is one of the leading global companies in Germany. In fiscal year 2005 Henkel Group had total sales of 12.0 billion euros with an operating profit of 1.2 billion euros.

BUSINESS ETHICS AND CORPORATE SOCIAL RESPONSIBILITY AT HENKEL

Business ethics at Henkel is characterised by three criteria:

- It is neither an end in itself nor an occasional, incidental activity, but a deliberate process focused on securing the future.
- It is a framework for each individual person as well as for the company as a whole.
- It aims to contribute to 'shareholder value'.

At Henkel we understand the concept of 'shareholder value' as the sum of all actions taken to steadily improve the competitive position of Henkel's businesses, thereby supporting profitable growth. In our opinion the pursuit of shareholder value is in the interests of shareholders and all other stakeholders. It ensures compensation payments, improves the long-term employment situation, brings in taxes for the state and assures our business partners of a stable and profitable business relationship.

At Henkel, shareholder and stakeholder value are two interrelated and mutually supporting elements of a sustainable corporate strategy. We are dedicated to sustainability and corporate responsibility.

If business ethics is understood as a point of reference and framework for our employees, who stem from the most varied cultural areas worldwide, then business ethics, as we conceive it at Henkel, has a functional character for management. A code of business ethics helps to guide the behaviour of our employees in keeping with our corporate strategy, and is especially helpful in doing so in ambiguous or undefined situations for which it is nearly impossible to provide explicit rules in advance. 'Linking people to strategy' is the term one of our American employees devised to describe this function of business ethics. This function alone suffices to ensure that business ethics makes a significant contribution to the company's current and future business success. In the light of this value function, the occasional criticism that business ethics is just a byproduct of business activity and a playground for managers infatuated by values, but lacking in operational responsibility, is unfounded and false.

The causal relationship between business ethics and business success is confirmed in practice. Recent studies have shown that employees worldwide favour companies that – in addition to appropriate compensation – are guided by established ethical rules. The same is true of customers, suppliers and all other stakeholders. The value of business ethics is also reflected in the valuation of companies by the financial community, as shown by the different sustainability rankings and the emergence of special ethical investment funds favouring companies with a distinct business ethics orientation.

In addition, similar considerations also apply to the evaluation of the attractiveness of countries and thus must be taken into account as location factors. Investors and companies prefer countries with clearly articulated ethical values that are also observed by the people and companies in these countries.

Today, Henkel is a company that has evolved from a multi-domestic position to a transnational enterprise with global presence. In the process, Henkel has gone through several stages of development. As the company has developed, our value system has advanced: from a national to a multinational level and ultimately to a globally valid and shared system. This value system includes operational and strategic targets as well as administrative and legal principles and is binding for all Henkel companies worldwide. It defines Henkel's corporate vision and values and currently has three major dimensions:

- Henkel's Code of Conduct.
- Henkel's Code of Teamwork and Leadership.
- Henkel's Code of Corporate Sustainability.

The implementation of these three dimensions documents a commitment by Henkel and its employees to clearly visible behaviour based on the company's vision and values. It also serves as a management platform for Henkel as a whole, one that pursues three clear goals:

- Building confidence.
- Creating a sense of belonging, a 'we' feeling.
- Creating a common focus on internal goals.

These three dimensions first of all serve as an inner frame of reference for all employees. However, the better this value system is applied and communicated to customers and suppliers, the better the goals of the management platform can reach external stakeholders. In this regard, the strong relationship of our value system to our corporate identity becomes evident.

Our vision and our values, our Code of Conduct, our Code of Teamwork and Leadership and our Code of Corporate Sustainability reflect our entrepreneurial and social responsibilities. They serve as mandatory guidelines for our company, a set of practical instructions governing our relationships with customers, suppliers and colleagues alike.

Vision

Business ethics is not something that can be driven into employees' heads overnight where it then becomes an internalised, dynamic management and control device focused on fulfilling predetermined goals. In fact the process more often takes several years and requires conscious, exemplary management leadership to be successful. If business ethics – as in the case of Henkel – is used as a framework for the companies' objectives, it is even more important to align the ethical principles with targets that remain valid for the long term and across cultures. These objectives are found in the company vision.

The Henkel Group's shared vision defines the company's purpose across all business units and defines the company's top objectives for employees, business partners and shareholders.

As Henkel evolved from a chemical specialist to become a company focusing on brands and technologies, Henkel's vision also had to be redefined. The challenge was to find clear wording offering a distinctive description of Henkel's business. In seeking this definition, we recalled the key to Henkel's success since its origins: making work easier for our customers and providing them with better results. This essential motivation of making things easier and better is still valid today. It is timeless and is valid for Henkel worldwide: for consumer goods as well as industrial goods, for our industrial customers as for trade partners and consumers.

Going back to the roots made it possible for Henkel to define a vision which will endure in the future: 'Henkel is a leader with brands and technologies that make people's lives easier, better and more beautiful.'

Based on this vision, we developed a new corporate identity for Henkel's different businesses, which uses the Henkel company name to emphasise membership of the global group.

With the choice of the claim 'Henkel – a brand like a friend', we also convey a certain rule of conduct for the employees and the company itself. This also helps to leverage the psychological strengths of the brand in general – namely building trust through reliability and quality – for the umbrella brand Henkel.

Trust is a company's single greatest asset. Trust can reduce transaction costs in businesses between customer and vendor, between a company and its employees, between management and shareholders as well as other stakeholders. Trust, however, can only arise if the company, its employees and its brands are consistent with respect to their language, symbols and behaviour in their interactions with people.

Trust emerges through transparency, awareness, proximity, coherence and quality and is confirmed when promises are kept. Where inconsistencies exist, it is difficult to persuade people that promises made will be fulfilled, because trust – which is the basis of every form of cooperation – diminishes. Avoiding such a possible loss of confidence is one of the most important targets that we pursue with our focus on business ethics.

This explains why Henkel adopted a new vision in 2001. Henkel has over 750 different brands. Consumers in more than 125 countries trust in brands and technologies from Henkel. It is a successful, multinational company growing splendidly. However, what was still missing was a binding element that could link all Henkel's worldwide activities, so that they could be visible and experienced emotionally, without detracting from growth and development. I am convinced that we have succeeded in creating this binding element with our current corporate vision.

Values

Today's economy is characterised by strong international competition. In such an environment, a company can only be successful if it has a common understanding with its employees of the manner in which the corporate vision is to be implemented.

At Henkel, we have found this common understanding through the definition of globally valid corporate values. They articulate Henkel's culture, which adheres closely to the principles of sustainable business practice. And they create an environment that is as productive as it is personally rewarding. In a second step, our vision and values were specified for implementation purposes in the Code of Conduct.

On the basis of our vision and our understanding of corporate responsibility, we derived 10 fundamental values:

1. We are customer driven.
2. We develop superior brands and technologies.
3. We aspire to excellence in quality.
4. We strive for innovation.
5. We embrace change.
6. We are successful because of our people.
7. We are committed to shareholder value.
8. We are dedicated to sustainability and corporate social responsibility.
9. We communicate openly and actively.
10. We preserve the tradition of an open family company.

In order to foster understanding for these values and thus support their implementation throughout the company, we set out the values in writing and communicated them vigorously so that they became established as a natural part of employees' relationship with Henkel. The essence of Henkel's values can be summarised as follows:

1. We are customer driven

We provide brands and technologies that (consistently) meet or exceed our customers' expectations. Our ability to understand and solve complex problems enables us to respond to our customers' specific needs. The quality of our products and dialogue with our customers are the means by which we establish long-term partnerships based on reliability, credibility and mutual trust.

2. We develop superior brands and technologies

Our strong brands and innovative technologies help to shape the future of the markets and the markets of the future. We achieve this through efficient management systems and use our knowledge and experience to obtain leading market positions for our brands and technologies worldwide.

3. We aspire to excellence in quality

We set correspondingly high quality standards in order to further strengthen the leading positions of our brands and technologies. We cultivate and foster quality awareness among our employees through ongoing training, information and motivation. The definition of first-class quality for our products comprises not only convenience and high product performance but also all-encompassing product safety and environmental sustainability.

4. We strive for innovation

By providing an environment and a flexible structure in which innovative thinking can flourish, we safeguard our competitive advantage in the long run. Our innovative strength and drive are based on research and development, extensive chemical and technical expertise, and a sound knowledge of customers, consumers, suppliers and markets. We take the requirements of sustainable business practice into account right from the start of the innovation process.

5. We embrace change

We anticipate changes well in advance. Therefore we are able to respond to changing circumstances by adapting our processes and structures rapidly and flexibly. This enables us to maintain the greatest possible efficiency at all times and in all parts of the economy. We are a dynamic learning organisation, driven by a worldwide system of active knowledge management.

6. We are successful because of our people

We value and respect our people. Their talents and skills are our strength. Our success is founded on the knowledge, creativity, social competence and high commitment of our personnel. In order to support this, we create an environment in which individual performance and teamwork can thrive. At the same time we expect outstanding performance and demand that our employees apply the highest standards of honesty and integrity in all their daily business conduct. We assist our employees in reconciling their dedication to their job with their private lives.

7. We are committed to shareholder value

We understand shareholder value in terms of a common objective to increase the value of our company. We constantly benchmark our performance against the best in the worldwide market in order to earn a competitive return for our shareholders. We optimise shareholder value by managing worldwide growth of our business operations responsibly.

8. We are dedicated to sustainability and corporate social responsibility

We are responsible and committed members of society within every country in which we operate. We are convinced that effective environmental protection and social balance are the foundations of our economic success. Sustainable development is a challenge involving the whole of society, for which we seek viable and permanent solutions in dialogue with all social groups.

9. We communicate openly and actively

We live out a culture of trust, mutual respect and openness – both within the company and to the outside. We communicate openly and actively, even when we have made mistakes. We acknowledge our duty to keep our employees, shareholders, customers, suppliers and the general public informed, and see it both as a challenge and an opportunity to further the integration and acceptance of our company.

10. We preserve the tradition of an open family company

The history and the future of our company are established on entrepreneurial foresight and a long-term operational perspective. The relationship between the company and the founding family is one of continuity, openness and mutual trust. The same is true of relationships with our public shareholders and our employees.

These principles as summarised above clearly demonstrate that the economic and the ethical understanding of values are inextricably linked. Although at first sight it may seem inconsistent to use economic and ethical value concepts in parallel, in point of fact we chose to do so with clear intent and purpose. It was only by emphasising the interdependence between the two value concepts that we could generate a comprehensive and understandable framework of rules and goals for our employees that takes the company's – and our employees' – economic and social responsibility into account. Seen in this light, the implementation of our corporate values has surely decisively marked the company.

Code of Conduct

Henkel's image and reputation as a company that operates in an ethically and legally appropriate manner is inseparable from the conduct of each single employee and the way we perform our work, everyday. Employees of Henkel are expected to respect laws and regulations, avoid conflicts of interest, protect the Company's assets, and show consideration and appreciation for the local customs, traditions and social mores of the various countries and cultures in which Henkel conducts business. In fulfilling our responsibilities within Henkel, we do not take ethical shortcuts. Improper conduct will never be in Henkel's interest.

From our vision and values, we derive a range of (concrete) rules of conduct for day-to-day use. At Henkel, these rules are codified in an internal Code of Conduct. Containing important guidelines of behaviour, this code is intended to guide all employees in their daily business but also in strategic planning and decision making processes.

The Code of Conduct is not intended to be a static instrument. It will be continuously developed and adapted to the ever-changing legal and economic environments that affect the ways that we conduct our business around the world.

Henkel's Code of Conduct has been revised by the end of 2005. The core thoughts of the current version will be presented in the following:

1. Observing laws and social norms

Henkel is represented in many product markets and many regions around the world and therefore operates subject to the laws and regulations of different legal systems.

Being a good corporate citizen means that all employees of Henkel comply with all applicable laws, rules and regulations in the communities in which they operate, while also respecting local traditions and other social norms. A failure to do so could seriously damage Henkel's reputation and result in other negative consequences.

2. Individual responsibility for the reputation of Henkel

The regard in which Henkel is held is substantially determined by the behaviour and actions of each individual employee, irrespective of the position held within the Henkel organisation. Consequently, improper conduct, even on an isolated individual basis, can significantly damage Henkel. Personal integrity and an elevated sense of responsibility help all of us to decide which response is most appropriate in a given situation. Answering the following questions can provide guidance:

- Is my action or my decision in keeping with relevant laws, standards and norms, and with the values and standards of Henkel?
- Are my actions and decisions free from personal conflicts of interest in all cases?
- Will my decision withstand public scrutiny?
- Am I, through my behaviour, contributing to the reputation of Henkel as a company that maintains high ethical and legal standards?

3. Respect for people

Henkel's continued success depends upon our commitment to develop and utilize the diverse talents and energies of all Henkel employees, throughout the world. Employees and prospective employees are assessed based upon principles of equality and fairness.

We strive to create an environment of mutual respect, encouragement and teamwork. We value a sharing environment that provides the opportunity for open communications, continuous learning and diversity: these are the sources of our strength, today and in the future. Our goal is to provide a workplace environment that attracts and retains highly talented and motivated people, while helping them to achieve their full potential, without regard to their differences or similarities.

Each of us is responsible for creating a workplace environment that rewards high performance and a commitment to excellence, as well as an atmosphere of trust and respect: a productive work environment. We also recognize our obligation to respect the personal dignity and guard the privacy rights of all of our employees, customers, service providers and suppliers.

Henkel expects its employees, customers, service providers and suppliers to respect these principles.

4. Safety, health and the environment

Henkel and each of its employees play an active role in making the locations in which we operate a good place to live and work. Protecting people and the environment, and conserving resources, have long been counted among our core values. Henkel has been and remains committed to sustainable and socially responsible development; the promotion of safe and healthful working conditions; and striving for sustained progress in the fields of safety, health and the environment.

5. Conflicts of interest

We demand of ourselves, and those with whom we associate, the highest ethical standards. Private interests and the interests of Henkel must be kept strictly separate. Consequently, all employees should avoid situations that may lead to a conflict between their personal interests and those of Henkel. Henkel employees, during contacts with existing or prospective customers, suppliers, clients and competitors, must act in the best interests of Henkel to the exclusion of any personal advantage.

6. Corporate citizenship and donations

As a responsible corporate citizen, Henkel makes financial and material donations in support of social institutions, environmental initiatives, education, science, health, sport, art and culture.

Henkel has defined the criteria for donations and support activities within the framework of its international sponsoring concept.

The criteria applied in relation to donations are essentially as follows:

- Need;
- sustainable effect;
- transparency, i.e. the recipients and the specific purpose must be known to enable monitoring of the proper appropriation of donations;
- no donations to political parties;
- no donations or support for organizations or institutions that do not pursue generally recognized and accepted objectives.

7. Treatment of business partners, public officials and other representatives

We expect our suppliers and service providers to respect our ethical standards, including the principles of the Global Compact, and to act accordingly.

Within the marketplace, Henkel enhances its standing through the quality and value of its innovative products and services. We make decisions on the basis of known economic criteria, within the bounds of relevant laws, standards and norms.

We are honest in our dealings with others, obeying all applicable laws and corresponding regulations governing fraud, bribery and corruption, and avoiding even the appearance of a conflict of interest.

8. Market and competitive behaviour

Henkel and its employees are unconditionally committed to the principles of fair competition and must comply with the antitrust and fair competition laws of the countries in which Henkel conducts business.

Although accurate legal assessment depends on the complexities of the laws concerned and the individual circumstances of each situation, there are nevertheless forms of conduct that typically constitute a violation of competition laws:

- Agreements with competitors and coordinated behaviour aimed at or causing a restraint or limitation on competition are forbidden.
- Relationships with our customers, suppliers and also patentees or licensees are governed by a number of legal regulations relating to fair competition. In accordance with these laws and regulations, Henkel employees will not act in any way that would restrict a customers' pricing freedom or interfere with supply relationships with their business partners (geographical, personal or material restraints). Henkel employees will not encourage illegal tying and resale arrangements.
- Owing to its market position in relation to certain products, Henkel also has to obey certain special rules. For example, abuse of a dominant market position may be deemed to have occurred in the event of differentiated treatment of customers without material justification, refusal of supply, the imposition of inappropriate purchasing/selling prices and terms and conditions, or tie-in transactions without any material justification for the demanded additional counter-consideration.
- While attendance at and participation in trade and professional association meetings, on behalf of Henkel, may be important to further corporate objectives, it is also recognized that attendance at such meetings can present a potential antitrust/fair competition

risk due to contacts with competitors during the course of the meeting. Henkel employees shall attend only meetings of legitimate trade and professional associations, conducted for proper business purposes. It is preferable that meeting minutes be taken and made available. Any benchmarking or comparative information supplied must be in full compliance with applicable laws and regulations.

9. Protection of assets and safeguarding of competitively sensitive information

Within their sphere of activity, all employees bear their share of responsibility for the protection of the tangible and intangible assets of Henkel. Physical or tangible assets include property such as Company products, equipment, facilities, vehicles, computers and software, bank accounts, stocks and bonds, charge cards, files and other records. Intangible assets include informational assets, such as information developed by employees or agents of Henkel that is not generally known to the public (i.e. business secrets and/or know-how), industrial proprietary rights, technologies, and other items of information that are of value, important and thus needful of protection. Information provided by suppliers, customers and other business partners might also require protection.

In this context, IT security plays an important part. All employees are requested to use the information systems only in an ethical, legal and courteous manner and to use the provided security tools e.g. encryption and security procedures e.g. password handling to protect the Henkel data sufficiently.

10. Avoidance of contractual risks

Henkel takes its responsibility to contractual partners seriously. To avoid misunderstandings and unintended consequences, the risk management system of Henkel requires that all employees who bear responsibility for the conclusion of agreements and contracts shall, prior to such conclusion, perform a careful assessment of the contractual duties and terms and of the risks that could arise from such agreement.

11. Insider dealing rules

'Insider trading' laws and regulations do not permit a person to buy or sell Henkel securities, such as stock, while having 'inside' or confidential information. Inside information should not be shared with anyone other than Henkel employees who have a need to know it and who are aware of their legal obligations in handling this information.

In general, 'Insider information' is information that is not readily available to the public and that an investor would consider important in deciding whether to buy or sell Henkel stock. While it can be information that could affect Henkel's stock price, it can also be information that might affect the stock price of another company that has a significant relationship with Henkel. In such instances, employees and officers shall refrain from:

- any trades involving insider securities, in particular, Henkel securities,
- passing on such information to third parties, and
- issuing recommendations to third parties as to the acquisition and/or sale of insider securities on the basis of such information.

In order to eliminate even the appearance of a breach of the regulations governing insider dealing, so-called 'Blocked Periods' have been instituted. Within these periods, a specially designated circle of officers/employees who typically have access to insider information in the course of their activities are forbidden to trade in Henkel securities.

12. Financial integrity

In order to maintain the trust and respect of our shareholders, employees, business partners, communities and government officials, our financial reporting must be correct and truthful at all times. All records and reports published for external consumption must be prepared timely and in line with all relevant laws and regulations.

In keeping with existing legal requirements, as well as internationally recognized accounting standards, Henkel's assets, financial transactions, operating positions, and cash flows must be accurately recorded and openly reflected in the Company's records and public documents. We conduct business consistent with all applicable laws and regulations in every place that Henkel conducts business. We, the employees of Henkel, strive to do the right thing.

13. Reporting violations, enforcement, sanctions

The provisions of the Code of Conduct represent the fundamental components of Henkel's corporate culture. They should, however, not be misinterpreted as providing a basis for demanding that Henkel adopt a certain mode of behaviour. Employees who violate any laws, regardless whether they are subject matters of our Code of Conduct or other Company policies may be disciplined up to and including termination of employment. Henkel supervisors may also be disciplined for failing to detect a violation in their area if, in the judgment of the Company, the failure resulted from inadequate supervision of employees.

The Company will not discharge, demote, suspend, threaten, harass, or in any other manner, discriminate against an employee who reports a violation. Henkel will also not tolerate any attempts whatsoever to prevent employees from reporting such matters.

With the Code of Conduct we want to make it clear to all employees that Henkel's reputation depends on each individual employee. The Code of Conduct provides us with a management instrument that clearly defines our expectations in respect of each individual employee's behaviour. Henkel does not demand anything from its employees that is not comprehensible to every individual or that does not appear to be correct on the basis of common sense. I see business ethics at Henkel as an ethical expression of what is normal, reasonable and honest, of discipline and reliability. These are all virtues that should be self-evident.

CODE OF TEAMWORK AND LEADERSHIP

In order to intensify the connection with our vision and values, the Code of Teamwork and Leadership was revised at the beginning of 2005. The objective of the revision was to describe the behaviour outlined in the Code of Teamwork and Leadership more precisely. By concentrating on the essence of the code's principles, we were also able to define more practical guidelines. The more complex leadership is, the fewer the incentives and the less likely it is that one will see such guidelines implemented on a daily basis. However, for a community of values in a company, it is vitally important that such principles of action are lived out by every employee at every location worldwide. Only in this way can we further develop our culture of trust, mutual respect and tolerance.

The Code of Teamwork and Leadership consists of six crucial points:

1. Inspiring trust

Leaders establish a relationship of mutual trust, shaped by respect and tolerance. Conflicts are openly addressed in an objective and factual manner.

2. Setting targets

Leaders formulate and communicate clear direction and strategy. They work with employees to set ambitious employee goals jointly, including strategies, activities and means to accomplish the goals.

3. Assigning tasks and delegating decisions

Leaders ensure clarity of direction and responsibility, as well as clear decision-making processes. When assigning tasks, the leader carefully considers employees' skills and abilities. Both leaders and employees continually develop their knowledge and skills to produce lasting and sustainable quality and efficiency.

4. Convince and motivate

Leaders produce an atmosphere in which new ideas are created, evaluated and implemented and one where everyone performs to the full. In doing so, the leader takes responsibility for ensuring that all the necessary information and knowledge is available and that employees are positive and committed to achieving their targets. Individual skills are developed, diversity is valued and cultural differences are respected.

5. Achieving targets and evaluating performance

Leaders pursue targets and allocate resources in support of strategic objectives. They provide ongoing coaching and development for employees to enhance performance, jointly implement any necessary adjustments, and evaluate performance based on results.

6. Leading by example

Leaders are role models in setting and achieving targets and living the Code of Teamwork and Leadership on a daily basis. They are positive, future-oriented and results-oriented. Leaders promote performance through coaching, employee development and fairly evaluating performance based on results. They are responsible for the success of the company and those they lead.

These guidelines serve as a means of binding all Henkel employees in shared responsibility. This is not only true of the relationships between supervisors and employees. Each employee is asked to demand these guidelines. It is critical to foster a culture that provides explicit feedback on the quality of the perceived teamwork and leadership shown by all involved. Each employee is expected to treat others as he or she wishes to be treated.

CODE OF CORPORATE SUSTAINABILITY

In 2005 Henkel also revised its Principles and Objectives of Environmental Protection and Safety, expanding these to include aspects of social responsibility. The new Code of Corporate Sustainability defines the principles of sustainable business practice at Henkel.

We recognise the need to harmonise economic, ecological and social goals. Our products and technologies are designed to make a valuable contribution to society and to further and support sustainable development continuously in all countries in which we operate.

Based on this understanding, we conduct a continuous and open dialogue with all social groups regarding our past achievements and future priorities. Our policy of doing business in an ethical and legal manner is inseparably linked with respect for human rights and for the customs, traditions and social values of the countries in which we operate. We welcome and support the volunteer work of our current and retired employees in many different areas, as such volunteer work reflects our understanding of responsible corporate citizenship.

Sustainable development is a shared responsibility of the worldwide community. Acting on this conviction, Henkel has declared its support for the International Chamber of Commerce's Business Charter for Sustainable Development and the United Nations' Global Compact, and has joined the chemical industry's international Responsible Care® initiative.

The Code of Corporate Sustainability will help us to manage our operations successfully in a sustainable and socially responsible manner throughout the Henkel Group. We believe that economically strong and successful enterprises are essential when it comes to achieving effective protection of the environment and social progress. Henkel is an economically strong and successful company. Aligning our operations to the rules of the Code of Corporate Sustainability allows us to further secure and develop the strong positions we hold in our markets. Foremost, however, we will be able to increase Henkel's contribution to sustainable development.

Our Code of Corporate Sustainability deals with nine elements. These can be broken down into three major areas of action:

1. The first area describes what we expect in the future from our personnel and their importance for the company. This is clear, for instance, in the principle of 'Individual responsibility and motivation'. It means that every employee should identify with the aims of the company.

   'Treatment of business partners and market behaviour' is another important component of this first area. We want to ensure that Henkel behaves in a fair way in international competition and makes decisions in accordance with sensible economic considerations and in compliance with relevant legislation and standards.

   Ultimately, the principle of 'Open Dialogue' derives from our corporate value: 'We communicate openly and actively'. We engage in dialogue with all our stakeholders, i.e. with employees, shareholders, customers, suppliers, neighbours and all other interest groups.

2. The second major area of action concerns our responsibility to run our plants and production processes safely. This relates not only to new processes and efficient production facilities, but also to transfer of technologies and knowledge within the Henkel Group. In this way we can specifically improve the safety and efficiency of products, plants and production processes. This is the only way to ensure that our overriding aim is achieved – the long-term success and continued existence of the company.

3. The third major area in the Code of Corporate Sustainability describes how business processes must be designed in order to implement these requirements of sustainable development efficiently. The principle of 'Management systems for clear responsibilities and continuous improvement' is also relevant here. Using integrated management systems, we implement standards throughout the Group and clearly assign responsibilities at all management and work levels.

PROCESS OF IMPLEMENTATION

If business ethics is to be employed as a management instrument, it requires conscious planning and implementation to ensure success.

For Henkel this process began with the spin-off of Cognis in 2001. With the disposal of the chemical sector, Henkel moved out of one of its substantial business activities and took a decisive step in its strategic repositioning. Accordingly, the business activities now focusing on brands and technologies needed to be captured in a new corporate vision for Henkel.

Following the redefinition of the corporate vision, the next step was to further develop the values and the Code of Conduct at Henkel as implementation guidelines for employees. Since the corporate values and the Code of Conduct were intended to be valid globally, this meant including legal regulations from numerous countries as well as taking a wide range of customs and conventions into account. To achieve this, Henkel uses an iterative process controlled by a steering committee consisting of representatives of the human resources department, corporate communications and the legal department and supported by management. The process also involves members of the Sustainability Council, who are an integrated part of Henkel's R&D departments, and representatives of internal auditing.

External developments, such as the addition of Paragraph 10 to the Global Compact (proscription of bribery), are relevant, too, especially if (as in this case) they are sustainable and valid globally.

Although planning and implementation can be separated from each other, early communication of the corporate vision and values at Henkel ensured that the discussion of the Code of Conduct was more focused, efficient and ultimately more valuable. This part of the process also entailed more intensive communication with employees in the various countries concerned in order to comply with cultural and legal requirements. This project alone took more than a year at Henkel and was completed once the final formulation of the Code of Conduct had been adopted.

To implement the Code of Conduct, Henkel does not only make use of multilingual translation, brochures and explanations on its homepage and other media. As we have learned in the past, the process of implementation is all the more successful if supervisors and employees discuss the revised Code of Conduct among themselves. Since the rules and guidelines are of a more general character, it becomes even more important to illustrate them with relevant examples appropriate to the specific location and culture. This also implies that management must constantly lead by example and serve as role models by acting in a manner always consistent with Henkel's corporate values and the Code of Conduct.

The same is true of the Code of Teamwork and Leadership and of the Code of Corporate Sustainability. The classical media were not the only way of communicating the Codes: the corresponding documents were made available to all supervisors worldwide so that the Codes could be presented to and discussed with employees. Furthermore supervisors were asked to derive concrete cooperative projects from the Code of Teamwork and Leadership.

CONCLUSION

The objective of Henkel's business ethics is to establish a framework for entrepreneurial action. When Henkel's employees embrace this framework, it becomes omnipresent throughout the company. It offers guidelines that do not always require detailed instructions, but allow room for individual initiative and entrepreneurial thinking, while ensuring that every employee has a clear understanding of ethical values and corporate goals.

By ensuring that its employees are aware of the importance of the company's values, Henkel's business ethics also pursues other objectives:

- legal compliance;
- leadership aligned with the company's objectives; and
- marketing that is outwardly focused, on stakeholders and shareholders.

Thus Henkel's business ethics plays a major role in securing Henkel's future in an increasingly complex and ever more rapidly changing world.

Ethical behaviour pays off in the long run, through improved public reputation, higher employee motivation and greater focus on pursuing the company's objectives.

The extent to which business ethics can contribute to a company's success ultimately depends on the company itself and its commitment to consistent implementation and use of ethical value systems. Our experience suggests that only an open corporate culture and an ethically value-driven management that leads by example will be able to respond successfully to the challenges of an increasingly globalised world. This in turn requires a stronger personal ethos, a sense of belonging to an ethical, global community, which is the very foundation of the global economy. The trend toward individualism will undoubtedly continue. All the more reason for us to encourage a revival of the sense of responsibility and the sense of duty – for the sake of our companies as well as for our society.

CHAPTER 19

A Company's Social Side

Markus Holzinger, Klaus Richter and Dirko Thomsen

O ver the past decade corporate social responsibility has been launched as a practical programme in many multinational companies.

Managers cannot be expected to ignore business rules and profit, of course. But a number of leading companies believe in the values of social responsibility and public trust. In their view, it is a mistake to justify the company's existence merely in terms of profit. Firms have discovered that moral problems are economic problems, be they the need to deal honestly with employees, suppliers and customers or the emphasis on environmental protection and responsible behaviour towards people in developing countries. 'Corporate social responsibility is now an industry in its own right, and a flourishing profession as well' (*The Economist*, 2005).

The main thrust of this chapter is the process of corporate social responsibility at Volkswagen. The text is divided into three parts. The first part contains a description of an assortment of

The ICCA Handbook on Corporate Social Responsibility Edited by J. Hennigfeld, M. Pohl and N. Tolhurst
© 2006 John Wiley & Sons, Ltd

responsible business practices generally implemented at Volkswagen. The second part questions historical responsibility. The example of the Memorial Work project exemplifies the management ethos of corporate social responsibility at Volkswagen. Finally the chapter addresses the question of learning business ethics. Learning has been a hot topic with managers. The background and the content of the module 'Corporate Ethics and Corporate Government', which has been developed at Volkswagen AutoUni, is explained.

CORPORATE SOCIAL RESPONSIBILITY AT VOLKSWAGEN

When companies strive to align their economic objectives with sustainable growth and human progress, this is referred to as corporate social responsibility (CSR). CSR is all about a company's responsibility to the local community and society at large. That includes attitudes towards human rights, the interests of the workforce and suppliers, and commitments to society. Volkswagen takes the view that for corporate social responsibility to become a reality, an ongoing increase in shareholder value must first be assured and that the long-term success of the company can only be guaranteed through corporate social responsibility.

In the early 1990s, Volkswagen reorganised its working-hour model to make it what is sometimes called a 'living company', thereby safeguarding over 30 000 jobs in Germany. This was made possible by the workforce's willingness to work longer hours when order books are full and shorter hours when work is in shorter supply. Wage levels were largely maintained. To provide long-term job security, Volkswagen has opted for what is known as a public–private partnership. The project concerned is called 'Autovision' and it fosters employment levels and growth, promotes change in regional structures, and encourages corporate relocation, spin-offs and training schemes. Since the project began in 1998, 4000 new jobs have been created in the Wolfsburg region alone.

Furthermore, the principles of sustainable development (see below) and environmental protection form an important part of the corporate culture at Volkswagen. A development process designed to bring lasting ecological and social benefits for both the company itself and for society as a whole is under way at the Group's various production sites. Thus, one priority objective in the product development sector is to cut average corporate fleet fuel consumption by 25% between 1990 and 2005, thereby also reducing carbon dioxide emissions. By 1998, a 15% reduction had already been achieved. In Germany, Volkswagen operates a recycling system to take back waste and residues from production plants and workshops, free of charge. All of the Group's European plants have been certified in line with EMAS[1] since at least 1995 and regularly conduct environmental audits. Lifecycle assessments are systematically performed as a product-specific element of the environmental controlling process. The company can thus continuously improve its fuel consumption and emission levels, its choice of raw materials and its recycling quota. The Group's ethical and social principles apply worldwide.

Actively involved in the Global Compact

In 2000 at the World Economic Forum in Davos, Switzerland, the Secretary-General of the United Nations (UN), Kofi Annan, called the Global Compact (GC) into being, bringing together private-sector multinational companies, UN sub-organisations and

---

[1] Abbreviation for Environmental Management and Audit Scheme. The statute (no. 1863/93) describes the guidelines for voluntary participation by commercial companies (from certain sectors of industry) in the European Union's unified system for introducing environmental management systems. As a more far-reaching version of ISO14001, it can be linked to an existing management system but requires, for example, the publication of a regular environmental declaration. EMAS guidelines relate to specific locations, ISO guidelines to the company as a whole.

representatives of governments, trade unions and non-governmental organisations (NGOs). The starting pistol was fired for the operational phase of the Global Compact in July 2000 in the course of a United Nations event in New York. The Compact is intended to be a value-oriented platform to serve learning, transparency and dialogue. It aims to encourage the participating companies to act responsibly towards society in social and ecological terms, i.e. to be a 'good citizen'. Initially, there were nine principles, including respect for human rights, non-discrimination in the workplace, the rejection of forced labour and child labour, the acceptance of the right to collective bargaining and conscientious environmental behaviour. An anti-corruption principle has also since been added.

Responsibility for complying with the principles contained in the Compact rests with a company's management. However, this will still not be monitored. The only obligation on the companies is to list their activities for the Global Compact objectives in a periodical progress report. As no specific preconditions are required for participation in the GC, it is astounding that only 1700 of the approximately 70 000 transnational corporations worldwide are participating in the Compact. Of these, 28 are German. The Volkswagen Group stated its commitment to the Global Compact at the 2002 World Conference on Sustainable Development in Johannesburg. A brochure on the subject was published and is still very much in demand. With the Group environmental policy, which commenced in 1995, and the 'Declaration on Social Rights and Industrial Relations' issued in 2003, Volkswagen is still complying with the 10 principles of the Global Compact at an extremely high level. The organisations and companies involved in the initiative exchange information at events known as Learning Forums. Volkswagen uses these forums, in so far as it is able, just as regularly as the 'Policy Dialogue'. Dialogue also takes place at the highest level. The Board of the Volkswagen Group is informed regularly about developments in the Global Compact and knows what demands are made of our company. However, Volkswagen is also directly involved, namely via the regular cooperation of the Group's external relations department in the German network, Friends of the Global Compact. Volkswagen participated actively in the debate on the acceptance of the tenth principle, i.e. counteracting corruption, and permit AIDS assistance projects in South Africa and Brazil to be investigated within the scope of so-called case studies. It is a matter of course to report regularly on the activities of the UN Initiative in the political news magazine, *p:news*, and maintain an Internet presence at www.globalcompact.org.

Model of sustainable development

In the explanatory text formulated on the Global Compact, Volkswagen developed a model of sustainable development, as aforementioned, on the occasion of the World Summit in 2002:

- At Volkswagen, the model of sustainable development is the benchmark for a long-term corporate policy that not only tackles economic challenges but also addresses ecological and social issues.
- Together, commercial success, far-sighted environmental protection and social competence enhance the Volkswagen Group's global competitiveness.
- The Volkswagen Group develops, manufactures and markets automobiles and services throughout the world in order to provide its customers with attractive solutions for their personal mobility.
- Volkswagen aims to make advanced technologies available around the globe while taking account of environmental protection and social acceptability considerations.
- Along with economic success, the primary objectives of Volkswagen's corporate policy include continuously improving

the environmental acceptability of its products and reducing its consumption of natural resources.

- Volkswagen is a company with German roots, European values and global responsibility. The rights, personal development, social security and economic participation of its employees are core elements of corporate policy.

- A spirit of cooperation and partnership forms the basis of successful collaboration between management and employee representatives – in Germany, in Europe and around the world.

- For Volkswagen, globalisation is a decisive factor in securing international competitiveness and safeguarding the future of the company. Modern and responsible corporate policy is responsible for making globalisation at Volkswagen environmentally and socially compatible. This same policy serves the long-term interests of Volkswagen's customers, stakeholders, employees and partners. Globalisation must not be based on exploitation.

- Volkswagen also actively promotes an environmentally and socially compatible approach to business among its suppliers.

- Wherever it operates, Volkswagen considers itself a partner of society and the political sphere.

Corporate values and guidelines: the basis of a new company culture

A set of seven company values and 14 company guidelines now stand for nothing less than tomorrow's company culture. The project was started at a meeting of Volkswagen senior managers in Shanghai in September 2002. This was not undertaken by external consultants, as is frequently the case today, but rather study groups of managers compiled the guidelines themselves. The result is a list of seven values, each having two guidelines intended to characterise future dealings with each other and with customers. Dr Bernd Pischetsrieder, chairman of the board at Volkswagen AG, raises it to the level of a constitution for the group of companies and its brands: 'If different groups of people found a state so that they are stronger and more successful together, they must establish what the common factors are. And then they must all abide by the constitution.'

So what characterises the Volkswagen Group, where are its strengths and what needs to be improved? According to Pischetsrieder, the essential thing is to maintain and extend two really great strengths across all the brands and companies: competence and enthusiasm for our products plus respect for the human dimension.

The details of the set of company values are as follows:

CLOSENESS TO THE CUSTOMER

The idea is to allow exemplary orientation towards the customer to grow out of traditional closeness to the customer. Pischetsrieder: 'Each of us should get to know our customers better, be interested in their motives, understand their habits and needs.' For example, by undergoing training at a dealer's premises.

MAXIMUM PERFORMANCE

Each one of us makes high demands of himself; this is the only way to achieve first class results. And: each one of us bears the responsibility for his own ability to work and employability and is supported in this by the company.

CREATE VALUE

Everyone must act in such a way that value in the group of companies is increased. Time, money and energy are only invested in activities that create value.

ABILITY TO INNOVATE

Carrying ideas right through the company with courage, toughness and persistence is just as important as the idea itself. Each employee should engage in a personal struggle to promote his ideas and should be open to the ideas of others. Pischetsrieder: 'Success is the greatest enemy of innovation. Only good employees with courage, creativity and imagination can counteract this.'

RESPECT

Respect for the work of others is essential for lasting success. Furthermore, the hierarchy only corrects decisions on competence in exceptional cases. Managers are required to find employees with the potential to outstrip them.

RESPONSIBILITY

Offering either too much or too little leeway is irresponsible. Courage, creativity and imagination are important prerequisites for using this room for manoeuvre. Pischetsrieder: 'Responsibility includes our relationship with the employees just as much as our relationship with the environment.'

SUSTAINABILITY

It is essential that the company takes the long-term goals it has approved into account in its daily work. Managers have the means and the duty to think beyond day-to-day issues and to organise.

For Volkswagen, social responsibility is a permanent challenge. Through numerous projects and innovations the company has shown how social, environmental and economic success can be combined with each other. Volkswagen belongs to Germany and Europe's pioneers in corporate social responsibility management. The company is co-founder of the corporate network 'CSR Europe' and its influence has been decisive in shaping this issue.

HOW DOES MORALITY COME INTO PLAY IN CORPORATIONS?

Why should morality play a role in corporations? According to traditional economic theory, society profits most from entrepreneurs when they pursue their particular interests. Regulated by the invisible hand – so the theory goes – this pursuit of their own entrepreneurial interests will ultimately serve the public interest as well. In that case, calls for moral integrity only appeal to this 'invisible hand', so that deliberation on morality ought to be left to private individuals and policy makers. We come across this same kind of exclusivity in the field of humanities in teachings stipulating that an action must be taken with no regard to self-interest if it is to be deemed moral.

Anyone reading a newspaper report on a large corporation's good deeds is likely to feel a twofold sense of conflict. If he has shares in the company, he will possibly appreciate the anticipated positive effect of the act on potential sales, but will inevitably ask himself if the intended aim could not be better achieved by way of sales promotions. If he views the report from a strictly moral standpoint, he will welcome the act while nonetheless invariably feeling that it smacks of economic self-interest, which ultimately detracts from its merit. Corporate ethics will never satisfy the purists.

Any attempt, therefore, to resolve the conflict between morality and commercial enterprise by means of exclusion, i.e. the exclusion of economic objectives or, conversely, the exclusion of public interests, is doomed to fail. It must be said, however, that the conflict between economics and morality is rooted more in the theory-based endeavour to achieve a theoretical basis, with as few conditions tied to it as possible, for the new economic teachings of an Adam Smith or the critical philosophy of an Immanuel Kant rather than being rooted in actual practice. Indeed, in practice, it has proven sensible not to categorically separate the two, but rather to link morality and enterprise. The Volkswagen example demonstrates the opportunities for corporate social responsibility inherent in a non-dogmatic and realistic treatment of the relationship between commercial enterprise and public welfare.

If we take a look at everyday practice, however, we can see that corporate social responsibility is not an issue devoid of problems. Needless to say, businesses will always attempt to gain a good reputation in the community where their customers and other groups they interact with are based. There is no significant difference between the reputability of the traditionally esteemed Hanseatic merchants and today's global players, for good reputation is one of the elements of product value and determines how much a customer is prepared to pay. In this respect, corporate social responsibility subscribes to the same commercial codes of practice as those of traditional merchants.

To be content with that, however, would mean applying morality too frugally. As so aptly portrayed in Molière's *Tartuffe* or Wilhelm Busch's *Hypocritical Helen*, good deeds demonstratively put on display will make people suspect hypocrisy and will thus have the opposite effect to that intended. Much the same goes for external pressure on corporations (in the form of regulations or customer boycotts, for instance) to act ethically. The issue here is not one of morality, but revolves instead around the distribution of power among the state, consumers and commercial enterprise. A morally relevant act is characterised by the fact that it is voluntary, i.e. optional.

The relationship between morality and success is not a causal one. When we look back at the lives of the morally good people we know, the picture that often presents itself is one in which virtue, recognition and affluence evolved over time and were not initially based on deliberate calculation and a desire to control the outcome. Striving for virtue as a means to achieve fortune and popularity will only reap the distrust of others. This is what happens to organisations that display a newly acquired sense of morality too quickly and too demonstratively. We prefer humility. In our particular context, 'doing good and talking about it' can serve only as a slogan for those who wish to solicit business sponsorship.

Volkswagen runs an educational measure which could be described as a corporate social responsibility scheme. However, it was never intended to be instrumentalised for PR purposes. That is why our 'Memorial Work' project in Auschwitz/Oswiecim could serve to exemplify plausibly how best to loosely tie in economic goals with corporate social responsibility.

When Volkswagen first began to look back and examine the history of its founding during the Nazi era, this undertaking presented no opportunity whatsoever for generating a competitive advantage. Correspondence received from Volkswagen dealerships and from buyers across the different world regions in 1986 urged us not to make a public affair of examining the history of the Volkswagen works during the Third Reich, given that the competitive disadvantages appeared all too clear.

Concerns about memories of the company's entanglement in this era and fear about incalculable reverberations on the market initially outweighed any confidence in our own intellectual and moral resources. Critical preoccupation with our own history involved risks for the owners, for management and for the workforce – especially given that this course meant a shift away from the consensus of refraining from raking up the past, which had characterised the post-World War II era until that time.

Since the mid-1980s, however, there had also been positive signs indicating that a shift of this kind would actually be a constructive phenomenon. On the occasion of its centennial anniversary in 1983, Daimler-Benz published a company history in which the era of the Third Reich was scarcely mentioned – receiving a unanimously critical response from the public and the media in Germany. Volkswagen's 50th anniversary (and likewise the anniversary of the City of Wolfsburg) was due to be celebrated in 1988. In a project headed by Klaus-Jörg Siegfried, the city archive had recently published two books on the history of the founding of the Wolfsburg community (Siegfried, 1988, 1993).

Thus, Volkswagen could expect the topic to be greeted with acceptance when the Group placed review of and discourse concerning its own past fully into the public domain in 1986, entrusting work on this to academics at the University of Bochum and Professor Hans Mommsen. This history of the company's foundation (Mommsen and Grieger, 1996) comprised 700 pages and provided the basis for a whole range of strategies for solutions in

1992 regarding humanitarian aid for the countries of origin of those forced to work at the plant during the war, individual compensation awards for forced labourers in 1998, and, likewise, construction of an international youth centre in Auschwitz in 1986.

Only extensive and public reflection on the scholarly, financial, legal and pedagogic dimensions of its history endowed the company, its executives and its workforce with the self-confidence needed to pursue the sensitive issues surrounding the organisation's own history.

One of the circumstances particularly conducive to Volkswagen's Memorial Work scheme was the fact that the company already had 20 years of experience with international youth exchange work under its belt. After World War II, the majority of the population in Wolfsburg – a community situated close to the 'Iron Curtain' – was made up of exiles from various regions now in Poland. Since integrating young people into the West was a concern for the company as a whole, these sections of the population were the ideal bridge to the East, a bridge to help us understand our Central European neighbours better.

Confidence in Auschwitz as a place of learning was also determined to a substantial degree by our cooperation partners, most notably the International Auschwitz Committee and its vice-president, Christoph Heubner, who came up with the concept for the gradual development of Volkswagen's pedagogical commitment in Auschwitz and oversaw the scheme from the first seminars held in 1987 to the maintenance work performed since 1992, and the joint projects and exchanges between Polish and German youth groups in Auschwitz and at other locations in Germany. Our Memorial Work project is a living scheme, shaped by the past while subject to evolution. Thus, it functions more like a self-organising system than a blueprint for achieving a particular target.

Here is a summary of the Memorial Work project in its current form: around 55 apprentices and trainees from Wolfsburg, Hanover, Emden, Braunschweig, Kassel and Zwickau do voluntary work at Auschwitz alongside students from schools in Bielsko-Biala, Chocianow and Polkovice. This work involves repairing fences or exposing roadways at the camp to reveal items such as spoons, shoe-heels, cigarette holders or coins. Over the course of 14 days, German and Polish adolescents share their lives with each other – at work, at home and at the International Youth Centre in Oswiecim/MDSM. They also take part in discussions with former inmates and peruse the archives with the aim of gaining insight into the lives of the victims and the perpetrators. They pitch in and help, building a gate, laying electric cables or installing a pneumatic test-bed wherever their professional skills are called for – at the centre, at the partner school or anywhere around town.

The Memorial Work project also involves a five-day return visit by Polish participants to the site where the German apprentices work. In addition to meetings and celebrations, these visits include discussion of the results of the participants' own memorial work, i.e. the personal significance of the assignment to the students and apprentices, the response they encountered from their families, friends, casual acquaintances or co-workers.

The cooperative work on individual assignments provides insight into an unfamiliar working world, while discussions and parties reveal differing patterns in the upbringing of both nationalities: 'The Poles aren't as . . . as I would have thought.' The project increases participants' sense of commitment to community work as well as helping to build self-esteem, e.g. when an apprentice realises that someone is waiting for his work. Apprentices looking back on what has been jointly accomplished in the course of the project clearly see how it has helped them develop as individuals. The apprentices acquire increasing reserves of tolerance and compassion as the work they do together culminates in success, as they find pleasure in their communal life and as their interest in the lives of their foreign co-participants develops.

Notwithstanding the retrospective success of the scheme, the concept does require explanation, since the reasons for its success are, likewise, reasons for the criticism it receives, i.e. the close proximity of corporate interests and the memorial work. How can morality and business be brought together at a site like this? While this is an essential question in academic terms, the question hardly arises in practice (Thomsen, 1999).

With a view to everyday practice, the proximity of the corporation first of all safeguards the life setting for memorial work as a link to the working world, to parents, friends or interest groups. Integration of this kind protects the site from 'museumification' and 'historification'. The proximity of the corporation means the Memorial Work project may not always be endowed with the 'political correctness' associated with seminar and school undertakings. It does, however, provide the actual pedagogical challenge of the project in the form of everyday conflict situations with colleagues, in the workplace and in recreational settings.

In this context, the organisation stands for a world where humanitarian principles must first be tested, especially in competition situations likely to arise in working life and on the job market. The organisation can provide the elements for a memorial that will help to turn good educational theory into an effective education course for adolescents. Taking a brief detour into the history of literature, we find that developments in positive educational novels always steer the reader to 'active' life concepts – Goethe's *Wilhelm Meister*, for example, or Gottfried Keller's *Green Henry*. The opposite path of societal education, on the other hand, is a very restricted one.

The company can also make use of the opportunity to moderate and defuse the competitiveness of life for the duration of the project – for one thing by producing comparative benefit: building inexpensive pneumatic test stations for a school or fitting an electric gate for the international youth centre. Thus, the youths learn that the know-how acquired in their working lives is useful outside the organisation as well.

The relationship between commercial enterprise and this kind of memorial work is eased further if we become aware that, in our context, the moral subject actually taking the action is not the corporation as a legal entity. Moral actions can only be taken by individuals within that entity. Just as church dignitaries are not forced to act according to religious motives, executives or other members of the workforce are not necessarily obliged either to act for reasons of economic interest. Realising that, irrespective of any theoretically based comparison of corporations and society, the individuals who people corporations are the same as those who people societies constitutes a bridge in the conflict between morality and business. Each and every employee is also a citizen, a parent, a child or a bowling buddy. It is imperative, therefore, that we address personal engagement in the workforce on a broad level where activities relating to corporate social responsibility are concerned, rather than confining intellectual justification for such activities to the decision-making competencies of the legal entity we call The Corporation.

The Memorial Work project bears fruit by affording participants practice in handling their own freedom in sensitive situations. The young people taking part learn to make independent judgements, they become aware of the impact history has on them and on their environment. They experience growth and the fact that it changes them – and, indeed, realise that this change arises solely from their own, independent thinking and doing. Many of the participants in the scheme end up committing themselves long-term to projects in Germany or Poland. In those cases, putting corporate social responsibility into practice will have literally achieved its self-imposed aims, with the corporation providing answers to the challenges facing society.

It is also possible to acknowledge a corporate social responsibility activity such as the Memorial Work project in the context of overall human resources development. Since corporations have stopped concentrating their entire focus on cheap labour and costly material investments, the workforce has no longer been expected to relinquish its brains, values, talents and inspirations (at least those not 'under contract') at the company gate. Instead, the organisation is undertaking development measures aimed at building and utilising all this positive potential, in spite of the possibility that those possessing such potential may eventually choose to leave the organisation.

Thus, the company stops being an isolated system concealed behind high walls. Social indicators and reference values penetrate into the company; conversely, the organisation radiates out into its social environment. In former times, this would have been interpreted as a worst-case scenario, a loss of planning control. These days, we are obliged to see this circumstance as an opportunity. Corporate social responsibility is one way of making creative use of such an opportunity.

And, on a final note, memorial work also refines the organisation's survival skills, since companies (as A.O. Hirschman illustrated in the 1960s) do not, as a rule, behave differently from political parties, interest groups or families. In economically good years, their performance tends to deteriorate. Conversely, however, this means that they have the potential to learn in times of crisis rather than being pushed out of the market by stronger competitors. Whether a learning process of this kind can lead an organisation back to its previous market strength will then depend considerably on the loyalty factor and on customer and employee opposition. This blend – of loyalty towards the 'Volkswagen family', on the one hand, and the capacity for critical opposition, on the other – has evolved out of the Memorial Work project (among other things). By the same token, the company itself also enjoys increased customer retention.

We can say that the Memorial Work project has played a significant part in shaping the company and learning culture at Volkswagen, as well as helping to build the individual characters of young employees. This is something we can establish in retrospect. Affirmation for our scheme would probably be less forthcoming today, however, if the Memorial Work project had actually set out in pursuit of this very objective in the first place. Irrespective of all its very real significance for the company's value, morality in the organisation cannot be clearly pinpointed. It is only because it cannot be planned and is not comfortably at home in liberal economic teaching nor enforceable by means of ethical rigour that it can impact positively on the company, on adolescents and on the society in which they live.

CORPORATE ETHICS AND CORPORATE GOVERNANCE MODULE AT THE VOLKSWAGEN AUTOUNI

Events perceived as crises, such as the destruction of our environment, massive cases of white-collar crime and the failure of the global economy to eradicate worldwide poverty have led, in particular, to calls for business ethics. We repeatedly find that business is not, as so often presumed, totally isolated from moral concerns. The new managerial approaches build on employees adept at reflection and communication, who are creative and who put their entire personality into what they do. Given the growing importance, at the operational level, of 'increasing managers' awareness about issues of value management in transcultural competence training courses' (Zimmerli and Palazzo, 1999), the Volkswagen AutoUni has designed a module for 'Corporate Ethics and Corporate Governance'. From the outset, it was clear in this module that corporate ethics has to 'deal with the rocky terrain of everyday corporate management . . . if something is to budge' (Jäger, 1992: 273).

The Volkswagen AutoUni

The Volkswagen AutoUni serves as a skills and cultural forum for the Volkswagen Group's technical and managerial elite, and aims for comprehensive development of the student's character and competence. It has developed into an educational institution recognised the world over, with broad-based research and instruction and a strictly postgraduate orientation. The Volkswagen AutoUni offers science-based continuing education in the interest of lifelong learning, and, following state accreditation (application currently being processed), will award internationally accredited academic degrees. The institution will set a new course in postgraduate education in Germany by expanding the previous concept of the 'corporate university'. It owes its special profile to taking the phrase 'corporate university' at face value; unlike the German state universities, whose scientific approach it uses as a basis, it is also *corporately* oriented. Constantly updated content provides a direct connection with the company (note the educational principles based on 'real cases'). In contrast to other corporate education institutions, however, the AutoUni will be a real university. The innovative forms of generating and disseminating knowledge developed through the corporate link are combined with an academic background. By interlacing economic practice, a source of numerous research issues, with scientific theory construction and applications, often lacking in real-world case studies, new knowledge potential for the Group will be revealed and lead to new forms of knowledge.

All courses are interdisciplinary. It appears increasingly certain that individual disciplines cannot fully grasp the complex world in which we live. Multidisciplinarity in the sense that the Volkswagen AutoUni is a scientific methodology promoting the plurality of perspectives in a productive dialogue and finally leading sustainably to higher quality solutions through syntheses. The basic standpoint of the Volkswagen AutoUni is that no subject can be fully tackled by a single discipline any longer, and that no problem can be assigned to a single department since the issues in the real and very complex world of today cannot be adequately addressed by isolated disciplines and specific departments.

The structure and contents of the module are geared to the specifications of the VW AutoUni. Concretely, 210 hours are allocated to each module, with a third of the learning units being taught in face-to-face taught classes and two-thirds online. Practical discussions of 'mini-cases' treat specific content in more detail.

As a branch of applied ethics, corporate ethics is not limited to the discussion and presentation of current theoretical disputes, but seeks answers to concrete issues in the context of economic activity. The aim is, therefore, to point to models for action and methods of corporate ethics using suitable case studies as illustrations.

Case studies, group work and discussion rounds reinforce participants' fundamental moral attitudes and social skills. The point is to increase people's awareness of ethical issues and promote creativity in order to open up new dimensions for possible approaches.

Leadership by character

The corporate ethics and corporate governance modules aim to increase managers' awareness of ethical issues in business. The initial level considers the new management self-concept. On the one hand, this self-concept is directed at deflating the myth of market self-regulation. Behind this myth is the belief that the market as a medium of social interaction already has moral content. 'The social responsibility of business', writes Milton Friedman (1970), 'is to increase its profits.' On the other hand, there is a presumption that one dimension of society, namely, coordinated agents acting solely in accordance with economic and instrumental reason, is not beset by ethical problems. As matters of social fact stand, however, this is patently not so. In industry, as in politics, one corruption scandal follows another in rapid succession.

Today's corporate leaders are not by any manner of means guided exclusively by economic and technological relationships.

Leading has become 'leading by character'. 'Go-getter' management has been superseded by the approaches of 'value management', which consciously aims to shape the company in relation to values. Management must be enlivened much more through the exemplification of ethically guided conduct with corresponding content. For these leadership characteristics, a manager has to have a sense of his or her own character.

At this point, the module explicitly discusses issues concerning leadership values. What types of conduct inspire confidence among followers of leaders? Participants define the value conflicts and dilemmas encountered in their everyday work. In order to discuss the provocative claim that leadership could also be viewed from the perspective of providing a service, we invite an abbot from Andechs Monastery to speak on 'Serving instead of ruling. A comparison between the organisational and management cultures in companies and monasteries'.

Corporate ethics at the organisational level and in society

The module is not restricted to the level of the individual, however. While individual ethics deal with individual actions and attitudes, institutional ethics and the development of social, economic, political and, in particular, legal structures are at issue at the organisational level. 'If you want an ethical code to prevail, you have to institutionalise it' (Bowie, 1992: 341). We discuss the role of codes of conduct. Module participants research the current in-house status of VW's corporate guidelines. What does it mean for a company that a common identity has to be brought to life? Can corporate values provide a foundation on which the company can build its identity and, thereby, a positive prevailing mood?

Here it is important to analyse and assess the different manifestations of corruption. Participants interpret the Enron scandal, for example. It becomes clear that the addiction to profit of individual managers is not the only cause of corruption-related disasters. Often, failure of the value systems and control mechanisms has a much greater impact. Evidently, corruption always emerges 'where the economic and civic virtues of individuals are "weak" ' (Ulrich, 2001: 322). Agents must be interrelated through a system of checks and balances.

Especially now that companies operate in the public eye, tainted fish or oestrogen in meat can lead an entire industry to ruin. Via an extensive and highly complex network of intersecting international, national, regional and municipal forms of communication, the public keeps track of industrial environmental scandals. 'The fragility of shareholders' and consumers' trust reveals the fragility of the legitimisation of globally operating corporations' (Beck, 2002: 130). Using the examples of Nike and Shell, we draw attention to the role of social responsibility on the part of global corporations and convey the sense that values give a company character.

Global ethics

In the age of globalisation, corporate ethics can no longer be limited to the narrow territory of the nation state. According to the corporate social responsibility approach, global corporations should pursue not only profit but a civic interest in political guidelines as well. Companies are expected to assume social responsibility in the cultural and political contexts in which they are based. If a company has cars built in China, then the work environment in that country becomes a matter of direct concern for that company's moral commitments, especially in the case of child labour.

Participants receive information on CSR management at various companies, analyse the differences between the programmes and try to relate these differences to those between countries and cultures. Cultural globalisation is not a uniform or consistent process. Corporate values can have very different political and cultural meanings in societies (Scherer and Steinmann, 1998). Given this insight, module participants study the relation between ethics and culture and consider the conflicts that can arise in a manager's everyday work.

It then becomes clear that the global arena constitutes the decision-making framework for contemporary management. Wherever managers operate, they must also assume responsibility for the consequences of their actions, particularly concerning other people and, indirectly, the environment as well. As the arena of economic activity becomes global, so does responsibility.

References

Beck, U. (2002). *Macht und Gegenmacht im globalen Zeitalter*. Frankfurt/Main.

Bowie, N.E. (1992). Unternehmensethikkodizes: können Sie eine Lösung sein, in H. Lenk and M. Maring (Eds.), *Wirtschaft und Ethik*, pp. 337–52. Stuttgart.

Economist, The (2005). 22 January, p. 3.

Friedman, M. (1970). The social responsibility of business is to increase its profits. *New York Times*, 13 September.

Jäger, A. (1992). Unternehmensethik und Verantwortung, in H. Lenk and M. Maring (Eds.), *Wirtschaft und Ethik*, pp. 268–84. Stuttgart.

Mommsen, Hans and Grieger, Manfred (1996). *The Volkswagen Works and its Labor Force During the Third Reich*. Düsseldorf.

Scherer, A.G. and Steinmann, H. (Eds.) (1998). *Zwischen Universalismus und Relativismus*. Frankfurt/Main.

Siegfried, Klaus-Jörg (1988). *The Life of Forced Laborers at the Volkswagen Works from 1939 to 1945*. Frankfurt/Main.

Siegfried, Klaus-Jörg (1993). *Arms Production and Forced Labor at the Volkswagen Works 1938 to 1945*. Frankfurt/Main.

Thomsen, Dirko (1999). Experience and pedagogical deliberation on memorial work with apprentices, in *Memorial Circular, The Topography of Terror*, pp. 25–31, Berlin; in English: *Contributions to Historical Social Studies – 31st year*. Vienna (2001).

Ulrich, P. (2001). *Integrative Wirtschaftsethik*. Bern.

Zimmerli, W.C. and Palazzo, G. (1999). Transkulturelles management, in A. Grosz and D. Delhaes (Eds.), *Die Kultur AG. Neue Allianzen zwischen Wirtschaft und Kultur*, pp. 139–44. Munich.

CHAPTER 20

In the Driver's Seat: Implementing Sustainable Management Around the Globe

Katja Suhr and Andreas von Schumann

SUSTAINABLE MANAGEMENT – A HISTORY WITH A FUTURE

Sustainable management has become a widely publicised buzzword. But what is it all about? What does sustainable management offer a company in addition to its communicative function?

Sustainable management focuses on an investment's effectiveness and ability to shape the long term. The goal is to contribute to shaping the prospects for progress, and hence for social evolution, in the medium and long term. Sustainable management means

The ICCA Handbook on Corporate Social Responsibility Edited by J. Hennigfeld, M. Pohl and N. Tolhurst
© 2006 John Wiley & Sons, Ltd

creating and consolidating future-proof management structures. Any company intending to invest in a location in the longer term is concerned about a stable environment. Questions of the qualification of local staff, quality of global suppliers, opportunities and risks of technology transfer, infrastructure and the political situation play an important role.

A cursory glance at economic history is sufficient to see that successful companies have always helped create durable structures in their environment. In the course of globalisation, however, new dimensions of structure-creating and sustainable management have evolved. First, a company's radius of action expands with advancing global networking and group formation. Second, there has been a sharp increase in the momentum of commerce at both national and international level, evident not least in faster market development, shorter product cycles and faster evolution of target groups. In addition, modern communication technologies like the Internet and mobile telephones make global exchange of information at a much faster rate possible.

In times of change, dynamism and increased pressure to adjust, it is easy to lose sight of the long term. Attention is concentrated on short-term success and seizing 'opportunities'. Issues that require staying power and unexploited potential are subordinated to the supposed need for a fast and flexible response. Sustainability strategies run the risk here of languishing as costly instruments of corporate communication instead of providing guidance as a critical success factor in a company's risk management and the management of its corporate environment.

The relevance of sustainability aspects within overall strategies is generally acknowledged nowadays. However, the ability to implement a visionary corporate policy efficiently, effectively, and at the same time pragmatically at different times and in different locations, remains a competitive advantage only a small number of companies actually utilise.

SUSTAINABLE MANAGEMENT BY INTERNATIONALLY ACTIVE COMPANIES: THE OPPORTUNITIES ARE THERE!

With its many facets and approaches, sustainable management offers many opportunities to companies. These range from:

- cost optimisation by reducing raw materials through
- creating employee loyalty by health care and training and
- quality assurance by qualifying suppliers to
- developing new market potential in developing and emerging countries.

But what does sustainable management look like in practice among globally active companies? What are its success factors?

In cooperation with Thomas Häusle and Alois Flatz, cofounder of the Dow Jones Sustainability Index, GTZ surveyed 20 internationally active German groups in various industries in 2005. The project team developed a typology of company approaches under sustainable management, which was based on the analysis of motivation, objectives, strategy development, implementation and management of the companies surveyed (see Figure 20.1).

TYPOLOGIES: FROM MINIMALISTS TO DRIVERS

The purpose of the following typology is to describe the status quo and degree of sustainable management in a company (see Figure 20.2). Second, this status review aims to identify directions

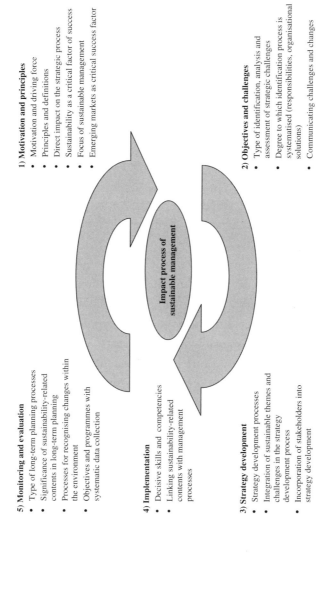

1) Motivation and principles
- Motivation and driving force
- Principles and definitions
- Direct impact on the strategic process
- Sustainability as a critical factor of success
- Focus of sustainable management
- Emerging markets as critical success factor

2) Objectives and challenges
- Type of identification, analysis and assessment of strategic challenges
- Degree to which identification process is systematised (responsibilities, organisational solutions)
- Communicating challenges and changes

3) Strategy development
- Strategy development processes
- Integration of sustainable themes and challenges in the strategy development process
- Incorporation of stakeholders into strategy development

4) Implementation
- Decisive skills and competencies
- Linking sustainability-related contents with management processes

5) Monitoring and evaluation
- Type of long-term planning processes
- Significance of sustainability-related contents in long-term planning
- Processes for recognising changes within the environment
- Objectives and programmes with systematic data collection

Impact process of sustainable management

Figure 20.1 Sustainability impact cycle

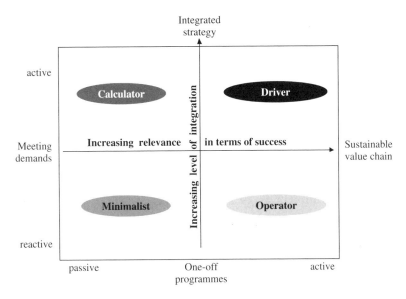

Figure 20.2 Typology matrix

and approaches that result in sustainable management integrated in corporate strategy and significantly affect corporate success.

Minimalists

Companies of this type do not attach particular importance to the theme of sustainability. Their concern with this issue generally begins and ends with protecting against risks and responding to external requirements. This is why sustainability-related contents are neither identified by those companies nor integrated into management processes.

Calculators

Sustainable management focuses on communication with the environment. Sustainability activities are strongly aligned with ratings and indices, rarely associated with related company-specific challenges. They are hardly ever integrated into the corporate strategy. Personnel responsible for sustainability are usually communication experts. Communication is often very broad, but at the same time also very general.

Operators

Operators traditionally take aspects of sustainability very seriously and their approach is based on operational needs (e.g. health, safety, environment, supply chain management). Despite this, commitment is not aligned directly with the core business. Sustainability strategies arise as parallel strategies. They are implemented consistently, but are unable to develop their full benefit for the overall strategy.

Drivers

Drivers show a high level of commitment to integrating sustainability aspects into the overall corporate strategy. This is why there is no separate sustainability strategy. They define their long-term challenges very clearly and aim for competitiveness at their worldwide locations. In addition, drivers have the power to implement strategies with a long-term orientation. They make an active contribution to sustainable development of their own company and the corporate environment. A positive corporate image is also very important for drivers, but in their case the image is based on their entrepreneurial actions. For drivers, integrating aspects of sustainability into corporate development leads to high credibility among staff, shareholders, suppliers and customers. In the dialogue with these various stakeholders from the specific corporate environment, drivers succeed especially in

- achieving *staff* advocacy, where staff at all levels can make their own innovative and creative contribution to a sustainably managed enterprise;
- achieving *shareholder* advocacy by being able to demonstrate savings through sustainably created products and processes;
- achieving *supplier* advocacy, by communicating credibly that they too can improve their quality and reduce their risks in the medium to long term by embracing sustainability;
- achieving *customer* advocacy, by ensuring that products and services are both customer-oriented and future-oriented.

One key advantage of this dialogue is that it is a very effective risk minimisation tool.

SUCCESS FACTORS FOR SUSTAINABLE MANAGEMENT: BECOMING A DRIVER

Resource-conserving processes, efficiency programmes, cost reduction programmes and environmental management systems are just a few of the current *ecological* instruments of sustainable management. Key *social* instruments include social programmes, labour standards, local gender programmes, staff training and health care. However, whether a firm succeeds in implementing sustainable management and becoming a driver is determined by its alignment with the history and tradition of a company, the nature of its products and services, the market requirements and the relevant local, national and international environment.

In addition to these specific requirements, the results of the survey, together with GTZ's global working practice, show there are four key success factors. These represent important milestones in becoming a driver.

1. **Integration instead of separation**

Mandatory integration of sustainability into a company's overall strategy is crucial for utilising the opportunities of sustainable management. Linking sustainability aspects with long-term corporate goals is decisive for the success, acceptance and credibility of sustainable commitment in both developing strategy and implementing this in management processes. The same applies to a company's extended management processes, since integration of economic, social and environmental elements throughout the entire value chain is an important factor for securing long-term corporate success. For example, involving suppliers in the quality discussion (qualification through training and upgrading, environmental management systems, quality management, technology and know-how transfer) makes it possible to ensure more intensive exploitation of the economic potential of the entire value chain. Here, for example, introducing social and ecological standards ideally has two functions: first as a quality assurance instrument, and second as a contribution towards participating in shaping the company's environment. The dynamism of globalisation itself calls for systematic integration of sustainability aspects into corporate strategy and management processes in order to reduce location-specific risks.

2. **Proactive management of the corporate environment**

The prerequisites for securing a company's long-term competitiveness include its integration into the local, national, regional and international environment. This includes dialogue with various groups in the company's environment. Participation in stakeholder dialogues, round tables and networks has the clear goal of playing an active role in shaping this environment.

Given the lack of stability in developing and emerging countries in particular, changes in a company's political, economic and social environment need to be identified.

A company's environment

- **Economic environment**: customers, staff, suppliers, competitors, trade associations.
- **Political environment**: political institutions, associations, chambers, parties.
- **Social environment**: NGOs, educational institutions, insurance companies, non-profit organisations.
- **Ecological environment**: location conditions, management of natural resources.
- **Cultural environment**: tradition, religion, values, intercultural understanding.

Examples of particular external challenges include global climate change, demographic developments, poverty, lack of energy and food security and HIV/AIDS. Understanding these changes and trends and integrating them into business processes is of the essence to utilise opportunities at the individual locations. Low-cost, long-term positioning of a company in the various markets is only possible through proactive shaping of the company's environment. Nuanced management of the environment with a medium- and long-term focus poses high demands in terms of creativeness and innovative capability, but dialogue between actors inside and outside the company makes the process manageable.

3. **Local adaptation instead of global blueprints**

The principle in implementing group-wide strategies is 'all business is local'. Adaptation to local requirements is a central success factor. Group-wide strategies provide a framework which defines the scope for local management. However, local adaptation of the strategies gives local managers the freedom they need to achieve direct benefits from sustainable management. Environmental factors are just as important as corporate management instruments in developing a group-wide strategy for sustainable management and adapting it to the local setting. The way a company handles environmental changes, such as the spread of HIV/AIDS, is crucial for its success. For instance, company-specific prevention programmes can equally be understood as acceptance of social responsibility and long-term personnel policy. They are accordingly a simple and readily comprehensible example of combining social responsibility and management processes with a long-term focus.

4. **Reducing complexity through prioritisation**
Given the broad scope of sustainability aspects, aligning activities with the company's core business becomes very important. Company-specific formulation of targets aiming at long-term stability in the company's environment poses high demands in terms of focus and prioritisation. A key success factor is focused concern with a small number of strategically important themes directly related to local corporate needs, rather than a comprehensive approach encompassing as many sustainability themes as possible.

BECOMING A DRIVER: THREE EXAMPLES FROM GTZ PRACTICE

Securing resources sustainably: profitable environmental management in the international supply chain

GTZ is implementing the 'Pruma – Profitable Environmental Management' project on behalf of the German government and in cooperation with suppliers in 20 countries. The project aims to implement measures in the operating practice of SMEs in developing countries that contribute sustainably to:

- reducing production costs;
- improving operating impact on the environment;
- promoting the organisational development of the firm.

Integrating these three areas – cost management, environmental management and organisational development – has short-term impacts on the economic situation of the firms involved and improves their market position in the long term. Pruma comprises the following modules:

- **Resource management**: training workshops on efficient use of raw materials and energy, and fundamental connections between product design, work planning and organisation, and production costs.
- **Good housekeeping**: training workshop on improved identification of inefficient, environmentally harmful use of resources, resulting in cost savings, as well as improving both environmental impacts in the firm and industrial safety. Good housekeeping can be used as a first step towards further environmentally oriented management activities.
- **Cost management**: in a series of training workshops entrepreneurs learn to reduce the costs of waste products – all outputs which are not part of the final product – systematically and continuously. They reduce the negative environmental impacts of their business, cut production costs and initiate a process of internal organisational development. Experience has shown that the process, which is designed for transparency, motivates staff to contribute actively to further improvements themselves.
- **Network meetings**: entrepreneurs meet regularly to develop cost-effective eco-friendly solutions and strategies for challenges in their everyday operations.

In the driver's seat?

Through their participation in Pruma, these firms have taken an effective step towards becoming a driver by giving clear priority to environmentally oriented management. Some 300 case studies from 20 countries and 50 industries document this impressively. Depending on the company size and the nature of the improvements, firms save between US$500 and US$150 000 per measure, with little or no investment. Payback times are less than one year in 55 % of the cases, and some 25 % of the measures pay off at once and result purely from organisational improvements. However, it is not only the positive economic effects that make a contribution to sustainable management; improvements to the ecological and social dimensions of the 'company as system' also play a part. The next step on the way to becoming a driver is to broaden consideration of the issues to include social components in the overall management of the enterprise.

Stakeholder dialogue for more quality: Common Code for the Coffee Community with the German Coffee Association

The Common Code for the Coffee Community (CCCC) is a joint initiative by the German Coffee Association and GTZ. It aims

- to **strengthen** the **competitiveness** of producers, the processing industry and traders in terms of quality enhancement and security (optimised production, management processes etc.); and
- to **promote sustainable production methods** to secure the long-term prospects of producers and traders.

The CCCC follows a holistic concept of sustainability, comprising a *social, ecological and economic dimension*. Criteria have been developed for each dimension to evaluate the performance of participants in terms of the requirements. Starting from the idea of a process of ongoing improvement, actors along the entire value chain and their environment (customers, competitors etc.) are led to a new and holistic understanding of quality. The initiative essentially comprises the following measures:

- developing a practice-driven code of conduct for globally sustainable production, processing and trading of raw coffee;
- developing implementation guidelines, an independent monitoring system and an evaluation concept;
- proactive environment management through structured multi-stakeholder dialogues;
- carrying out pilot projects to implement and apply the Common Code.

In the driver's seat?

The key success factors of the initiative are integrating aspects of sustainability into the entire value chain and proactively structuring dialogue with all participating stakeholders. The vice president of the German Coffee Association, Annemieke Wijn from Kraft Foods, stresses specifically that sustainable coffee cultivation is ultimately more efficient for everyone involved. As businesses progress to become drivers, it will be important to maintain the momentum of the initiative in the future to ensure that the economic benefits of sustainable management can continue to evolve for all participants in the value chain.

Local personnel policy: HIV/AIDS workplace policy with DaimlerChrysler in South Africa

In 2001 the incidence of HIV among employees of DaimlerChrysler South Africa (DCSA) was still completely unknown. However, it could be assumed that the incidence among staff in the company matched that in the urban centres of South Africa, where one in every four to six people is reportedly infected with the virus. On this basis, some 500 to 1200 of the roughly 3000 staff at the Daimler plant in East London would be infected with the virus. Besides the tragic social consequences, the economic consequences of AIDS, such as the loss of trained and qualified staff, rising absenteeism, shrinking human resources and falling productivity are risk factors for every company.

Together with GTZ, DaimlerChrysler built up a comprehensive work programme over the next few years, including the following goals:

* **Improvement of health information**, education and communication regarding HIV/AIDS in order to reduce stigmatisation in the workplace, improve preventive behaviour and achieve a higher take-up rate for health services.
* **Improvement** of the effectiveness and quality of the **medical care networks** for company staff with regard to TB and HIV/AIDS.
* Support for adequate and cost-effective **adaptation** of the company insurance systems **to the characteristics of the disease**.
* **Sharing experience** of HIV/AIDS prevention at work.

In the driver's seat?

Four years on, examples of the positive impact of this scheme include a 56% drop in the mortality rate. Furthermore none of the babies of the HIV-positive mothers in care were infected with HIV and there has also been a significant reduction in incapacity for work. Overall the programme has accordingly made a substantial contribution to the automotive company's medium-term security in its South African environment. The combination of a long-term perspective and rapid response to direct changes in South Africa made it possible to reduce the economic risks. The workplace programme is an important and pragmatic milestone on the way to becoming a driver in terms of the automotive group's South African environment. As the company continues its progress to become a driver, involving subcontractors in the workplace programme and utilising the South African experience for other DaimlerChrysler facilities will play an important role.

COMPANY PROFILE

The Deutsche Gesellschaft für Technische Zusammenarbeit (GTZ) GmbH, a company owned by the Federal German government, is active globally in the field of international cooperation. Taking a variety of approaches, GTZ makes a structural contribution with partners from politics, the private sector and civil society in over 130 countries in Asia, Africa, Latin America and Eastern Europe. GTZ's activities cover a broad spectrum, from advisory services to government and economic promotion right through to environmental and resource management.

Agenz bundles GTZ's global competencies and supports internationally active companies as they move towards sustainable management.

For further information see www.gtz.de.

CHAPTER 21

What Gets Measured Gets Done

Anita Roper

*W*hen Alcoa began to formalise its approach to sustainability in the late 1990s, it became apparent that this would only be successful if the company set ambitious goals, measured progress toward those goals and reported publicly on that progress. This 'what gets measured gets done' approach has resulted in significant environmental, social and economic achievements and a sustainability strategy that aligns the interests of all stakeholders.

Sustainability is not new to Alcoa, although in the past we did not always use this term. For many years, we strove for excellence with a focus on improving our understanding and management of the economic, social and environmental effects we created within communities where we had a presence.

Today, our vision is to be the best company in the world. This vision, combined with our values, principles and systems,

The ICCA Handbook on Corporate Social Responsibility Edited by J. Hennigfeld, M. Pohl and N. Tolhurst
© 2006 John Wiley & Sons, Ltd

provides a solid foundation for integrating sustainability into our operations.

Our sustainability goal is to achieve financial success, environmental excellence and social responsibility simultaneously. We aim for that success through partnerships that help us deliver net long-term benefits to our shareholders, employees, customers, suppliers and the communities in which we operate.

To achieve this, we need to engage our stakeholders, set short- and long-term goals, implement initiatives to reach those goals and be the best company in each community.

This belief has underpinned our work with communities to gain a better understanding of how Alcoa affects their economies, societies and environments. It has focused us on integrating sustainability into our decision-making processes and establishing mutually agreed goals and performance measurements.

This is not without challenges, and there is not always agreement between various stakeholders on the value of our involvement. Stakeholders sometimes bring conflicting expec- tations, experience and objectives, and we must work with them to seek understanding, reasonable balance and agreement.

We must also engage with a wide array of stakeholders, as we have operations in more than 40 countries, which are at varied stages of the economic, environmental and social development cycle. We strive for a global view that accommodates local viewpoints, using our values and principles as guideposts while being sufficiently flexible to take local conditions and stakeholder expectations into account.

All of our stakeholders demand an organisation that is accountable and transparent. To meet this expectation, Alcoa has created frameworks and processes that codify our sustainability approach and permit us to manage and measure our internal and external efforts in achieving sustainability.

2020 STRATEGIC FRAMEWORK FOR SUSTAINABILITY

Alcoa has a long history of using metrics as a means to drive change within the company. In 2000, we established our 2020 Strategic Framework for Sustainability, which is supported by clear, publicly declared targets for measuring progress toward our vision for 2020. These targets are supplemented by environment, health and safety (EHS) goals and complemented by our existing financial goals.

The framework began in 1999 when a worldwide team analysed environmental trends from 1900 to the present and predicted environmental trends for the next 20 years. Short-term (interim) goals were established for business planning purposes, and long-term (strategic) targets were set to provide directional guidance for the locations and businesses. Goals and targets were discussed and agreed upon with business leaders and technical experts throughout the company. We also expanded our metrics system to collect the data needed to measure performance against our interim and strategic goals and to track trends.

Progress was excellent. Within four years of the framework's implementation, we had a surge in ISO14001 management system certifications at the location level, a 50% reduction in land-filled waste, almost 30% lower water use, a 25% cut in greenhouse gas emissions, major reductions in other air emissions, a dramatic drop in spills and other environmental incidents and 90% fewer non-compliance issues, to mention but a few of our achievements. The process continues to work because the data system allows us to set clear goals, track our progress and analyse data to identify where additional focus is needed.

Without a system to measure the appropriate data, it is difficult to focus employee attention properly, to make everyone aware of the importance of the issues, and to demonstrate management commitment to getting the job done properly. We have concluded that most, and perhaps all, people want to do the right thing... but they need to have a clear understanding of what the right thing is and how best to go about doing it. Alcoa's 2020 Strategic Framework is a process to help us ensure that clarity for all employees and provide timeframes that allow employee creativity and innovation to be brought to bear on the issues.

We will continue to measure our progress, convert the data into useful information and use that information to manage our performance.

INTERNAL PROCESSES

To take advantage of opportunities for embracing sustainability, an organisation also needs to integrate this thinking into its internal processes – governance practices, manufacturing design and processes, employee and business systems and business opportunities. These are critical to help set goals and measure progress toward attaining them.

Metrics system

In 1988, Alcoa initiated a process to collect and display current, detailed information on safety and make it available to all employees. We have expanded the original data system to include incident management, and we now use the system for all environmental, health and safety data collection, incident management and reporting.

We can use the system at any time to determine current safety statistics, including accidents or near misses that occur anywhere in the world on a particular day. We can also view detailed reports on incidents, review the corrective action plans or status of a corrective action and evaluate our progress toward our environmental, health and safety goals. The system is an excellent management tool, which has helped us facilitate our rapid progress in these areas.

As part of our commitment to openness and transparency, we began publishing real-time safety data publicly on www.alcoa.com in 2003 to provide timely insight into our performance on this critical measure.

We continue to work on determining which regional or global metrics are required to guide us toward achieving sustainability, particularly in the more complex and difficult-to-measure social aspects of our operations.

Audit

Alcoa's goal is the same through both its internal and external audit processes: to maintain world-class transparency and accountability in our operations.

External auditors review our financial performance thoroughly, and we publish these results in our annual report. We also have an autonomous, global Internal Audit Department (IAD). This group is responsible for providing financial, information technology and environmental, health and safety audits in all Alcoa locations around the world. The group assesses risk across the company, applies audit resources to address those risks, and develops recommendations to close any gaps detected in the course of an audit. IAD is also charged with implementing the Alcoa Self-Assessment Tool, a type of self-audit that is required to be performed at least once every 18 months by all Alcoa locations and administrative processes worldwide.

Alcoa Business System

Alcoa's operating system is known as the Alcoa Business System (ABS). It is characterised by three overarching principles: make to use; eliminate waste; and people linchpin the system.

In practice, this means:

- Defining precisely our customers' requirements.
- Pre-specifying the activities, the pathways and the connections necessary for meeting those customer requirements and refusing to vary from them.
- Safeguarding what we have pre-specified with built-in tests to identify and solve problems that might threaten our predetermined outcomes.
- Enabling every Alcoa employee to recognise and trace problems back to their root cause and eliminate them – not through the use of elite, discrete teams of problem solvers, but through the disciplined, immediate, relentless participation of the people occupying the affected pathway.

This system provides the most efficient way to eliminate waste by enabling us to supply customers, on demand, with defect-free products at the lowest cost and with the highest degree of safety.

Ethics and Compliance Line

One of the ways we monitor and measure our performance in adhering to our values and business conduct policies is our global Ethics and Compliance Line. This line offers employees and other concerned parties an anonymous channel to express concerns and raise issues about workplace activities and business practices. Employees are also encouraged to use the line to obtain interpretation of laws or regulations, seek clarification of Alcoa policies or procedures or simply ask for advice on proper actions.

The compliance line is available to Alcoa employees world-wide, with local toll-free compliance lines answered in the caller's native language, where possible. We also offer an ethics and compliance email address (anonymous, if desired) and a postal address to submit written inquiries. Every concern or request for advice is addressed and responded to without reprisals. We have a target response date of 18 calendar days contingent upon the seriousness and number of issues raised.

The issue is reviewed immediately when an employee calls or sends written notice. Matters considered to pose an immediate threat to the personal safety of employees, Alcoa property or the community are sent to predetermined emergency contacts who begin an immediate investigation and institute corrective action when necessary. Non-emergency issues are sent to a regional liaison officer for review and forwarding to the appropriate location or business unit for investigation. Once an issue is resolved, a written report on the investigation and any corrective measures is submitted to the regional liaison, who then responds to the employee; this is done through the service provider to maintain employee confidentiality.

Through this process, we have established a sophisticated network of contacts across the global organisation. The regional liaisons, typically the general counsel for the region, have access to an up-to-date list of contact people at each location or business unit designated to investigate any issues at their facilities. This clear hierarchy helps us meet our goal of an 18-day maximum timeframe to respond to anyone reporting an issue.

We have also had success in using an outside vendor to receive the initial calls, emails and letters. The vendor can staff the line 24 hours a day, seven days a week in any part of the world and in most languages, using a data maintenance system to track each issue as it moves through the process. However, if budgets and staffing allow, doing this work in-house has certain advantages. The vendor is locked into accepting and fielding all calls to the line, even if they pertain to non-compliance issues. If Alcoa employees staff the line, we would have greater leeway in asking the caller questions to confirm if the issue has substance before forwarding it to the regional liaison.

The metrics we use to evaluate the compliance line fall into two categories – activity (quantitative) and effectiveness (qualitative).

Activity metrics measure whether the process for receiving and handling calls is in place and working. The parameters include the number of calls received, whether each call was answered within three minutes, if the translator was on the line in three minutes and whether the caller received a response in 18 days, to name but a few.

The metrics for effectiveness are more complex. We can survey employees to ask if they know about the line, whether it's useful, if their issues are being addressed properly, etc. Other qualitative measurements include the following:

- How many issues raised could be verified/substantiated?
- How many disciplinary actions or terminations occurred due to verification of the issues reported?
- What was the volume of calls in which an employee sought advice before acting, thus perhaps preventing an issue from arising later?
- How many calls resulted in a process or procedural change or an improvement being implemented on the basis of the investigation?
- What costs were reduced or eliminated (if any) by implementing a process or procedural change due to a call?

We have found that most employees are comfortable using the compliance line, but there are regions where providing a reporting tool like the Ethics and Compliance Line is not culturally acceptable at this stage in the country's development. Where it is culturally acceptable, the line is a very effective means to facilitate detection and correction of problems. It is also used as one way to keep management aware of what is occurring in their respective businesses with regard to ethics and compliance issues.

EXTERNAL PROCESSES

In this age of information access and global connection via the Internet, stakeholder expectations have become increasingly complex and sophisticated. These expectations have moved from 'trust me' to 'tell me' to 'show me' to 'involve me'.

Concurrently, the issues stakeholders are most concerned about have evolved from primarily economic and environmental matters to encompass social responsibility and governance. Performance expectations have also evolved from regulatory compliance to stewardship, and with this has come the call for increased transparency and accountability.

Community trust is invaluable in resolving disputes and issues, and Alcoa understands that trust is built when stakeholders see that we are open to hearing their concerns and working with them to address environmental, social and economic issues. From deploying a community framework to engaging the community early in greenfield developments, we are strengthening our relationships with key stakeholders by listening to their expectations and setting goals and introducing measurements to address them.

Alcoa Community Framework

In 2001, we launched the Alcoa Community Framework to help our locations facilitate and measure ongoing relationship building and communications with employees and community stakeholders.

The framework allows for great local flexibility and results in community engagement through a variety of means. These range from simple briefings, discussion forums on specific issues, open houses, plant tours and tree plantings to active participation by community members in the development of our locations' environmental improvement plans.

For example, our US locations conduct individual community assessments to gain a better understanding of each location's role in the community and how best to work with stakeholders to address the needs of both Alcoa and our neighbours. Once an assessment is completed, the location develops a roadmap spelling out how it will deal with issues and stakeholders. Actions include forming community advisory boards, building relationships with local officials and media, leveraging employee engagement in the community and contributing to the facility's long-term economic sustainability.

These US locations are subject to a metrics assessment that evaluates eight categories of performance on a four-step scale: community assessment; events; effective government relations; effective media relations; effective contributions and employee involvement; community consultation; participation on statewide teams; and value added.

Each plant receives guidance on how to move from the starting point to full engagement in each category. The quarterly results are shared and reviewed with the business unit presidents, group presidents and other senior Alcoa management to ensure high performance is achieved and sustained. A similar system is used at many of our locations throughout the world.

In Australia, all locations have established community consultative networks that bring together Alcoa and community representatives. They work together on important issues, including sustainability, environmental effects, local employment and Alcoa sponsorship and partnership programmes. Locations have also developed other programmes for community engagement.

For example, our operations in Victoria established 'Alcoa in the Community' committees made up of a diverse range of employees, from management to union delegates. The committees proactively pursue community partnerships, approve sponsorship requests, act as ambassadors for the company and promote volunteering in the workforce.

We also work with Victorian communities to develop environmental improvement plans for each location. Community members participate in developing the plan, sign off on the plan, monitor our progress in achieving targets and review the plan annually.

In addition to our ongoing community engagement through the Alcoa Community Framework, we involve the local community when we plan to build new facilities and expand or upgrade existing ones.

Greenfield project – Iceland

In 2004, Alcoa began construction of an aluminium smelter with a capacity of 346 000 metric-tons-per-year in eastern Iceland, our first new smelter in 20 years. We saw the project as an opportunity to improve our approach to greenfield development by seeking the stakeholder perspective and using the feedback to improve design and performance.

Other developers had been considering an aluminium smelter and hydroelectric project in eastern Iceland for more than 20 years when Alcoa and the government of Iceland agreed to build the facility. The previous projects, which never materialised, had already triggered expectations and concerns within the communities affected. We recognised a need to engage stakeholders in a meaningful way to understand these expectations and concerns and to build trust. Working closely with Landsvirkjun, the developer of the hydroelectric facility, we decided to structure a process to help the projects be designed, constructed and operated in a manner that would strike a balance between environmental, social and economic considerations and improve long-term performance.

To that end, Alcoa and Landsvirkjun jointly identified and worked with a broad coalition of external stakeholders to develop sustainability objectives, indicators, performance targets, metrics and a public reporting process.

An advisory group comprising more than 30 stakeholders from Alcoa, Landsvirkjun and numerous governmental, educational and non-governmental organisations was central to the initiative. Participants included local, national and international stakeholders, representing both advocates and opponents of the project. The group decided its purpose was to look forward – not backward – and develop indicators to measure the performance of the hydro facility and smelter against sustainability targets.

The advisory group identified almost 50 indicators and more than 70 associated metrics, which continue to be developed and refined. Each indicator was categorised as one of the following:

- Direct – Alcoa (or Landsvirkjun) has sole accountability for the respective performance (e.g., plant air emissions).
- Indirect – Alcoa has some level of influence; however, other stakeholders also influence performance (e.g., the number and proportion of jobs in key economic sectors nationally and in the local community).
- Induced – The project will affect changes in the community; however, Alcoa has limited ability to affect the outcome (e.g., the number of cultural events per year in east Iceland).

Examples of indicators and metrics include the following:

- Environment

  - Indicator: number of species
  - Metric: changes in population

- Social
  - Indicator: number of apprentices/trainees
  - Metric: turnover in apprentices/trainees
- Economic
  - Indicator: regional wealth
  - Metric: change in income levels

Baseline conditions and data were recorded as part of the process, and Alcoa and Landsvirkjun established specific performance targets and developed monitoring protocols. Both companies are fully committed to publicly reporting and communicating monitoring results.

Greenfield project – Guinea

Alcoa, which has had a mining presence in Guinea since the late 1960s, is planning an alumina refinery with a capacity of 1.5 million metric-tons-per-year to be built in partnership with the country's government and Alcan.

The proposed location for the refinery is Boké prefecture, an underdeveloped portion of the country comprising small villages without running water and electricity, where most of the local population is illiterate. While the refinery would bring substantial economic benefits to the local community, Alcoa wanted to evaluate the environmental and social effects as well through a sustainability impact assessment.

We started dialogue with the local villages via community meetings at the onset of the initial project feasibility study. While we didn't have a lot to tell the residents initially, we committed to keep them informed and to work to minimise our presence during the environmental assessment and exploratory drilling. Rumours had already spread within the area about the choice of a site, and our actions in keeping local people informed built a level of trust for when the decision was made.

Because there was minimal information about Boké prefecture's biodiversity, we engaged Conservation International (CI) to conduct an initial biodiversity assessment and planning (IBAP) project. An IBAP integrates biodiversity information and conservation planning into the earliest stages of a project's design and implementation using a science-based approach.

CI, with assistance from Guinée Ecologie (a Guinean environmental non-governmental organisation), conducted a biodiversity rapid assessment, examining the flora and fauna of several sites within the Boké prefecture. The scientific team included experienced tropical biologists from both foreign and West African institutions, including eight Guinean experts.

In some cases, the assessment represented the first biological survey in nearly 50 years. While the habitats surveyed appeared heavily impacted by human activity, several important species were observed, including a rare crab species recorded at only one other site globally, various species on the Red List of Threatened Species and numerous species never previously recorded in Guinea.

CI, Guinée Ecologie, Alcoa and Alcan presented the findings from the survey at a multi-stakeholder workshop, where an action plan for conserving biodiversity in the Boké prefecture of Guinea began to be formed.

By working with independent non-governmental organisations and a strong technical team, we ensured a fair and objective assessment of the refinery's environmental impact and continued to build trust with the local community.

We will apply Alcoa's global standards for environmental, health, safety, audit and various other issues to further measure and control our impacts. In addition, we will undertake work consistent with the environmental and social standards of the International Finance Corporation (IFC), which is part of the World Bank.

Greenfield project – Juruti

In the heart of the Amazon, a proposed bauxite mining project is serving as a microcosm of sustainability. How can Alcoa extract and refine bauxite from the pristine Juruti region of Brazil yet leave behind enhanced environmental conditions once the project is completed? How can the project have a positive effect on the local community both economically and socially without altering the region's unique culture and heritage?

In an effort to find the answers, Alcoa conducted and sponsored extensive surveys, studies and field research, which identified the region's current environmental, socioeconomic and cultural components.

Outcomes of this initial work included detailed environmental maps of the area showing archaeological sites, protected areas, headwaters and more. Other surveys identified current conditions state of the physical environment (water streams, soil, groundwater, etc.), the region's plants and animals and the people of Juruti. The survey of the local people included their economic activities, quality of life, cultural and historical heritage, archaeological heritage and other parameters.

Due to controversy arising from non-Alcoa projects in the Amazon, Alcoa deepened its understanding of potential social impacts in the short, medium and long run through two key stakeholder and community opinion surveys to evaluate present and future concerns.

To engage the community, Alcoa held three public meetings to discuss the project's implementation. The first public meeting in the city of Juruti attracted 6000 people. The second took place in Santarém, with 1000 participants. Seven hundred people attended the last meeting in Belém.

To prepare for the hearings, Alcoa organised about 70 pre-public hearings. Many were held in a customised boat, which travelled about 300 kilometres of local rivers to reach citizens living along the watercourses. During the meetings, Alcoa used to foster involvement and increase understanding. In addition Alcoa established a partnership called *Rádio Margarida* (The Margarida Broadcast) with a non-governmental organization in Pará, which also included art teachers. Before holding pre-public meetings, Alcoa visited the communities to be introduced to community leaders and to invite the citizens to the event. After the meetings, critical points were consolidated and used to support and improve the forthcoming studies.

Alcoa also printed 21 000 communication instruments for distribution in the community. These included posters, personalised invitations, comic books, the *Viva Comunidade* newsletter, calendars and folders. The company also ran an advertising campaign; this included 500 commercial advertisements, four mini billboards, 15 banners spread over strategic parts of the city and 100 screenings of a corporate video. Complementing this work was a press initiative, including press conferences, gatherings and interviews.

A preliminary licence for the project was granted following the hearings, allowing construction to begin.

Expansion – Pinjarra

By combining a state-of-the-art environmental impact assessment with an innovative community engagement process based on a sustainability framework, our Pinjarra refinery in Australia received government approval in just seven months to increase annual production by about 600 000 tons.

Initially, community sentiment about the upgrade was somewhat sceptical. Engagement with this stakeholder group became critical to ensure regulatory bodies approved the expansion, and the resulting consultation and engagement process was built upon the refinery's existing community consultative network.

A community workshop brought together a broad cross-section of the community that had a direct interest in the Pinjarra efficiency upgrade. The 40-plus stakeholders involved in the workshop included representatives from the local community, neighbours, residents, local business owners, local and state government and the Alcoa project team and management.

The main purpose of the community workshop was to establish a stakeholder reference group (SRG) to work with the Alcoa team on environmental, social and economic aspects of the proposed efficiency upgrade project.

The SRG played an important role in representing the views of the local community on an ongoing basis during the project. In particular, the SRG:

- Became a major consultation point for the company to discuss and refine details of the proposal with stakeholders.
- Reviewed the various parts of the project important to stakeholders.
- Advised Alcoa on how the stakeholders believed environmental, social and economic issues should be recognised, managed and supported.
- Reviewed the draft environmental protection statement submitted to the Environmental Protection Authority.
- Advised Alcoa on how best to provide information to the broader community.
- Helped provide information on the project to the local community and community groups.

As part of the ongoing consultation activities for the proposed upgrade, an open house was held to give the local community a better understanding of the wide range of issues relating to the proposed project. Alcoa representatives and SRG members attended the event to talk about the proposed project and answer questions from the community. Information about the environmental, economic, social and other general aspects of the project were on display.

Following the project's approval, the chairman of the Environmental Protection Authority of Western Australia called Pinjarra's community engagement model an example of a 'best practice'.

Expansion – Wagerup

We have not always been successful in our community engagement efforts. Our refinery in Wagerup, Australia, had been poised for expansion for several years. However, the level of scrutiny and criticism from the media, community and government concerning odours, noise and other emissions from the facility had slowed down the expansion effort.

In response, we invested some 30 million Australian dollars in a comprehensive odour, noise and emissions reduction programme. This reduction programme was independently audited and found to have been highly effective in reducing emissions and odours from the refinery. An extensive ambient emissions monitoring programme was also undertaken to provide the community with the best possible information and to raise community confidence about air quality in the area surrounding the refinery.

Wagerup also began working with the surrounding community and government officials to address health concerns and land management issues that had arisen during efforts to develop a compatible land use framework in the area surrounding the refinery. A tripartite group (community, government and Alcoa representatives) was set up to provide advice on issues related to the environmental licence for the refinery and the environmental monitoring. Initiatives to provide greater information on ambient air quality included a trained odour response team to provide rapid response and follow-up on odour complaints. Wagerup also partnered with a local university and relevant government agencies to work with the surrounding community to identify and resolve issues associated with the refinery's operations, particularly land management, and to build confidence and capacity.

This engagement and a major two-day community open forum laid the groundwork for an even more comprehensive stakeholder consultative process as part of the assessment for a major expansion proposal for Wagerup. This community engagement process drew on the experience of the successful community engagement model developed for the Pinjarra upgrade project. Through these efforts, we took significant steps to rebuild our relationship with the community around Wagerup.

Gaining the trust of these stakeholders will require constant efforts to ensure that the refinery can be considered a good neighbour that contributes to sustainability in the region.

LESSONS LEARNED

So far, we have learned many lessons on our sustainability journey. Key points for organisations to consider when embarking on their own sustainability and engagement strategies include the following:

- Always adhere to your vision, values and principles.
- Set goals and measurements to focus attention, establish importance and show management support.
- Build internal and external ownership for specific initiatives by starting engagement early before key decisions are made.
- Ensure engagement is representative and inclusive.
- Establish partnerships and align goals and objectives at the outset.
- Define clear objectives, roles, responsibilities and boundaries for engagement and keep focused on the objectives.
- Listen and be responsive to local needs.

- Be aware of the local culture.
- Know that there never seems to be enough time.

Organisations today can no longer be self-contained, inward-focused entities. They first need to acknowledge they have an impact on the community and then begin to assess that impact, address stakeholder issues, set goals, measure progress and report on that progress.

What gets measured gets done, and what gets done is good for both the organisation and the community.

PART III

RANKING AND AUDITING

CHAPTER 22

The 'Good Company Ranking' of the *Manager Magazin*

Arno Balzer and Michael Kröher

BASICS

The *manager magazin* (mm) 'Good Company Ranking' is the first systematic assessment of the corporate social responsibility (CSR) practices of German and European large companies. The resulting ranking list is more than an assessment of the companies' efforts in the fields of sustainable and ethically responsible personnel management, environmental conservation and community service. Indeed, it evaluates these aspects of CSR in their direct relation with the companies' commercial success. Thus it can be said that the Good Company Ranking examines the extent to which investments in CSR are conducive to the company's basic goals of profitability and business growth.

With a circulation of more than 125 000, mm is Germany's leading monthly publication for decision makers in the business

The ICCA Handbook on Corporate Social Responsibility   Edited by J. Hennigfeld, M. Pohl and N. Tolhurst
© 2006 John Wiley & Sons, Ltd

community; its average over-the-counter sales figures (including bookstores in train stations and comparable sales outlets) are higher than those for all other German business magazines. And according to data collected in December 2005, mm is quoted in other media more often than its competitors.

manager magazin can therefore be seen as an opinion leader in the field of German-language business journalism. What's more, the publication has a strong, decades-long tradition of critical investigative reporting supported by independent research, particularly when it comes to large companies. Among many other achievements in keeping with this tradition, throughout the 1990s mm followed very closely the discussion regarding corporate governance that eventually culminated in the set of regulations developed by the so-called Cromme Commission.

Thus such issues as entrepreneurial ethics, social responsibility and the moral behaviour the financial markets and of large companies as they conduct their day-to-day business have come to play a central role in the articles and reporting of mm.

Following the establishment of the 'Cromme Code' in 2002, the editors took on the task of addressing other aspects of ethical business management and corporate social responsibility, illuminating them with substantiated, sustained, transparent journalism.

There was discussion about potential topics suitable for independent, autonomously prepared rankings. The magazine had set new standards in the methodology of rankings in the 1990s, e.g. with its evaluations of the annual reports of companies listed on the (German) stock market. Every two years this ranking, 'The Best Annual Reports', is conducted by a jury of experts on behalf of mm, and published in the February edition of mm.

INITIAL SITUATION 2003/04

English-language publications on the fundamentals of corporate citizenship (CC), CSR and corporate responsibility (CR) in general (e.g. Gopalkrishnan, 2000 and Anderson, 1989) began appearing around the turn of the century. In December 2001, the OECD held a round table discussion on the subject (Nourick, 2001) in Paris with international participants. Subsequently the topics of CC and CSR began appearing more often on the agendas of business congresses and association conventions throughout continental Europe. The first German-language treatments of these subjects appeared in publications issued by companies and associations such as the Bertelsmann Foundation; individual companies (e.g. Henkel, Bertelsmann, Deutsche Post etc.) established task forces to address the relevant tasks in a systematic manner. The results of these efforts were then reported in company publications.

The 'Freedom and Responsibility Initiative' of the DIHK (German Chamber of Industry and Trade) concerned itself with CSR and CC, and initiatives on the subject were also launched by the BDI (Federation of German Industries) and BDA (Confederation of German Employers' Associations).

In the year 2003 the German-language *Handbook of Corporate Citizenship* was published by André Habisch, a professor at the Catholic University of Eichstätt (Habisch, 2003). At the end of that same year, Christian Schwalbach, professor of management at Berlin's Humboldt University, announced the first international scientific congress on the subject of corporate social responsibility.[1]

Thus it was only fitting that mm – in cooperation with the Hamburg business consulting company Kirchhoff-Consult, which had also provided consulting and organisational assistance for mm in preparing the ranking of annual business reports – worked out a concept in early 2004 for an independent ranking, autonomously researched and compiled, that would evaluate the success of the CSR management of individual companies.

---

[1] International CSR Congress at Humboldt University, Berlin, on 14–15 October 2004, under the direction of Professor Joachim Schwalbach.

The ranking list offered mm readers exclusive insights into an area of business management and culture that previously had been largely unknown. At the time, no assessment of CSR activities or of CSR management within companies existed in the German-speaking world.

OBJECTIVES, UNIQUE FEATURES

The *goals* of the planned CSR ranking were exclusively journalistic ones.

The business ethics and the social responsibility of companies were to be evaluated, and the results published in a consumer medium. The report would include objective criticism of the management of the companies assessed, and positive examples would be listed and presented as potential 'role models', as it were.

The result would be an overview of the general situation in the German business community, as well as in individual sectors (companies listed on the stock market, with various levels of sales volume, etc.).

However, the *most important unique feature* was that the ranking would *not* be an 'open competition' individual companies could enter into or apply for.

Both the selection of the companies and the evaluation of their CSR management was carried out independently by the creator of the ranking list – using verifiable data, according to objective criteria, and for purely journalistic purposes.

A second unique feature was *general assessment of the success* of the companies' CSR management. This means: What was to be evaluated was not the mere idealisation of a good CSR concept, not the intention of becoming or being perceived as a good corporate citizen, but the actual business success achieved by implementing these concepts.

Success would neither be measured solely by compliance with social and ethical standards, nor solely in the protection of human rights, the absence and prevention of corruption, etc. Instead, the ranking would also evaluate materially measurable business success – i.e. increase in sales volume, profit, stock price, EBIT margin, total shareholder return, cash flow, equity ratio, etc.

This was done in order to avoid rewarding 'corporate charity' conducted in the form of generous cultural or sports sponsorships. Instead, the goal was to reward CSR management that comprehends the costs incurred in implementing the necessary measures as an investment which should and must lead to ongoing, verifiable improvement in corporate profits, and that views ethical behaviour and corporate responsibility as a strategy to increase the value of the company.

A third unique feature was the *internationality* of the ranking list. In the age of globalisation, and of corporations with worldwide operations, it makes no sense to limit the evaluation to German companies. Firms headquartered in Germany are always in competition with foreign companies – on the product market level, the level of financial markets, etc. Thus an international comparison was deemed most appropriate to achieve the desired goals.

PARTNERS AND ASSOCIATES

In addition to the initiators – the editorial offices of mm and the Kirchhoff-Consult company of Hamburg – the German branch of the international auditing firm Deloitte also came on board as a further sponsor of the CSR ranking. Deloitte agreed to provide experts (e.g. specialists to evaluate the environmental protection activities of companies within the framework of the CSR ranking) and to host the necessary meetings of the various advisers.

SELECTION AND METHODS

Sampling

On the basis of an autonomous selection of candidates (see above: Unique features), the basic sample of companies was determined as follows:

• All companies listed on the DAX 30 stock market index.
• All companies listed on the Stoxx stock market index (with the exception of those also listed on the DAX 30).
• A selection of 10 additional German companies from the industrial, retail, financial services and service sectors, which either already possess established intensive CSR management (e.g. Bosch GmbH, Bertelsmann AG), or are companies one would expect to have engaged in CSR management due to their role in German society (e.g. Deutsche Bahn AG, DZ Bank) or on the international marketplace (Boehringer Ingelheim GmbH, RAG).

The resulting sample totalled 80 participants.

Method

In the second quarter of 2004, a letter was sent to the selected companies requesting them to submit any and all written materials that could provide information about the objectives, scopes, implementation and evaluation of their CSR measures, in particular in the areas of:

• human resources;
• community service;
• environmental protection;

- financial strength/performance;
- communication of CSR measures – both internally and externally.

The partners and associates (see above: Partners and associates) established special task forces for each of the above-specified criteria.

Material submissions

The materials submitted included not only special CSR reports, but also environmental reports, business reports, internal papers and other publications.

In addition, the *websites* of the companies were evaluated, along with reports on the CSR activities of the companies that had appeared in independent consumer media (archive research). In individual cases, additional CSR management materials were requested from the management boards of the companies; in some cases, also from the PR and IR departments.

EVALUATION: CRITERIA, WEIGHTING AND BENCHMARKS

The CSR management of a company comprises tasks in several areas, and they must all be taken into consideration before generalisations can be made about social responsibility and ethical leadership. At the same time, the planned ranking was intended to analyse and evaluate individual aspects in detail. The partners and associates devised the following structure for the assessment of individual aspects of CSR.

Human resources

Data and facts on the following aspects were evaluated:

- Compensation (total and relative) and salary structure.
- Personnel development.
- Achievement of potential.
- Ethics and commitment.

Community service

Data and facts on the following aspects were evaluated:

- How community service activities are managed relative to the company's general strategy.
- How the CSR programme is anchored in the company.
- Degree of innovation in community service activities.
- How the company's initiatives are integrated in and perceived by society.
- How the company generates awareness and understanding for the themes of its CSR programmes.

Environment

Data and facts on the following aspects were evaluated:

- Company performance on environmental issues.
- Environmental aspects of the value-added chain.
- Ecological innovations.
- Integration of environmental aspects within business processes.

Financial strength/Performance

Data and facts on the following aspects were evaluated:

- Equity ratio.
- EBIT margin.
- Total shareholder return.
- Growth and volatility of cash flow.

Communication/Transparency

Data and facts on the following aspects were evaluated:

- Scope, contents, verifiability, topicality and feasibility of external publications on the subject of CSR.
- Scope, contents, verifiability, topicality and feasibility of internal publications on the subject of CSR.

Weighting

A total of 100 points could be awarded for each of the 80 selected companies.

However, different point values could be awarded for each of the individual sub-evaluations – with the result that the individual criteria had varying influence on the ultimate assessment. The maximum number of points for each of the individual criteria:

- Human resources 25 points.
- Community service 25 points.
- Environment 20 points.
- Financial strength/Performance 15 points.
- Communication/Transparency 15 points.

The points were awarded by the respective special task force for each of the individual criteria.

Benchmarks

The individual evaluation criteria listed above were evaluated by each respective special task force according to the same standards; i.e. each individual sub-evaluation had the same importance as the other detailed evaluation criteria.

ADVISORY BOARDS AND DECISION MAKING

In addition to the special task forces charged with evaluating the data and assessing the individual companies according to the disciplines listed above, there was an independent jury.

The members of the jury were (in alphabetical order):

- Dr Arno Balzer (chief editor of mm).
- Peter von Blomberg (acting chairman of the board of the German chapter of the anti-corruption initiative Transparency International).
- Professor Wolfgang Grewe (acting partner for Germany at the Deloitte auditing company).
- Klaus Kirchhoff (chairman of the board, Kirchhoff-Consult).
- Helmut Maucher (honorary president of Nestlé).

The jury was assisted by the heads of the various special task forces: Kaevan Gazdar (expert for human capital, 'Human resources' task force), Professor Dr André Habisch (head of the Centre for Corporate Citizenship, Eichstätt, 'Community service' task force) and Sam Vaseghi (Deloitte, 'Environment' task force). The areas of financial strength/performance and transparency were handled by special task forces under the leadership of Klaus Kirchhoff.

The special task forces informed the jury of the points they had awarded. A preliminary ranking was prepared on the basis of these points, and it was submitted to the jury for a plausibility and validity check. Following discussion with the heads of the special task forces, the final ranking was prepared.

The decisive meeting of the jury took place in Frankfurt in late November 2004.

FINDINGS

The final ranking list looked like this:[2]

1. BP (74.3 points)
2. Anglo American (72.0)
3. Deutsche Post (71.7)
4. BT Group (71.2)
5. Royal Dutch Petroleum (70.1)
6. Deutsche Telekom (69.8)
7. Nokia (68.1)
8. Royal Bank of Scotland (67.3)
9. BASF (66.8)
10. Henkel (66.0)

At the lower end of the ranking were such companies as Deutsche Börse, Assicurazioni Generali, Fresenius Medical Care, DZ Bank and the Edeka Group, with points ranging between 30.7 and 14.8.

DISCUSSION OF THE FINDINGS

The most surprising findings were as follows:

Two companies from relatively 'dirty' industries (oil and energy in the case of BP; mining and raw materials in the case of Anglo American) were at the top of the list, while comparatively 'cleaner' companies with 'modern', less socially controversial business models

---

[2] The complete table including rankings in the five individual disciplines is documented on the Internet, www.manager-magazin.de/unternehmen/csr/.

performed more poorly (e.g. financial service providers, the telecommunications industry, retail companies etc.).

The reason given for this was that in these 'winning' industries a number of public occurrences in the 1980s and 1990s led to the establishment of comprehensive CSR management – as part of risk management, as it were.

Following crises such as those of the Brent Spar oil platform in 1994, many oil and mining companies professionalised and systematically restructured their CSR activities – in most cases with the help of task forces set up specifically for this purpose. As a result, these companies already possess the relevant experience, and have built up a tradition of CSR management.

British companies performed considerably better than candidates from all other nations: four of the top 10 companies are headquartered in Great Britain. The number rises to five if one includes Royal Dutch Shell, which is registered in both the Netherlands and Great Britain.

The reason given for this was the traditionally strong role CSR plays in British companies. The terminology of corporate responsibility, according to Edward Bickham, executive vice president at Anglo American, is part of the 'flesh and blood' of his company's managers. 'These ideas are built into the company's DNA', he said (Kröher, 2005: 84).

In response to the environmental scandals, this tradition was very quickly and effectively professionalised in the 1980s. 'We learned a lot from these conflicts', said Graham Baxter, vice president for CSR at BP. 'We understood that we can only achieve sustainable profitability by systematically running our company as good corporate citizens' (Kröher, 2005: 85).

German companies performed comparatively well, with four German companies among the top 10 (Deutsche Post, Deutsche Telekom, BASF and Henkel). Aside from the British and German companies, only one other European firm ranked among the top 10, namely the Nokia group of Finland (7th place). French, Swiss,

Italian, Spanish and other European companies listed on the Stoxx achieved much lower scores.

The reason given for this fact was the relative significance issues of corporate citizenship have had in Germany as compared with the above-mentioned countries – due to the traditionally strong role of the trade unions, but also the importance of environmental groups and other non-governmental organisations since the 1980s.

PUBLICATION

The findings of the study and the ranking itself were published in a major article entitled 'Good Company Ranking' in the February 2005 issue of *manager magazin* (Kröher, 2005). Since then, the term 'Good Company Ranking' has become established as a logo for the *manager magazin* CSR ranking.

The article was also published online (www.manager-magazin.de/unternehmen/csr/), along with the detailed results, i.e. the points awarded in the five individual disciplines which the special task forces and the jury used to evaluate each of the companies.

FOLLOW-UP AND CONSEQUENCES OF PUBLICATION

The 'Good Company Ranking' was discussed intensively within most of the companies evaluated. All in all, the findings found broad acceptance.

Many queries were subsequently placed to the editorial offices of *manager magazin* – regarding details of the evaluation, but also regarding conclusions to be made as a result of the ranking, e.g. with regard to the respective competitors.

From the point of view of mm, this dialogue showed that in conducting and publishing the 'Good Company Ranking', the magazine had once again fulfilled its goal of critical reporting – also when it comes to issues of ethical business management and the social responsibility of companies.

In June 2005, *manager magazin* hosted a round table discussion on the subject of CSR management in Germany. Held at the Petersberg conference centre in Bonn, the event was attended by top managers from the German companies that had performed best in the 'Good Company Ranking', including Klaus Zumwinkel (chairman of the board of Deutsche Post), Ulrich Lehner (chairman of the board of Henkel), Gunther Thielen (chairman of the board of Bertelsmann), Claus-Michael Dill (chairman of the board of Axa Deutschland), Alfred Tacke (chairman of the board of Steag) and others.

Excerpts of the round table discussion appeared in the August 2005 edition of *manager magazin* (*manager magazin*, 2005).

NEXT STEPS, FUTURE GOALS

manager magazin intends to conduct its 'Good Company Ranking' in a similar manner and with similar criteria every two years, and publish the findings in the February edition of every 'odd' calendar year (e.g. February, 2007, February, 2009).

In the next evaluation – data analysis in the second half of 2006, publication in February 2007 – the sampling will be increased to 100 companies, with a similar ratio of international companies as in the previous study.

Other improvements, particularly in the area of the scientific methodology, are already being planned by the partners and associates. There is also discussion of expanding the jury to include renowned personalities from the scientific, social and political communities.

References

Anderson, Jerry W. (1989). *Corporate Social Responsibility*. Boston: Quorum Press.

Gopalkrishnan, R. (2000). *Teaching International Business Ethics: Corporate Social Responsibility*. London: International Business Press.

Habisch, André (2003). *Corporate Citizenship – Gesellschaftliches Engagement von Unternehmen in Deutschland*. Berlin: Springer Verlag.

Kröher, Michael O.R. (2005). Tue Gutes und profitiere davon, *manager magazin*, February, pp. 80–6.

manager magazin (2005). Wie sozial können Unternehmen sein? August, pp. 86–93.

Nourick, Shari (Ed.) (2001). *Corporate Social Responsibility – Partners in Progress*. Paris: OECD Press.

CHAPTER 23

The Caux Round Table: Taking CSR from Aspiration to Action

Stephen B. Young and Frank Straub

HISTORY

The Caux Round Table (CRT) was first convened in 1986 by Frits Phillips and Olivier Giscard d'Estaing at Mountain House in Caux, Switzerland. Attractively perched high on the Alps above Lake Leman, Mountain House had served as a venue for gatherings intended to reconcile French and German leaders after World War II. These gatherings were facilitated by volunteers such as Frits Phillips who were part of the Moral Re-Armament movement for change and reform. The dialogue helped increase confidence in a European identity among the French and German participants, a confidence that led to the creation of the European Coal and Steel Community, which united former ethnic adversaries behind a programme of common interest.

The ICCA Handbook on Corporate Social Responsibility   Edited by J. Hennigfeld, M. Pohl and N. Tolhurst
© 2006 John Wiley & Sons, Ltd

In 1986 Frits Phillips sought to replicate such a positive outcome from dialogue, this time between Japanese, European and American business leaders. Together with his colleague Olivier Giscard d'Estaing, he invited leading industrialists from Japan, Europe and the United States to meet at Mountain House for a discussion on trade restrictions already imposed or threatened in response to Japan's rapid economic development and success in manufacturing for export. The group resolved that good, constructive business practices should not be constrained by politicians, that such political constraint prevented wealth from being created for the benefit of humanity, but also that companies had an obligation to conduct their business affairs with honour and integrity.

Participants in the discussions agreed to meet annually to keep their resolve alive and fresh. Thus, the Caux Round Table was established.

On his retirement, Frits Phillips was succeeded as convenor of the CRT forum by Ryuzaburu Kaku, then chairman of Canon Ltd. Mr Kaku brought to the ongoing dialogue a philosophy of business management that he referred to as *Kyosei*. He advocated *Kyosei* as a guide to decision making to help businesses be not only profitable but also constructive contributors to society. The key premise of *Kyosei* is that business and society exist in a mutually supportive, living and organic relationship. Without good business, society remains deprived and offers only limited opportunities to its members; without good society, business lacks good employees, financial investment, eager customers, robust laws and a cultural tradition of trust and reliance.

Mr Kaku argued that business must foster its relationships with various supporting constituencies if it wanted to maximise its profitability.

In early 1992, Mr Kaku presented his strategic management philosophy to a meeting of business leaders in Minneapolis, Minnesota. He received a warm and empathetic response. At that time, Robert MacGregor, who had championed efforts by the business communities in Minneapolis, Kansas City and Chicago to improve inner-city conditions, was working on a project to publish a set of guidelines for conducting business. The resulting Minnesota principles reflected both the stakeholder approach of American teaching on business ethics and the old Yankee/Calvinist, New England traditions of community stewardship, which had been handed down in several leading family-run companies such as Dayton-Hudson in Minnesota.

In summer 1992, MacGregor travelled to Mountain House for the CRT Global Dialogue together with Charles M. Denny, CEO of ADC Telecommunications, and several other Minnesotans. They proposed that the CRT participants should draft a global set of principles incorporating *Kyosei* and the substance of the Minnesota guidelines. Several Europeans suggested that any proposed set of principles should also incorporate the ethical concept of 'human dignity' best expounded in the social teachings of the Roman Catholic Church, particularly in papal encyclica such as *Centissimus Annus*.

The European proposal was accepted and two years later, in 1994, the Caux Round Table Principles for Business were published. This set of guidelines for business decision making embraced *Kyosei*, the concept of human dignity and the American concern for stakeholder relationships. The CRT Principles for Business comprise seven general principles and a set of obligations for each of six distinct stakeholder constituencies: customers, employees, owners and investors, suppliers, competitors and communities. These Principles represent the most comprehensive set of guidelines on ethical and social responsibility available to businesses today. They are furthermore the only such set of guidelines drawn up by business leaders.

Drawing on intuitive analyses of human interdependency, such as *Kyosei* and the concept of human dignity, the CRT Principles for Business embrace the key ethical teachings of the world's religions. Informed by the revelations of the Koran, the insights of Confucius, the Laws of Manu and the prayers of Shintoism, they envisage streams of ethical responsibility and obligation flowing in parallel lines towards a common purpose: justice.

But business is not exclusively a moral enterprise. It is this-worldly and very materialistic in its ambitions. Accordingly, principled business decision making must both reconcile and integrate ethical sensitivity and profitability. The first CRT Principle for Business states that business must be profitable in order to make its necessary and special contribution to society, namely the creation of wealth. Being profitable is as much an obligation incumbent on business as is serving stakeholders with fairness and wisdom.

Management's leadership skills are challenged by the need to reconcile the conflicting demands of ethics versus short-term profit, customer demand for low prices versus employees' demands for higher wages and owners' demands for high returns. No calculus exists to provide easy answers, and manifold are the temptations to take short cuts that promise selfish advantage but also harbour a risk of third-party harm or loss.

The proper calling of business leadership is an arduous one indeed.

By the late 1990s, CRT participants had recognised that offering a set of principles could be only the first step in improving the moral quality of global capitalism. Efforts were therefore made to develop a comprehensive decision-making framework to help business executives shoulder their various and conflicting responsibilities. Phase two of the CRT's work in promoting more ethically and socially responsible business practices had begun.

In spring 2000, the CRT's Global Governing Board established a working group to investigate the development of metrics in order to help managers implement the Principles for Business. The approach suggested initially reflected the tests applied to companies by socially responsible investment funds and the Global Reporting Initiative. Under this semi-inquisitorial approach, company outputs are measured against defined standards of good conduct, and companies that manufacture alcohol products or weapons, sell tobacco or invest in Myanmar are judged to have failed to meet the minimum standards of responsible conduct.

Members of the CRT working group, however, were not satisfied with an approach that does not sit comfortably with management skills and management obligations. Business managers are responsible for setting and achieving goals. The incentives to which they respond with a personal commitment to act are forward-looking and geared to intended results. Managers cannot work well in a retrospective environment where their achievements are second-guessed from the perspective of outsiders or with the benefit of hindsight after new concerns have come to the fore. Market behaviour is prospective in nature, with the needs of others being taken into account in advance as part of the entrepreneurial risk.

The goal of the CRT working group being to encourage implementation of the CRT Principles for Business, there was clearly a need for a framework that business managers would recognise as being user-friendly.

The CRT working group therefore turned its attention to the achievements of the quality enhancement movement of the 1980s. This movement had succeeded in translating previously intangible dimensions of quality into tangible management objectives by means of a rigorous analytical process of continuous improvement, which resulted in better quality, more satisfied customers and, in many cases, lower production costs.

The CRT working group proceeded to develop a self-assessment and improvement process based on the approach used for the Malcolm Baldrige Award application process in the United States. To apply for a Malcolm Baldrige Award for quality, a company has to evaluate itself using three criteria: (i) its approach to quality; (ii) how it deploys this approach in attaining specific management objectives; and (iii) the results it achieves in respect of each such objective.

By June 2002, the CRT working group had drafted a set of 275 questions to serve as a framework for assessing the extent to which a company: (i) used the CRT Principles for Business as its fundamental business approach; (ii) deployed its assets and staff to ensure implementation of the CRT Principles; and (iii) what practical results it had achieved. The 275 lines of inquiry in the CRT's new CSR approach to management include all the data items covered by the Global Reporting Initiative and many more besides. The CRT's approach is broad-based, encompassing all the dimensions of the seven general principles and the interests of all six fundamental stakeholder constituencies. See Appendix to this chapter.

The new CRT process could equally be described as taking an inventory of strategic assets – those assets of a company that enable it to achieve high levels of *Kyosei*, human dignity and stewardship. Indeed, under the CRT approach, acquisition of such strategic assets also helps the company to generate sustainable profits, there being a strong affinity between profitability and responsible conduct. The CRT approach to business decision making is described more fully in the book *Moral Capitalism* by Stephen B. Young, global executive director of CRT.

Then CRT chair, George Vojta, suggested that the proposed inquiry, inventory and improvement process could be of great interest to boards of directors. The information acquired through the inquiry process would enhance the ability of company boards to supervise the strategic growth of their enterprises. Vojta also suggested that a short inquiry form would be less onerous for busy senior managers. The working group quickly drafted a short executive summary of the inquiry questionnaire.

The CRT recommendations evolved into a governance process for every company committed to corporate social responsibility. Good governance rests on two pillars – diligent inquiry into facts and values and the setting of proper goals and objectives.

In Japan the CRT governance methodology was introduced under the name 'CSR Innovation System' in order to appeal to

Japanese business leaders more open than ever to the need to rethink Japanese business practices. Outside of Japan, the governance methodology is being marketed as 'Arcturus' – the name of a star – with a view to focusing attention on the need to aim high when setting goals for business performance.

ARCTURUS/CSR INNOVATION SELF-AUDIT

Once the working group had developed a preliminary version of the Arcturus/CSR Innovation, CRT launched so-called 'beta tests' in order to determine just how this tool might contribute towards enhancing management practices within practical applications of the CRT Principles for Business.

Beta tests were conducted in Japan, the US and Europe. In Germany, the first test of Arcturus ethical inventory was carried out in 2004 by BLANCO, a private company and leading manufacturer of kitchen technology and catering and medical systems. BLANCO has sales of €293 million and 1700 employees. The company has been an active member of the Caux Round Table since 1994.

Anyone addressing the issue of business ethics soon realises that although there is no shortage of theory, hardly any practical tools are available to facilitate ethical decision making in the business context. Infusing ethical theory into practical business realities is precisely what the Arcturus management approach aims to achieve. This makes the CRT a possible spiritual home for all those in business who acknowledge corporate social responsibility as being a relevant dimension of business success.

Being ethical in their personal conduct and leading by personal example are important requirements for individual senior managers, but these factors alone are not strong enough to penetrate large and complex organisations and infuse in them the values set out in an abstract code of corporate conduct. So much fine-tuning is required to ensure consistent ethical conduct throughout an organisation that only a systematic approach using a practical tool like Arcturus can offer hope of success.

The CRT self-audit tool Arcturus not only allows for a valuable comparison to be made between the inside view of your company and the view held by external stakeholders. Arcturus can also expose shortcomings in your organisation and indicate what needs to be done to rectify them in terms of appropriate behaviours, practices and motivations.

One compelling reason to audit your company is that ethical behaviour pays. The correlation between enhanced profitability and a high standard of conduct has been demonstrated by several surveys, including research conducted by the Institute of Business Ethics in the UK.

Even the mere fact that a company has committed to self-assessment in terms of corporate social responsibility has a positive impact on the motivation of its employees and on the perceptions of that company held by external stakeholders such as customers, suppliers and the public at large.

For its beta test BLANCO engaged in a first collaboration with a university in order to implement its Arcturus self-audit. University students, not BLANCO employees, conducted interviews with stakeholders to provide a basis for assessing BLANCO's degree of compliance with the CRT Principles for Business. BLANCO found that arranging for external moderators for the interviews and external documentation of the results not only ensures greater objectivity in the self-assessment process but also lends greater credence to the results.

BLANCO's beta test was supervised by Professor Noll, Professor of Ethics at Pforzheim University, and conducted by four masters degree students with Tim Ortmann in the lead position. The students translated the Arcturus questions from English into German and modified some questions in the original American draft to take account of specifically German needs.

Any ethical assessment – whether self-administered or by a third party – must take local laws and practices into account. The business environment in Germany is not the same as in the United States or Japan, with differences particularly noticeable in terms of environmental and employee protection.

The BLANCO beta test took about four months to complete. The first step in the process required the president of BLANCO to complete the executive survey version of Arcturus. Completing this survey took only about three hours and provided a benchmark for later use with respect to the ratings assigned to BLANCO by the various stakeholders. In the BLANCO case, the scores given by the president in the executive survey turned out to be very close to those given by the stakeholders. This concurrence was not particularly surprising as BLANCO's president, Frank Straub, who is also the grandson of the company's founder, Heinrich Blanc, had served the company for almost 30 years and was very familiar with the company's situation and culture.

The Arcturus process was implemented in the following steps and generated the following results.

The audit team considered that the initial rating system proposed by the Arcturus instruction manual, which entailed rating the ethical performance of a company using only one numerical value, was not sufficiently comprehensive to reflect the complexity of ethical interrelations within that company. The team therefore developed and used an additional four-point scale to rate the results of the audit:

1. Good ethical awareness and compliance.
2. Possible areas of future ethical conflict.
3. Critical practice or unethical behaviour.
4. Insufficient data or no statement possible.

In addition, the student audit team adapted the Arcturus questionnaire to the German business context and to the special situation within which mid-size companies such as BLANCO operate. The team thus developed a four-point framework for analysing a company's ethical awareness:

1. Identifying relevant sub-groups within each stakeholder category.
2. Defining and executing process steps.
3. Extracting ethically relevant results.
4. Evaluation of results.

These four steps were expanded to encompass a more detailed set of issues before the Arcturus questionnaire was used with stakeholder constituencies. The following example illustrates the analysis of the stakeholder category 'employees'.

1. **Identifying relevant sub-groups within the stakeholder model**
   The study should consider only those stakeholders that fall within the relevant sub-groups. Once the relevant sub-groups of stakeholders have been identified they are clustered prior to analysis. The stakeholder category 'employees', for example, is acknowledged as a heterogeneous group encompassing a range of value and management cultures. The category therefore has to be subdivided into sub-groups with similar backgrounds and viewpoints, such as blue-collar workers and white-collar workers. Other differentiations made included the different business units (kitchen technology and catering and medical systems) and different locations. These distinctions are needed in order to fully and thoroughly understand the results.

2. **Defining and executing process steps**
   For the stakeholder group 'employees', the Arcturus student audit team first scheduled a kick-off workshop with part of the management team to review the questions and define areas requiring more detailed investigation. Extensive interviews were then conducted with the staff executives, the works councils of the various business segments, the health and safety officer,

and the employees working in the various plants. Finally, the questionnaire results from the different plant and office locations were reviewed in the presence of a supervisor. This process was considered to ensure sufficient sensitivity to the different points of view encompassed within the stakeholder category 'employees'.

3. **Extracting ethically relevant results**

Following collection of the data, the student audit team extracted the results ethically relevant to the audit. These ethically relevant results were then divided into matters concerning the employee as an individual and matters concerning the employees as a constituency within the company. In the case of the former set of matters, the factors considered to be of major importance in the ethical treatment of this sub-group included information sharing, inclusion in performance enhancement review and levels of job satisfaction. In the latter set of matters, those concerning employees as a constituency, the predominant factors identified included cooperation with the works council and the day-to-day working culture.

4. **Evaluation of results**

In our example of the 'employees' as a stakeholder category at BLANCO, the student audit team found that the employees were respected and kept well informed of decisions affecting the company as a whole. There was evidence of an honest effort by the company to promote trust and transparency, people were generally approachable and open to constructive criticism, and management was rated as being cooperative and sensitive towards the employees' needs. The company also valued, encouraged and enabled self-development and learning on the part of its individual employees.

As was the case with the stakeholder category 'employees', the student audit team subsequently found that BLANCO generally scored well in good ethical problem solving across all stakeholder groups. An example of this ethical sensitivity is the company's 'three bottles of wine' rule for accepting gifts from external sources (suppliers, contractors, etc.), which has long been in place and has been forcefully communicated to employees. These positive results could be interpreted as stemming from the values that have long been part of BLANCO's traditionally strong, family-driven corporate culture.

However, the Arcturus audit also revealed a few sensitive areas with potential for future ethical conflict. These areas were identified mainly where no specific rules of conduct had been laid down. For example, in contrast to the 'three bottles of wine' rule, the company has no written rule defining limits on gifts made to external contacts. The student audit team recommended action in these minor areas and highlighted the need for management awareness of the possibility of future abuse.

The audit detected no critical violations of ethical practice. In a few isolated areas, time and resource constraints prevented the award of a final rating. The use of an independent, external auditing team ensured that the results were objective. However, although more objective in making assessments than insiders would be, any external team obviously lacks the deeper insight normally held by the company management. For this reason, a combination of both an internal audit team and at least one external moderator is recommended for future ethical audits.

When the Arcturus beta test was completed, the results were presented to the senior employees, the board of non-executive directors, the shareholders and the Caux Round Table. The audit results were subsequently made public at an event held in Stuttgart in January 2005, attended by over 100 people.

An active commitment to business ethics is more highly appreciated today than ever before – both inside and outside a company. Paying attention to a corporation's social responsibilities is especially well accepted by the media. Doing good and then talking about it is therefore a contribution to the reputational capital of a business. The positive response to undertaking an ethical audit is another example of how being ethical pays.

APPENDIX: CAUX ROUND TABLE ARCTURUS CORPORATE SOCIAL RESPONSIBILITY INQUIRY PROCESS GLOBAL REPORTING INITIATIVE

Guide to using Global Reporting Initiative (GRI) report items when completing the CRT Self-Assessment and Improvement Programme

CRT PRINCIPLES FOR BUSINESS IN SELF-ASSESSMENT AND IMPROVEMENT QUESTIONNAIRE FORMAT

CRT Principle 1: Responsibilities of Business
1.1
1.2 GRI 6.59, 6.95, 6.96
1.3 GRI 6.48, 6.49, 6.50, 6.60, 6.61, 6.69, 6.70, 6.71
1.4 GRI 6.37, 6.38, 6.39, 6.40, 6.41, 6.42, 6.43, 6.46, 6.47
1.5 GRI 6.58
1.6
1.7

CRT Principle 2: Economic and Social Impact of Business
2.1
2.2
2.3 GRI 6.44, 6.53, 6.74, 6.75, 6.76, 6.77
2.4 GRI 6.45
2.5
2.6
2.7 GRI 6.51, 6.53

CRT Principle 3: Business Behaviour
3.1
3.2
3.3 GRI 6.22, 6.63, 6.65
3.4
3.5
3.6
3.7

CRT Principle 4: Respect for Rules
4.1 GRI 6.36, 6.85, 6.86, 6.88, 6.89
4.2
4.3 GRI 6.72, 6.73, 6.78, 6.79, 6.80, 6.81, 6.82, 6.83, 6.84
4.4
4.5 GRI 6.25, 6.55, 6.92, 6.93
4.6
4.7 GRI 6.90, 6.91

CRT Principle 5: Multilateral Trade
5.1
5.2
5.3
5.4
5.5 GRI 6.56, 6.57
5.6
5.7

CRT Principle 6: Environment
6.1 GRI 6.1,6.2, 6.4, 6.5, 6.6, 6.9, 6.11, 6.12, 6.13, 6.14, 6.15,
    6.16, 6.17, 6.18, 6.19, 6.20, 6.21, 6.22, 6.23, 6.24, 6.28, 6.31,
    6.32, 6.33, 6.35
6.2 GRI 6.30
6.3 GRI 6.66, 6.67, 6.68
6.4
6.5 GRI 6.25, 6.27

6.6
6.7 GRI 6.3, 6.7, 6.8, 6.10, 6.29, 6.34

CRT Principle 7: Illicit Operations
7.1
7.2
7.3
7.4
7.5
7.6
7.7

Index

Index compiled by Terry Halliday